Let the Good Times Roll

PROSTITUTION AND THE U.S. MILITARY IN ASIA

Let the Good Times Roll

PROSTITUTION AND

THE U.S. MILITARY

IN ASIA

Saundra Pollock Sturdevant and Brenda Stoltzfus

THE NEW PRESS,
NEW YORK

Published in the United States by The New Press, New York
Distributed by W.W. Norton & Company, Inc.
500 Fifth Avenue, New York, NY 10110

Library of Congress Cataloging-in-Publication Data

Sturdevant, Saundra Pollock.
    Let the good times roll : prostitution and the U.S. military in
Asia / Saundra Pollock Sturdevant, Brenda Stoltzfus.
       p.   cm.
    Includes bibliographical references.
    ISBN 1-56584-025-9 (cloth).—ISBN 1-56584-049-6 (pbk.)
     1. Prostitution—Asia.   2. Sex oriented businesses—Asia.
3. Military bases, American—Asia.   I. Stoltzfus, Brenda.
II. Title.
HQ231.85.A5S78   1993
306.74′2′095—dc20
                                               92-53736
                                                   CIP

1st Edition
Book design by Bethany Johns Design

Established in 1990 as a major alternative to the large, commercial
publishing houses, The New Press is intended to be the first full-
scale nonprofit American book publisher outside of the university
presses. The Press is operated editorially in the public interest,
rather than for private gain; it is committed to publishing in
innovative ways works of educational, cultural, and community
value, which despite their intellectual merits might not normally be
"commercially viable."

CONTENTS

DEDICATION

To the women who have worked in the clubs, who are working in the clubs, and who will work in the clubs.

To Adul de Leon who, as one of the leaders of Gabriela (a national coalition of women's organizations), was deeply committed to organizing and empowering the women selling their sexual labor all over the Philippines. The work on this book was informed by her presence as a friend and colleague. From the beginning, Adul was part of the search, both internal and external, to discover how to organize and empower prostituted women. Adul died of cervical cancer in the Philippines on March 17, 1991. We miss her very much.

PREFACE

This book grows out of the work of Brenda Stoltzfus and Saundra Sturdevant during the mid to late 1980s. Brenda spent five years in the Philippines as a member of the Mennonite Central Committee (MCC). Charged with assessing the possibilities of working with the women who work in the bars next to Subic Naval Base, Brenda did intensive work in Tagalog in Manila and then moved to Olongapo. There she frequented the bars, getting to know the women who worked there.

Two years later, Buklod, a drop-in center for women who work in the bars, was founded. Buklod, which means "bonding" in Tagalog, is a joint project of Gabriela, a national coalition of women's organizations in the Philippines, and the National Council of Churches in the Philippines. It now has a staff of seven Filipinas, four of whom are originally from the bars, and has added a night-care center.

Saundra Sturdevant began her professional life with a Ph.D. in Modern Chinese History from the University of Chicago. She began to photograph professionally in the early 1980s when she lived in Beijing and worked for the Foreign Languages Press. Since that time she has continued to photograph in China and other East and Southeast Asian countries, and in Central America. From 1986 to 1988, she was the Quaker International Representative for East Asia, an American Friends Service Committee (AFSC) position in Hong Kong during these years. One of the main issues that she focused on during that time was women's labor and, as it developed, the selling of sexual labor outside U.S. military bases in the region.

In July 1988, Saundra was able to hold a conference in Naha, Okinawa, in which two women each from the southern part of Korea, Okinawa, Japan, the Philippines, and the West Coast of the United States participated. The conference focused on the sale of women's sexual labor outside U.S. military bases in the region, and it was at this conference that Brenda and Saundra first met. This collaborative effort followed.

Saundra and Brenda spent March through September 1989 doing the fieldwork for this book. In each country, they lived three to five minutes from the bar area. The accommodations were minimal but adequate. In Olongapo and Tong Du Chun, women working in the bars lived next door and/or in the immediate neighborhood. Shopping for food in the local open markets provided an integration into the community and gave opportunities to initiate conversations. Most of the time was spent observing the activity in the streets and clubs, taking photographs, and relating to the women working in the clubs, the GIs, and sometimes the pimps and bar owners.

The work was made possible through the help of local women's and labor organizations in these three countries. In the Philippines, Buklod Center assisted the work in Olongapo, with Brenda interviewing women. Several of those women assisted

Saundra in gaining access to the clubs for photographing and by agreeing to be photographed in their homes.

One woman, Lita, whom Brenda had known since she first started working in the bars at age fourteen, took Brenda and Saundra to her home province in Samar to photograph and collect data. Brenda interviewed this woman and her mother. Another woman, Madelin, took them to her house in a resettlement area outside Manila called Sapang-Palay, where an entire squatter community in Manila had been moved during Ferdinand Marcos's time.

In Korea, My Sister's Place, a center that works primarily with Korean women who are married to GIs, supported by them, or working in clubs servicing GIs, assisted the work. Staff from My Sister's Place made introductions to women willing to tell their stories, interviewed these women in Korean in consultation with Brenda, and provided some initial translation. Because the center is not in the bar area of Tong Du Chun, Saundra made her own contacts for photographing by spending time in the bar area. She was able to gain access to some clubs and women's rooms in addition to photographing on the streets.

In Seoul, with the help of local labor organizations, it was possible to visit and take photographs in small garment factories similar to those where some of the women had worked before going to the clubs. Also, with the help of rural grass-roots organizations, it was possible to visit and photograph in a farming area similar to those where the club women had come from.

Work on Okinawa was exceedingly difficult. There is no women's center on Okinawa. Brenda and Saundra made all their own contacts in the Kin bar area next to Camp Hansen, a Marine base. Photography was very difficult due to the involvement of the *Yakuza* (the Japanese Mafia) in the sale of sexual labor.

In every club there was a large sign saying "Photographing is prohibited." If anyone tried to take pictures, the response was direct and immediate: all the lights would be turned on and male Okinawan muscle would surround the offending party. If the issue could be settled quickly, no problem. If not, the offending party would be pushed out the door onto the street. The bar owners and managers sought to prevent either U.S. Military Police or Okinawan police from entering the bars. They were quite successful.

Then there was the fact that since very few women Marines were stationed at Camp Hansen, Saundra and Brenda did not blend into the mass of people in the bar areas. In a number of clubs, the Filipinas were told not to talk with either of them. In other clubs, when they entered, the ago-go dancers were told to put on the bottoms and tops of their bathing-suit costumes.

In short, it was almost impossible to take photographs inside the clubs, and using a camera on the streets had to be done with some care as well. By speaking Chinese, Saundra was able to take photographs inside one club owned by an Okinawan woman who had lived in Taiwan. This hard-rock bar did not employ Filipinas—undoubtedly a factor in the owner's decision.

Brenda was able to make contact with the Filipinas working there through her Tagalog. Because the bar owners quickly became suspicious, Brenda spent time during the afternoons in a tailor shop in the bar area where many of the Filipinas went to chat before going to work. After having built relationships with some of the women, she was able to explain the project and several agreed to be interviewed.

Although there was no direct aid for the work on Okinawa, strong support from individuals in the women's movement and the community was critical. Their friendship, suggestions of how to proceed, invitations to dinner, and sharing of their lives sustained us in many, many ways. These networks also enabled Saundra and Brenda to obtain the use of a house in Kin belonging to a hundred-year-old Okinawan woman.

The women who were interviewed and photographed were told how the material would be used and they gave their permission. Most chose to speak openly, but a few chose to hide their identities by changing their names and not being photographed. In one case—that of a traditional abortion technique done through massage in which the fetus is effectively torn from the lining of the uterus and the woman expels it through hemorrhage—the *hilot* (a traditional woman healer) performing the abortion and the woman undergoing the procedure requested only that their faces not be photographed. That was complied with.

A Euro-American woman photographing on the streets and in the bars with one or two cameras hanging around her neck stood out. This was obviously the case at night with a strobe unit going off and was heightened by the fact that Saundra appeared again and again with her camera. However, the atmosphere on the streets and in the bars was one of partying, with a number of bar owners or managers giving permission to photograph. The few requests not to take pictures were immediately complied with.

In each country, Brenda used a tape recorder to conduct the interviews. In the case of the Philippine and Okinawan stories, Brenda did the interviewing in Tagalog. Because the voice of the interviewer would not be heard in the final version, if questions were asked in the process of the interview, the interviewee was requested to reiterate the question in her response. Following the initial interview, Brenda transcribed and discussed the transcript with the interviewee. If necessary, corrections and additions were made.

In keeping with the goal of providing a venue for the women to speak about their lives, it was important to minimize the role of the interviewer. The approach varied with each woman. In some cases Brenda began the interview by asking the woman to tell her story and did not pose another question until the very end. Linda, for example, filled up three ninety-minute tapes without Brenda's asking a single question except "Would you like to stop for dinner?" In most cases, once a woman got started, Brenda only needed to listen and occasionally ask questions in the interest of clarity or to encourage expansion of some aspect of the story. At the end of the interview, each woman was asked what she would like to say to the readers of the book. Some women took the opportunity to make a statement; others said it was all there in their stories.

When dealing with matters of content, Brenda attempted to phrase questions in as neutral a way as possible. However, complete neutrality and objectivity are not possible. In the Philippines the fact of the prior relationship between Brenda and the interviewees was a factor, whether large or small, in how the women told their stories. The authors' bias is that this relationship, where trust had been established, has resulted in the women speaking very freely about their lives. In Okinawa, however, the women also spoke with surprising openness. This could be attributed in part to the cathartic effect of telling one's story to someone who speaks your language and is sincerely interested in your life.

Translation of the Philippine and Okinawan stories is fairly direct. Translation always raises the problem of awkwardness versus keeping as close to the meaning in the original language as possible. The authors' bias was toward keeping the original meaning even if the terminology is not necessarily what one would use in English, while also trying to allow the story to flow smoothly. It is important to keep in mind that these are oral herstories that have been transcribed, not written literature.

With the Korean interviews, the translation process was less direct. Staff at My Sister's Place helped with some of the initial translations, perhaps enough to see what direction the interviews were taking. Upon returning to the U.S., Korean colleagues did the full translation of the tapes and Brenda edited.

Editing was done for reasons of length, the flow of the story, and redundancy. Words were not put in any woman's mouth. If something was implied but not said and seemed necessary for a clear understanding, it is bracketed.

In addition to the photographs and interviews, Brenda and Saundra collected data on the economic, political, and social system in the bar areas from observation and conversations with people on the scene, the Social Hygiene Clinics, U.S. military personnel, and the local groups and centers mentioned above. This material provides the basis for the introductions to the bar scene in each country and is a starting point for the final chapter of analysis.

The primary documents in this book are the women's life herstories and the photographs. The introductions are to assist the reader in placing the stories in the larger social, political, and economic context of each country and region. The final chapter begins the process of pulling together threads from the stories and other sources into an interpretive analysis, but it is not a comprehensive academic analysis— deliberately not so. To provide a comprehensive and structured analysis would be to take away from the voices of the women and, in fact, to perpetuate the kind of domination already endured by them from various quarters. Such theorizing and analyzing would best be done by the women, themselves, who sell their sexual labor. We look forward to that day.

Brenda and Saundra would like to give special thanks and acknowledgment to family and friends who gave the support and assistance necessary to complete this work. Special thanks to: Yu Bok Nim and Faye Moon of My Sister's Place; Suzuyo Takazato; Bill and Maxine Randall; Miyagi Harumi; Shigemi and Miyoko Kamiyama; Alma Bulawan, Linda Cunanan, Emma Catuyong, Elsa Ruiz, Fely Gloria, Perla Escanuela, Lily Morada, and Mahlou Bautista of Buklod Center; Rattlesnake Productions; Lois Miller and Freeman Miller; Priscilla Stuckey and Dennis Kauffman; Deward Hastings; Morrie Camhi. Special thanks also goes to the staff at The New Press, especially to our editor David Sternbach and to Kim Waymer in production for their respect and the sensitivity with which they handled this work. Thanks also to Bethany Johns Design for their work on the book.

Funding for this project was received from: The L. J. Skaggs and Mary C. Skaggs Foundation, The United Church of Canada, The United Methodist Church Global Ministries, Berkeley City Arts Fund, Mennonite Central Committee, and donations from friends.

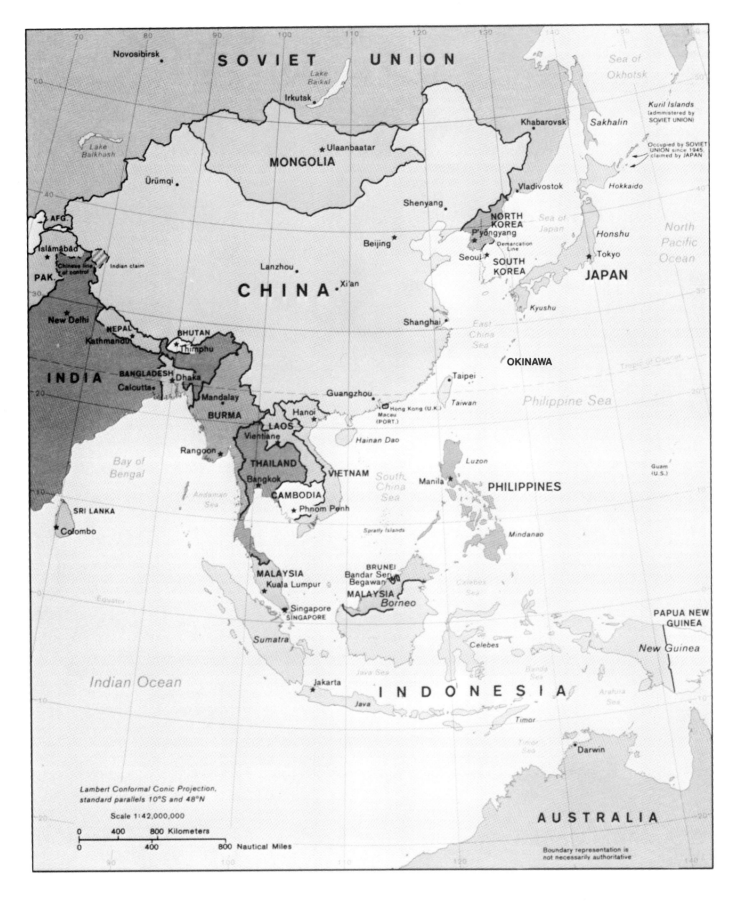

FROM AMERICAN LAKE TO A PEOPLE'S PACIFIC

Walden Bello

Pacific Command

Perhaps the best way to comprehend the U.S. presence in the Pacific is to describe it as a transnational garrison state that spans five sovereign states and the vast expanse of Micronesia. The U.S. Pacific Command is an integrated and extremely secretive complex composed of mobile forces and fixed bases over which the host states in the western, central, and south Pacific exercise merely nominal sovereignty.

This complex is massive: 330,000 servicemen and women, half of them deployed in the western Pacific; about 300 bases and facilities; half of the U.S. Navy's ship strength; two-thirds of the U.S. Marine Corps; two Army divisions, one of them forward deployed in South Korea; and several fighter wings of the U.S. Air Force.

But in conveying the imperial reach of the U.S. presence, numbers cannot match Admiral George Steele's Kiplingesque description of a typical day in the life of the Seventh Fleet, the prime instrument of American power:

On a given day in the Seventh Fleet, one can find several ships well east of Japan entering or leaving the Seventh Fleet area of responsibility. An anti-submarine warfare exercise is in progress on Tokyo Bay. An aircraft carrier with her destroyer-screen and a submarine are exercising in the Okinawa operating area, while another carrier task force group is visiting Mombasa, Kenya. An amphibious exercise involving ships and submarines of Ready Group Bravo is in progress on the coast of Korea . . . and ship visits are in progress in Hong Kong; Beppu, Japan; Kaohsiung, Taiwan; Manila; Sattahip, Thailand; Singapore; Penang, Malaysia . . . Patrol planes of Task Force 72 are conducting ocean surveillance in the Indian Ocean in support of the carrier task force group there and range along the Asian mainland at a respectful distance on the lookout for unusual happenings . . .[1]

The northern anchor of this complex is Japan-Korea; the southern anchor is the Philippine base complex; and Micronesia is the great rear area. Traditionally, this Pacific garrison state has been used for power projection into Northeast Asia, the Chinese heartland, and Southeast Asia. More recently, it has also served to project U.S. power to the Persian Gulf and Indian Ocean.

Japan is, to use Joseph Gerson's description, the "keystone" of the U.S. military structure, its contributions consisting not only of numerous bases and facilities but also of its military, which is supported by the third-largest military budget in the world; its pro-U.S. political leadership, which has so far obediently subordinated its foreign policy to U.S. strategy; and its industry, which now provides the Pentagon with critical high-tech components such as advanced microchips for weapons systems.[2]

The U.S. military contingent in South Korea is the only U.S. military presence on the Asian mainland. Although Washington has pronounced the traditional policy of containing the Soviet Union and China no longer operative, there are no plans to withdraw the 40,000 U.S. troops, with their on-site nuclear firepower. Currently, their task is to impose the forty-four-year-old division of the Korean nation and make it difficult to achieve reunification except under terms favorable to South Korea and the United States.

The Philippine installations, Subic Naval Base and Clark Air Force Base, are probably the U.S.'s most valuable from a strategic standpoint, being centrally located to project power to Northeast Asia, the Chinese and Indochinese mainland (their central function in the 1950s and 1960s), and the Indian Ocean and Persian Gulf (their main role from the 1970s onward). The furious eruption of Mount Pinatubo, which lies less than ten miles from Clark, forced the U.S. to give up the air base; it appears, however, that Washington is negotiating an agreement with the Philippines for continued use of the Subic facilities, which it has long considered indispensable for the projection of America's naval power to the Indian Ocean.

Micronesia in the central Pacific serves as a rear zone supporting the forward U.S. military presence in the western Pacific; a fallback area in the event of a withdrawal of U.S. forces in the Philippines; and an experimental site for the development of missile systems. At least sixty-six nuclear devices were exploded on the Marshall Islands from the late 1940s to the early 1960s, making nomads out of islanders who had to be relocated and subjecting many others to radioactive fallout.[3]

Aside from being employed for power projection to the Asian mainland and Indian Ocean, the bases have served as springboards for U.S. intervention in the internal affairs of their host countries. For instance, Clark and Subic have provided both overt and covert support for government troops conducting operations against insurgent forces in the Philippines. The most publicized example of U.S. intervention in Philippine affairs from the bases occurred in December 1989, when Phantom jet fighters from Clark flew "intimidation missions" against rebel troops seeking to overthrow the government of President Corazon Aquino. In the southern part of Korea, the infamous Kwangju Massacre in May 1980 was perpetrated by South Korean troops who were "released" at a critical time by the U.S. commander of the U.S.-Republic of Korea Combined Command.[4]

The transnational garrison state has spawned a subeconomy and subculture that has had distorting effects on the larger economy and culture of the host societies. Much of the estimated $500 million pumped into the Philippines by the U.S. bases, for instance, has spawned a subeconomy whose main components are the purchase of sexual labor, entertainment, smuggling of arms, drugs, and extortion. Contrary to the Pentagon's propaganda of the "beneficial" economic impact of the bases, these are hardly the pillars on which one might build a healthy economy. In the southern part of Korea, Okinawa, the Philippines, and Thailand, the degradation of women forced into sexual labor is institutionalized in a multimillion-dollar entertainment industry that enjoys the blessing of the U.S. military hierarchy, which considers sexual recreation vital for the "morale" of troops.

The conversion of Micronesia into a closed "strategic colony" of the U.S. destroyed the once-thriving economy of the islands and converted them into welfare states living almost entirely on government appropriations from Washington. Washington's subsidies spawned a massive colonial bureaucracy that, in some islands, includes half of the adult population. It is not surprising that, with extreme economic dependence on the U.S., the central Pacific territories have opted for a continuing colonial link with the U.S. in the form of a "Compact of Free Association." It is also not surprising that, cut off from their traditions and bereft of a productive relationship to their lands and waters, teenagers throughout Micronesia have turned to suicide in alarming numbers.

In Search of Enemies

For over forty years, the U.S.'s forward military strategy was legitimized by the ideology and strategy of "containing Soviet-inspired communism." Containment gave the U.S. military and alliance strategy a coherence and legitimacy that withstood both the Sino-Soviet split as well as the U.S. defeat in Vietnam. But ever since Mikhail Gorbachev took the Soviet Pacific Fleet off Washington's enemies' list, Pacific Command has been a garrison without a clear mission. Confronted by increasing popular clamor at home to match base closings and troop reductions in Europe and the U.S. with similar cuts in the Pacific, Defense Secretary Richard Cheney announced in 1990 a 10 percent reduction in U.S. forces in the western Pacific. But more military energy has gone into the task of looking for new, credible foes than to formulating plans for a substantive reduction of forces.

In line with the strategic perspective laid down by *Discriminate Deterrence*, the 1988 document produced by the Presidential Commission on Long-Term Integrated Strategy, Pacific Command has tried to reorient the U.S. posture from the Soviet threat to the so-called "terrorist threat" from the Third World.

President Kim Il-Sung, of course, has "most-favored-enemy" status in the eyes of the U.S. military. As Admiral Charles Larson, commander-in-chief of Pacific Command, recently claimed in testimony before the U.S. Congress, "North Korea poses the greatest immediate threat to regional stability."[5] The recent controversy over North Korea's nuclear reactor at Yeongbeon stems less from genuine concern over North Korea's ability to manufacture a nuclear bomb than from the U.S. search for a credible regional threat.

But the search for a substitute enemy does not end with Kim. Indeed, it would be hard to sell the view that the main purpose of the massive American presence is to deter the non-nuclear army of an isolated country whose main allies, China and the Soviet Union, have thrown in their lot with South Korea and the U.S.

There are other active candidates. In arguing for the maintenance of U.S. bases in the Philippines, for instance, some defense analysts claim that these outposts would be necessary to check the future ambitions of China and Indonesia. "Indian expansionism" has also been mentioned as a threat not only to South Asia but also to Southeast Asia. Indeed, General Dynamics—one of the Pentagon's top contractors—singled out India as one of the key targets for the next generation of cruise missiles. In a fifty-two-page briefing paper, the company "outlined a scenario for the year 2000 in which India and Pakistan are spoiling for a war over Kashmir. The U.S. would intervene to prevent an Indian nuclear strike against Pakistan and use 307 cruise missiles to neutralize targets in India."[6]

But for an increasing number of Pacific Command's top officers, the threat does not come from the Third World but from Japan. In an interview that official Washington criticized as "indiscreet," Major General Henry Stackpole, commander of Marine forces in Japan, told the *Washington Post* that the objective of the U.S. military presence in that country was to prevent Tokyo from beefing up "what is already a very, very potent military." Already, he claimed, the Japanese had "achieved the Great Asia Co-Prosperity Sphere economically, without guns." Thus, "No one wants a rearmed, resurgent Japan. So we are the cap in the bottle, if you will."[7]

Stackpole's comments did not so much reflect an opportunistic search for a suitable enemy as manifest a profound psychological unease over the reality that the massive American military presence has, in fact, provided a protective umbrella for the rapid integration of the Asia-Pacific region around the economic needs of Japan.

Japan's Economic Hegemony

The Asia-Pacific region is unique in the sense that whereas the U.S. dominates it militarily, Japan has mastered it economically.

Japan is now the region's most important trading partner. Although the U.S. remains the number-one market for most economies in the region, Japan is pushing hard as an import absorber and should outstrip the U.S. within the next few years. In 1989, it took in $70.3 billion of the region's imports, compared to the $101.3 billion absorbed by the U.S. On the other hand, Japan's exports to the region came to $92.4 billion, whereas the U.S. exported only $67.9 billion.[8]

Japan is now the most dynamic investor in the area, accounting for $41.5 billion in direct investments as of 1989, in contrast to the U.S. figure of $32 billion. Half of the Japanese total poured in between 1985 and 1989, reflecting the appreciation of the yen and the consequent search for cheap labor among Japan's conglomerates.

Although U.S. capital remains important in the area, many businesses, cowed by the Japanese competition, have practically ceded the area as a Japanese economic sphere of influence.

Japan is now the area's main source of technology, particularly high technology. In 1987, the value of Japan's exports of high tech to the East Asian and Southeast Asian economies was twice that of the United States.[9]

Japan is the principal bilateral aid donor to the region, providing $4 billion a year, or more than twice the U.S. level. The bulk of Japan's loan and grant program is, in fact, targeted at the Asia-Pacific region, for according to K. Matsuura, director general of the Foreign Ministry's Economic Bureau, "[W]e shouldn't simply throw away money in random directions. Aid must be steered to places where it will bring long-term benefits back to its donor."[10]

It is not only Japan's regional economic domination but also its global reach that creates concern in the United States. However, given its tight integration with Japan, it is the Asia-Pacific region that could trigger a significant expansion of the Japanese military, in the event that regional instability coincides with worsening relations between Japan and the United States.

Although the current policy of the Liberal Democratic party mainstream that dominates Japanese politics is faithfully to uphold the U.S.-Japan alliance, in which the Japanese more or less dutifully subordinate their foreign policy in return for U.S. military protection, there is an increasingly powerful right-wing nationalist lobby for independent remilitarization.

Shintaro Ishihara (*The Japan That Can Say No*), who favors scrapping the U.S.-Japan Security Treaty, speaks for an increasingly influential current within the Liberal Democratic party. Also plugging for a more independent path and an expansion of Japan's military might are the Japan Defense Agency (JDA), the powerful armaments industry created by the JDA's "Buy Japan" policy, and the top brass of the Japan Self-Defense Forces. Reflecting the feelings of the generals is General Hiroomi Kurisu, former chairman of the joint chiefs of staff, who wants a bigger military because "Japan needs the power to protect Japanese interests in [its neighboring] countries."[11]

Japan's military potential is, indeed, great. It now has the third largest navy in the world; as a matter of fact, its surface fleet is larger than the U.S. naval contingent in the western Pacific.[12] Its defense budget is already the world's third largest, yet it spends only slightly over 1 percent of its GNP on defense—in contrast to the U.S. figure of 5.8 percent. If Japan were to spend more for its military and devoted, say, even just another 1 percent of its $2.3 trillion GNP to defense spending, the result would be rearmament—and regional destabilization—on a massive scale.

Moreover, Japan's superiority in the cutting-edge high technologies like semiconductors, electrooptics, high-performance computing, digital imaging, and superconductors can enable it to achieve a breakthrough to high-technology weaponry that would allow it to leap over the nuclear stage.[13] But even without a "technological leapfrog," says one analyst, Japan would have some rather significant advantages in an era of three-way (U.S.-Soviet Union-Japan) military parity:

First of all, the Japanese might be able to use their advantage in production technology to produce weapons more quickly and cheaply than their rivals. They might be able to use flexible production systems to bring the low-cost advantages of mass production to the specialized production of advanced military systems. Furthermore, Japan's reliability advantage could prove to haunt both its economic competitors and its military enemies. While U.S. weapons systems incorporating all the latest electronic equipment continued to malfunction, the Japanese might achieve decisive superiority with slightly less sophisticated but more reliable systems. If Japan could produce the 100 percent reliable system, would the United States and the Soviet Union be able to keep up?[14]

The more the Japanese see themselves being pushed around by Washington to achieve the latter's strategic priorities, as was the case in the Persian Gulf War, and the more Americans blame Japan for the U.S.'s economic ills, the more attractive the path of an independent security policy will appear to increasing numbers of Japanese. Indeed, survey findings showing that most Americans now rate Japan as the most serious threat to the well-being of the U.S. are matched by poll results showing that more Japanese teenagers see the U.S. rather than the Soviet Union as their most likely enemy in a future war.[15] It is a sign of the times that one of the most popular comic strips in Japan today is the saga of a Japanese nuclear submarine that defies the U.S. Pacific Naval Command and declares a "war for Japan's true independence."[16]

One cannot, in fact, assume that the still-dominant antiwar sentiments among the Japanese will be permanent, or that they will be strong enough to resist the drive of the independent militarization lobby.

An Alternative Security System

The unraveling partnership between Japan and the U.S. presents the Asia-Pacific region with perils as well as possibilities. The deepening rift creates the risk of a new, extremely destabilizing arms race—if not a "long, miserable Cold War," to cite one projection.[17] But, combined with the regional ferment and flux triggered by the end of the Cold War, the increasingly divergent thrusts of the two countries also present the opportunity for peoples of the region to take advantage of it to carve out more autonomy, more space for the realization of a regional future that is radically different from the projects of both the U.S. and Japan.

The creation of an alternative security framework to replace the now-obsolete containment paradigm must build on significant past success at a subregional level. The Reagan administration's military buildup in the early and mid eighties provided the impetus for the emergence of antinuclear and antimilitary movements throughout the Asia-Pacific region. The movement, which was loosely called the Nuclear-

Free and Independent Pacific Movement (NFIP), registered significant victories, including New Zealand's banning of visits by nuclear-armed and nuclear-powered warships; the virtual disintegration of ANZUS (Australia-New Zealand-U.S.) alliance; the creation of the South Pacific Free Zone by eleven South Pacific states; the upholding of their nuclear-free constitution by the people of Palau, despite strong U.S. pressure on them to scrap it; and the emergence of a strong antibases movement in the Philippines, which also has a nuclear-free constitution.

Three features of the Pacific antinuclear movement stand out: first, the solid intertwining of principles of demilitarization, denuclearization, and nonintervention; second, vigorous trans-border alliances among third world peace movements; and between first world movements (Japan, U.S., Australia, New Zealand) and third world movements (Philippines, South Korea, Micronesia, South Pacific); and third, successful tactical alliances being forged between popular movements and governments (the NFIP movement and the governments of Vanuata and New Zealand). Indeed, so legitimate and popular is the concept of a demilitarized region that some governments have rhetorically espoused it, even without significant popular pressure: the conservative governments of Malaysia and Indonesia, for example, have urged the Association of Southeast Asian Nations (ASEAN) to become a nuclear-free zone.

The time is ripe to channel subregional energies into the drive to create a regional denuclearized and demilitarized zone. The principle mechanism to achieve this end would be a multilateral treaty for demilitarization and denuclearization that would involve as signatories the U.S., Japan, member states of the former Soviet Union, China, and all other Asia-Pacific countries. This treaty would institute, among other things, a ban on nuclear testing in the Pacific; a prohibition of the storage and movement of nuclear arms in the region; a ban on chemical and biological weapons; withdrawal of foreign bases from the western Pacific; the pullout of U.S. troops from the Korean peninsula; significant cuts in standing armies, air forces, and navies; deep reductions in naval deployments; a ban on research and development of high-tech weaponry; and tight limits on the transfer of conventional arms via sales or aid.

The fundamental aim of an alternative security framework would be to move regional conflicts from resolution by force and intervention to resolution by diplomacy. Thus, accompanying the sanctions must be diplomatic mechanisms for the resolution not only of superpower disputes but also regional conflicts like the Cambodian civil war and the dangerous disputes over the Spratly islands in the South China Sea.

Drawing on their earlier experiences of forging tactical alliances with selected governments at the subregional level, nongovernmental and people's organizations and movements would need to craft a successful strategy of winning over Asia-Pacific governments and isolating the U.S., which, being the only true pan-regional military power at this point, would be the state most negatively affected by a denuclearization agreement (though China and the former Soviet Union might also prove recalcitrant). Endorsement of the effort by the Southeast Asian governments, coordinated with a regional mass campaign against Japanese remilitarization and pressure from the Japanese peace forces, would contribute to neutralization opposition from the Japanese government, whose Self-Defense Forces still have a major problem with internal and external legitimacy.

The next few years will be a period of flux in the relations among nations in the Asia-Pacific region. The year 2000 may see either a new era of balance-of-power politics characterized by increasing tension between the U.S. and Japan or a qualitatively new Pacific that is denuclearized and significantly demilitarized, as well as more independent. The outcome will depend greatly on the courage and willingness of progressive forces in the region to use that rare window of opportunity for change offered by the end of containment.

1. Admiral George Steele, "The Seventh Fleet," *Proceedings of the U.S. Naval Institute*, January 1976, 30.

2. See Joseph Gerson, "Japan: Keystone of the Pacific," in *The Sun Never Sets*, eds. Joseph Gerson and Bruce Birchard (Boston: South End Press, 1991), 167–96.

3. See Glenn Alcalay, "U.S. Nuclear Imperialism in Micronesia," in *On the Brink: Nuclear Proliferation and the Third World*, eds. Peter Worsley and Kofi Buenor Jadjor (London: Third World Communications, 1987).

4. Many people consider the Kwangju Uprising the spark of the modern Korean democratic movement. It is estimated that two thousand Koreans were killed by elite troops of the Republic of Korea army under the control of the U.S. command.

5. Admiral Charles Larson, Statement before U.S. Senate Armed Services Committee, Washington, D.C., 13 March 1991, 5.

6. Seema Sirohi, "U.S. Arms Makers' Post–Cold War Scenarios," *Pacific News Service*, 15–19 April 1991.

7. *Washington Post*, 27 March 1990.

8. Richard Cronin, *Japan's Expanding Role and Influence in the Asia-Pacific Region: Implications for U.S. Interests and Policy* (Washington, D.C.: Congressional Research Service, 7 September 1990), 75–76.

9. Ibid., 9.

10. K. Matsuura, "Administering Foreign Aid: The View from the Top," *Economic Eye* (Spring 1989), 12–13.

11. Quoted in "Beneath Talk of a New Partnership with U.S., Serious Tensions Grow," *Los Angeles Times*, 11 December 1990, H3.

12. Ibid.

13. Steven Vogel, *Japanese High Technology, Politics, and Power* (Berkeley: Berkeley Roundtable on the International Economy, March 1989), 98–99.

14. Ibid.

15. "Beneath Talk of a New Partnership . . .," *Los Angeles Times*, 11 December 1990, H3.

16. Ibid.

17. George Friedman and Meredith Lebard, *The Coming War with Japan* (New York: St. Martin's Press, 1991), 403.

Walden Bello is executive director of the Institute for Food and Development Policy and coauthor with Peter Hayes and Lyuba Zarsky, of *American Lake: Nuclear Peril in the Pacific* (London: Penguin, 1987).

IT TAKES TWO

Cynthia Enloe

"Since U.S. occupation troops in Japan are unalterably determined to fraternize, the military authorities began helping them out last week by issuing a phrase book. Sample utility phrases: 'You're very pretty' . . . 'How about a date?' . . . 'Where will I meet you?' And since the sweet sorrow of parting always comes, the book lists no less than 14 ways to say goodbye.''—Time, 15 July 1946[1]

On a recent visit to London, I persuaded a friend to play hooky from work to go with me to Britain's famous Imperial War Museum. Actually, I was quite embarrassed. In all my trips to London, I had never gone to the Imperial War Museum. Now, in the wake of the Gulf War, the time seemed ripe. Maybe the museum would help me put this most recent military conflict in perspective, see its continuities with other wars, clarify its special human, doctrinal, and technological features. I was in for a disappointment.

It was only the British experiences of the "great" wars that were deemed worthy of display. Malaya, Aden, Kenya, the Falklands—those British twentieth-century war sites didn't rate display cases. In fact, Asia, Africa, and the Caribbean didn't seem much on the curators' minds at all. There were two formal portraits of Indian soldiers who had won military honors for their deeds, but there were no displays to make visible to today's visitors how much the British military had relied on men and women from its colonies to fight both world wars. I made a vow to go to the Gurkha Museum on my next trip. The only civilians who received much attention in the Imperial War Museum were British. Most celebrated were the "plucky" Cockney Londoners who coped with the German blitz by singing in the Underground. Women were allocated one glass case showing posters calling on housewives to practice domestic frugality for the cause. There was no evidence of the political furor set off when white British women began to date—and have children with—black American GIs.

Still my friend's and my disappointment with the museum's portrayal of Britain's wars did serve to make us wonder what a realistic curatorial approach would be. What would we put on display besides front-line trenches (at least they showed the rats), Cockney blitz-coping lyrics, and unannotated portraits of Sikh heroes?

Brothels. In my war museum there would be the reconstruction of a military brothel. It would show rooms for officers and rooms for rank-and-file soldiers. It would display separate doors for white soldiers and black soldiers. A manikin of the owner of the business (it might be a disco rather than a formal brothel) would be sitting watchfully in the corner—it might be a man or a woman, she or he might be a local citizen or a foreigner. The women might be white European, Berber, Namibian, or Puerto Rican; they might be Korean, Filipina, Japanese, Vietnamese, African-American, or Indian. Depending on the era and locale, they might be dressed in sarongs or miniskirts topped with T-shirts memorializing resort beaches, soft drinks, and aircraft carriers.

In this realistic war museum, visitors would be invited to press a button to hear the voices of the women chart the routes by which they came to work in this brothel or disco and describe the children, siblings, and parents whom they were trying to support with their earnings. Several of the women might compare the sexual behavior and outlooks of these foreign men with those of the local men with whom they had been involved. Some of the women probably would add their own analyses of how the British, American, French, or United Nations troops came to be in their countries.

Museum goers could step over to a neighboring tape recorder to hear the voices of soldiers who have patronized brothels and discos while on duty abroad. The men might describe how they imagined these women as being different or similar to women from their own countries. The more brazen might flaunt their sexual prowess. Some of the soldiers, however, probably would talk about their feelings of loneliness abroad, their sense of what it means to be a man when you're a soldier, the possible anxieties about meeting the expectations of one's officers and buddies as far as sexual performance is concerned.

War—and militarized peace—are times when sexual relations take on particular meanings. A museum curator—or journalist, novelist, or political commentator—who edits out sexuality, who leaves it "on the cutting-room floor," gives the audience a skewed and ultimately unhelpful account of just what kinds of myths, anxieties, and inequalities are involved fighting a war or sustaining a militarized form of peace.

It is for this reason that the oral histories and photographs contained here are so vital. They help us to make sense of the dependence of the military on particular presumptions about masculinity in order to sustain soldiers' morale and discipline. Without a sexualized "rest and recreation" (R & R) period, would the U.S. military command be able to send young men off on long, often tedious sea voyages and ground maneuvers? Without myths of Asian women's compliant sexuality would many American men be able to sustain their own identities of themselves as manly enough to act as soldiers? Women who have come to work as prostitutes around American bases in Asia tell us how a militarized masculinity is constructed and re-constructed in smoky bars and in sparsely furnished boardinghouses. If we look only at boot camps and the battlefield—the focus of most investigations into the formation of militarized masculinity—we will not be able adequately to explain just how masculinity is created and sustained in the peculiar ways necessary to sustain a military organization.

The women who have been generous enough to tell their stories here reveal how sexuality is as central to the complex web of relationships between civil and military cultures as the more talked about security doctrines and economic quid pro quos. Women also remind us of how difficult it is sometimes to map the boundaries between sexual relations and economics. This doesn't mean that all sexual relations, even those commercialized by a prostitution industry next to a military base, can be reduced simply to economics. The women who tell their stories to Saundra Sturdevant and Brenda Stoltzfus are less concerned with parsing analytical categories than with giving us an authentic account of the pressures, hopes, fears, and shortages that they must juggle every day in order to ensure their physical safety, hold on to some shred of self-respect, and make ends meet for themselves and their children.

These stories also underscore something that is consistently overlooked in discussions of the impact of military bases on local communities: the fact that local women working in brothels and discos mediate between two sets of men, foreign soldiers and local men. These two are rarely talked about simultaneously, but the women who have taken part in this project know that they must be. These women detail how their relationships with local male lovers and husbands created the conditions that make them vulnerable to the appeals of the labor-needy disco owners. Unfaithfulness, violent tempers, misuse of already low earnings, neglectful fathering—any combination of these forms of behavior by the local men with whom they were involved became the major launching pad for work as a prostitute. This means, too, that children have to be talked about. Most of the women who speak here have children—some fathered by local men, others by foreign soldiers. Prostitution and fathering: the two are intimately connected in these women's lives.

This is not, of course, to argue that local men are the root of the commercialized and militarized sex that has become so rife in countries allied to the United States. Without local governments willing to pay the price for the lucrative R & R business, without the U.S. military's strategies for keeping male soldiers content, without local and foreign business entrepreneurs willing to make their profits from the sexuality of poor women—without each of these conditions, even an abusive, economically irresponsible husband would not drive his wife into work as an Olongapo bar woman. Nonetheless, local men must be inserted into the political equation; the women here make that clear. In fact, we need to widen our lens considerably to fully understand militarized prostitution. Here is a list—probably an incomplete one—of the men whose actions may contribute to the construction and maintenance of prostitution around any government's military base:

husbands and lovers
bar owners, local and foreign
local public-health officials
local government zoning-board members
local police officials
local mayors
national treasury or finance-ministry officials
national-defense officials
male soldiers in the national forces
local male prostitution customers
foreign male soldier-customers
foreign male soldiers' buddies
foreign base commanders
foreign military medical officers
foreign national-defense planners
foreign national legislators

Among these different men there may be diverse masculinities. Women in Okinawa, Korea, and the Philippines describe how they had to learn what made American men feel that they were manly during sex; it was not always what they had learned made their Korean, Japanese, or Filipino sexual partners feel manly. Sexual practice is one of the sites of masculinity's—and femininity's—daily construction, but that construction is international. Tourists, colonial officials, international technocrats and businessmen, and soldiers have long been the internationalizers of sexualized masculinity. Yet the entire R & R policy and its dependent industry only work if thousands of Asian women are willing and able to learn what American military men rely on to bolster their sense of masculinity: bar owners, military commanders, and local finance-ministry bureaucrats depend on Asian women to be alert to the differences among masculinities.

Each of these groups of men, therefore, is connected to one another by the women working in the base-town bars. But they also may be connected to one another quite directly. For example, Australian researcher Anne-Marie Cass has found that at least some Filipino male soldiers are adopting what they see to be an American form of militarized masculinity. The men most prone to this practice are those in the Scout Rangers, the elite fighting force of the Philippine Constabulary. They act as though the American film character Rambo epitomizes the sort of attributes that make for an effective combat soldier: "a soldier in khaki or camouflage, sunglasses or headbands, open shirt, bare head, and well armed, lounging in a roofless jeep travelling down a Davao City street, gun held casually, barrel waving in the air."[2] One consequence of this form of borrowed, intimidating masculinity, according to Cass, was that local prostitutes servicing Filipino soldiers performed sexual acts with customers that they otherwise would have refused to engage in.

A woman who goes to work in a foreign military brothel or disco finds herself negotiating among all these mainly male actors. She has direct contact, however, with only some of them. She never hears what advice the foreign base commander passes on to his troops regarding the alleged unhealthiness or deviousness of local women. She never hears what financial arrangements have been made between local and foreign medical officials to guarantee the well-being of her soldier-customers. She rarely learns what a soldier who wants to marry her and support her children is told by his military chaplain or superior officer. She does not have access to the discussions among foreign legislators when they decide not to hold hearings on their government's military prostitution policies. Consequently, she makes her assessments using what information she has.

Much of it comes from the women with whom she works. As these interviews reveal, the relationships among women working in the bars are not always supportive or sisterly. The environment does not encourage solidarity. There has been collective action—for example, protests among bar workers in Olongapo against being forced to engage in boxing matches for the entertainment of male customers. But, despite growing efforts by local feminists to provide spaces for such solidarity, collective action remains the exception. Most women rely on a small circle of friends to accumulate the information necessary to walk the mine field laid by the intricate relationships among the several groups of men who define the military prostitution industry. They teach one another how to fake orgasms, how to persuade men to use condoms, how to avoid deductions from their pay, how to meet soldier-customers outside of their employers' supervision, how to remain appealing to paying customers when they are older—their valued status as a virgin, a "cherry girl," long gone.

Readers will be listening to these women tell their stories at a time when the end of the Cold War and the frailty of industrialized economies are combining to pressure governments in North America and Europe to "downsize" their military establishments. The U.S. Department of Defense has announced the closing of military bases at home and abroad. One of the apparent lessons of the Gulf War in the eyes of many American strategists is that the United States now has the administrative capacity rapidly to deploy large numbers of troops overseas without maintaining a costly and often politically risky base in the region. Simultaneously, Mount Pinatubo in the Philippines has spewed its deadly ash so thickly over Clark Air Force Base that even this facility, which until recently the Bush administration had wanted to keep, now appears to be too uneconomical. All this points to a rollback in the numbers and size of American bases overseas. It might be tempting, consequently, to listen to Asian women's stories as if they were tales of a bygone era.

That would, I think, be a mistake. Large bases still exist in Okinawa, southern Korea, and the Philippines. Even with some cutbacks, the number of American men going through those bases on long tours and on shorter-term maneuvers is in the thousands. Governments in Seoul, Tokyo, and Manila have made no moves to cancel the rest-and-recreation agreements that exist with Washington—agreements that spell out the conditions for permitting and controlling the sort of prostitution deemed most useful for the American military. Nor has the no-prostitution formula in Saudi Arabia adopted to fight the Gulf War—a formula imposed on the United States by a Saudi regime nervous about its own Islamic legitimacy—been adopted anywhere else.

Listening to women working as prostitutes is as important as ever. For political analysts, it will provide information for creating a more realistic picture of how fathering, child rearing, man-to-man borrowing, poverty, private enterprise, and sexual practice each play vital roles in the construction of militarized femininity and masculinity. For antibase campaigners, it will shake confidence in relying only on economic approaches to base conversion. Marriage, parenting, and male violence all will have to be accepted as serious items on a political agenda if the women now living on wages from prostitution are to become actors, not mere symbols, in movements to transform foreign military bases into productive civilian institutions. Listening is a political act.

---

1. Quoted by Anne Farrer Scott, "Women and War," *Hungry Mind Review* (Summer 1991): 23.

2. Anne-Marie Cass, "Sexuality, Gender and Violence in the Militarized Society of the Philippines," unpublished paper prepared for the Australian Sociological Association Conference, Brisbane, 12–16 December 1990, 6.

Cynthia Enloe is Professor of Government at Clark University and author of books including, *Does Khaki Become You?* (London: Pandora Press, 1988) and *Bananas, Beaches & Bases: Making Feminist Sense of International Politics* (Berkeley: University of California Press, 1990).

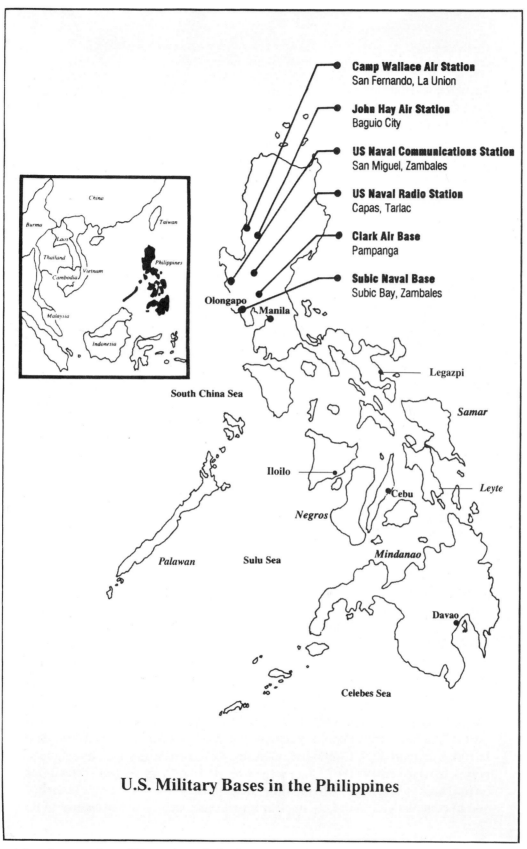

U.S. Military Bases in the Philippines

After the eruption of Pinatubo, all the bases were closed except Subic Naval Base.
The exchange rate in the Philippines in 1989 was $1 = P20.

Subic Naval Base viewed from
Olongapo City Cemetery. Subic is home
port for the U.S. Seventh Fleet. With
three floating dry docks and the best-
trained indigenous labor force in the
region, it is a centerpiece for the U.S.
presence in the Pacific.

The Philippines

GATHERING THE DUST:

THE BASES ISSUE IN THE PHILIPPINES

Aida F. Santos

In a land that straddles an earthquake belt, is smack in the middle of the path of typhoons, and cradles more than a hundred volcanoes, a volcanic eruption should be expected as simply one of those things. Catastrophe, both human-made and otherwise, feeds on the daily life of Filipinos. In fact, we have a cultural idiosyncrasy that baffles the westerner. We laugh at our own miseries; we turn disasters to jokes. So when Mt. Pinatubo started to come alive, and with such fury, after six hundred years of dormancy, Filipinos saw the joke immediately: "What the antibases activists were not able to do in two decades, Mt. Pinatubo did in one day."

What began as a grandiose show of fire and fury turned out to be an awesome series of volcanic eruptions that would affect a significant part of the island of Luzon, including the metro Manila area, and even other nearby Asian neighbors. Thousands of hectares of agricultural land lay in complete devastation, villages buried under tons of lahar or mudflows, thousands of families rendered homeless.

For Filipinos, whose classic repertoire of yuletide songs includes that which speaks of "dreaming of a white Christmas" in a tropical setting, this was an eerie, gray substitute. The green and brown landscape was turned into a glacier of ash and debris. It is a sight that inspires awe, fear, and a sense of hopelessness all at once.

But what makes Mt. Pinatubo politically significant is the fact that it is located between three provinces in Central Luzon—Pampanga, Zambales, and Bataan. In these three areas stand, respectively, three facilities that aptly symbolize the neocolonial power structures in the country: the United States' Clark Air Base, Subic Naval Base, and the mothballed Bataan Nuclear Plant (the last built by Westinghouse). In July 1991, after months of considering the possibility of leaving Clark, the U.S. government officially announced its withdrawal from there, ostensibly due to the extensive damage wrought by the continuing eruptions of Mt. Pinatubo. The other, smaller facilities—Camp John Hay, the Rest and Recreation (R&R) center in the mountain city of Baguio; Wallace Air Station in La Union; Camp O'Donnell in Tarlac; and San Miguel Communications Facility in Zambales—were closed down early in 1991, in accordance with the constitutional mandate that terminated the U.S.–Republic of the Philippines (R.P.) Military Agreement in September 1991.

Prior to Pinatubo, the Philippine government's stand on the annual compensation package for the continuation of the U.S. base facilities, with or without Clark Air Base, was pegged at $825 million annually and not to exceed seven years. Everything changed, the reports have it, when Pinatubo erupted. Manila's ash fall was Washington's silver lining. In plain terms, the U.S. panel argued that since it would need big resources to rehabilitate the areas of Clark and Subic, it could only make a compensation offer from "an economic point of view."

Historical Background

The U.S.-R.P. Military Base Agreement (MBA) technically expired on 16 September 1991. This signals the termination of forty-four years of overt U.S. military presence in the country. Signed in 1947, a year after the U.S. colonial rule officially ended in the archipelago, the MBA has always been regarded as a bugbear of the supposed independent status of the Philippines. It has always been referred to as a case of "special relations" between the two countries.

Foreign military installations in the country have been a continuing factor in the nation's checkered colonial history. Subic Naval Base was originally put up by the Spanish colonial government from 1896 to 1898, then ceded to the U.S. after Spain lost to the new colonial ruler in a mock battle that saved the face of the Spanish colonizers. During the brief but harsh period of Japanese occupation, Subic was operated by the Japanese invaders beginning January 1942, then regained by the Americans in World War II. U.S. Marines who fought in World War II trained at Subic, which was then considered the largest training facility in the world. Located on the South China Sea side of Luzon island, some eighty kilometers west-northwest of Manila, Subic is self-contained and is reputedly one of the best harbors in the world. The base proper and related sites occupy over 24,000 hectares, that is, 13,780 of land and 9,525 of water. Subic is a primary port, providing training and logistics support for the U.S. Seventh Fleet and offering the best ship repair technical facilities and human resources in the Pacific area.

The facility at Clark, originally called Fort Stotsenberg, began as a U.S. Army Cavalry station in the final stages of the Spanish-American War in 1898. Clark eventually covered 63,103 hectares, consisting mainly, before Pinatubo erupted, of arable agricultural land. Clark served as the only tactical operational U.S. Air Force installation in the entire Southeast Asian region, with a full defense capability that accommodated the largest U.S. military transport planes serving the entire Western Pacific. Antibases and antinuclear advocates believe from confidential sources that Clark had 200,000 square feet of ammunitions and weapons storage space. It served as an essential link to the Pacific-Indian oceans airline system. Both Subic and Clark provided operational support during the U.S. invasion of Vietnam and, more recently, the Gulf War.

Opposition to the bases has a long history, but it was under Ferdinand Marcos's rule that this opposition took a heightened form as one of the causes underpinning the popular anti-Marcos movement. From this broad-based movement, which tackled various social, political, and economic issues, arose a more specific antibases-antinuclear movement.

The movement believes that these facilities are the most blatant symbol of foreign intervention in the country. This intervention, however, is not merely confined to the presence of the U.S. military facilities. Antibases advocates believe—and rightly so—that the bases have been used by U.S. administrations as leverage in their political and economic intervention in the Philippines.

The MBA has been one of the cornerstones of the neocolonial relationship between the U.S. and this country, along with the Philippine Trade Act (or the Bell Trade Act), the Tydings Rehabilitation Act, and the Military Assistance Agreement, which were all passed into law immediately before and after the country was given independence by the U.S. in 1946. These treaties were publicly presented as U.S. support for the postwar rehabilitation of the Philippine economy, then a shambles.

In reality, these treaties only made legal the imbalances in the power relationship between the two supposed allies and friends. They institutionalized the new colonial relations and made a mockery of the so-called independence and sovereign state of the new nation. This "special relationship" turned out to be special for U.S. interests; for Filipinos, it was a slow economic death.

The Bell Trade Act, for example, which was in effect up to 1974, coupled the unlimited entry of American imports with the export of raw agricultural products and mineral ores to the U.S. Particular Philippine products, though—such as sugar, cordage, tobacco, and coconut oil—were subjected to quotas, thus providing ample protection to American agricultural producers. More onerous was the equal rights or parity amendment, which allowed U.S. citizens and corporations the same rights as Filipinos in the exploitation of Philippine natural resources. The act also fixed the exchange rate of the peso to the dollar. The result was that it became necessary to protect American economic interests in the country.

The MBA was part of the United States' self-appointed role as world policeman against what was termed the "specter of communism." The signing of the bases agreement of 1946 gave the U.S. free use of twenty-three base sites for ninety-nine years, renewable after expiration. Subsequent renegotiations reduced the number of years. Signing of the Military Assistance Pact, which allowed the U.S. to furnish arms, ammunitions and supplies, training and personnel to the Philippine armed forces, followed. All in the name of peace and order, or in more sophisticated lingo, in the name of "national interest." The Joint U.S. Military Advisory Group (JUSMAG) was set up and paid for by the Philippine government, supposedly to provide advice to the local army, constabulary, air force, navy, and intelligence services of the Armed Forces of the Philippines (AFP).

Resistance to foreign colonial interventions is as old as the country's colonial history, which began with Spain's aggression in the late 1500s. And although the local ruling elite supported this political and economic schema of the new colonial order, a number of local communities revolted. The most noted opposition came from the Hukbalahap, originally an armed movement against the Japanese invasion of the 1940s. After the Japanese were defeated and thrown out of the country, the Huks continued to oppose the imposition of foreign domination in the country. A segment of it joined the peasant organizations that were fighting for land reform. (Unfortunately, very little is said about women's participation in the Huk movement, a significant patriarchal oversight in the writing of Philippine history).

The military campaign against this organized resistance to the government necessitated the buildup of the AFP, whose main task was to dismantle all forms of opposition to the new order. Central Luzon—where Subic and Clark are located—became the battleground. Eventually, the organized resistance of the Huks and peasant organizations was suppressed when the Philippine government launched its massive pacification campaign. The Pentagon equipped and trained the local military to dismantle all forms of opposition, including that of the local communist movement. It was the civilians who actually bore the brunt of this militarized pacification.

Continuing through the 1960s and 1970s, and spanning all the administrations from Roxas to Marcos, any and all forms of opposition were labeled as subversive activities and communist-inspired. One Philippine president, Diosdado Macapagal, not too long ago, admitted publicly that the Central Intelligence Agency (CIA) had always played a role in the country's presidential elections. Communism was the big threat, and the success of socialist revolutions in other countries was painted as an evil design that must not contaminate the Philippine democracy, the show window of American legacy in the Southeast Asian region. The old ill winds of the Cold War and the McCarthy era were useful to the agenda of neocolonialism. Hand in hand with its U.S. military advisers, the AFP designed and implemented its counterinsurgency campaigns.

A Question of Sovereignty

It becomes understandable, then, that the question of the U.S. military bases in the country has been a central issue in the nation's political and economic sovereignty, in an interweaving neocolonial design of a historical vintage. U.S. officials in the 1990–91 bases negotiations were unabashed in their candid linking of renewal of the treaty with foreign economic assistance to the Philippines. The Aquino administration saw this as a boost to the Philippine economy, and Ms. Aquino pronounced that "[we] can expect easier access to more aid and assistance from other countries if the bases treaty is ratified."

Raul Manglapus, who headed the Philippine negotiating team, is perceived in popular and academe-based activist circles as a true-blue "Amboy" (American boy). Manglapus et al. tried to sell the Filipino people the line that the treaty was in their interests. To some Filipinos, whose sense of hopelessness about the economic downturn has become a part of the Pinoy psyche, have repeatedly argued that the compensation from the U.S. base facilities has helped, and would continue to help, the sagging economy, especially in the baselands. But everyone knows that with or without the treaty the Philippine economy is sick, so sick that the promised U.S. economic assistance in the bases "compensation" package can do little about it. Others say the Manglapus-Armitage proposed agreement was an unabashed sell-out, a classic case of cash register diplomacy.

Despite the recent changes in geopolitical configurations and the thawing of tensions between what has become the former Soviet Union and the western powers, Washington and the Pentagon continued to insist on keeping the bases in the Philippines, purportedly as a stabilizing factor in the region. "Mutual security" has been a selling point emphasized by probases adherents, including the Aquino government.

Officials of the Armed Forces of the Philippines and the Department of Defense made threats about the future of the Philippine military if the base treaty were rejected. They argued that the modernization of the armed forces would be placed in jeopardy. The U.S. supplies the AFP with arms and weapons in the latter's counter-insurgency program against leftist revolutionaries and the Moro National Liberation Front (MNLF)—a campaign that inevitably harms noncombatants and destroys civilian villages all over the country. Countering these claims, human rights advocates insist that the counterinsurgency campaigns of the AFP are not simply aimed at the communists and Moro separatists. In fact, these campaigns are aimed against legal people's organizations, including legitimate trade unions and other groups critical of the government. Nationalists see these threats as barefaced subservience of the Aquino government to the vested U.S. interests in the country. Moreover, the United States' supplying of arms to the AFP constitutes outright U.S. intervention in Philippine internal affairs.

Anti-Americanism for various reasons and of various shades has reportedly arisen, especially in what used to be the bastion of Americanism. In the cities of Angeles and Olongapo, citizens have openly made disparaging remarks about the actions of the base authorities. Even the staunch probases Olongapo City Mayor, Richard Gordon, had a war of words with the commanding officer of Subic when the latter refused to allow Pinatubo evacuees access to the base at the height of the more deadly eruptions. In a dramatic move, Gordon refused Commander Mercer's truckload of apples as a contribution to the evacuees. Mercer probably thought that Gordon could be bought off by a truckload of the fruit that ordinary poor Filipinos associate with Christmas—but even Gordon isn't that mercenary!

In Angeles City, residents claimed that the U.S. personnel who had opened the water reservoirs inside Clark to save the baseland from the rainwaters coming from Mt. Pinatubo, were responsible for the collapse of three major bridges, the destruction of a portion of the expressway, and the lahar that destroyed the city. Local discontent further rose with news reports of the possibility of nuclear-related accidents and leaks that could be triggered by Pinatubo's volcanic activities. The U.S. base facilities have always been suspected of storing nuclear weapons. The haste with which U.S. personnel were made to evacuate Clark in the first days of Pinatubo's eruptions fueled the claim further, even as U.S. base authorities insisted on their "no confirmation or denial" policy. These are some of the items in the so-called special relations between the U.S. and the Philippines.

Bases: Bane or Boon?

Pinatubo rendered one aspect of the bases question moot and academic. However, with Clark, Subic, and other smaller installations finally to be closed down, it is still useful to review the claimed economic benefits that the Philippines supposedly derived from the bases.

The presence of the U.S. military facilities in various parts of the country has had a socioeconomic impact in the communities around them: businesses arose, and goods and services catering to the needs of U.S. personnel and their dependents expanded. To run the base facilities, Filipino workers were hired.

What is most noticeable, and the most significant economic activity around the baselands, particularly in Olongapo and Angeles, has been prostitution. There is virtually no industry except the "entertainment" business. And while the Olongapo mayor, in a magazine interview, claimed that "there are no prostitutes in Olongapo," around Clark and Subic the total number of R&R establishments during the first quarter of 1990 was registered at 1,567 and 615, respectively.[1] A survey done by a women's research institution estimated some 55,000 prostituted women, registered and unregistered, in Angeles and Olongapo alone. These figures do not include child prostitutes.[2]

It must be said that it is not only U.S. military personnel who have contributed to the expansion and perpetuation of the R&R business in these areas (before the devastating Pinatubo eruptions, there were easily 100,000 military personnel and their dependents stationed at the two bases). The local populace has as much a role in this as do the clients of the women. Local authorities on many occasions have admitted the importance of taxes and fees that local business operators, along with the number of foreign-owned establishments, provide to the coffers of the two cities.

Before Pinatubo, political tensions had heightened in the area around Clark. This was due primarily to the fact that the underground revolutionary movement through the Communist Party of the Philippines' New People's Army (NPA) had begun to flex its muscles and to target U.S. base personnel. The U.S. military response was to prevent its personnel from leaving the base. Houses built by businessmen in Angeles for lease to base personnel remained unoccupied for many months. A number of bars showed signs of falling income, and women waited at the gates of Clark in a desperate bid to earn something.

What Pinatubo did was further dramatize this situation and make clear how imperative it is to wean the local economy from depending on the bases. This dependency over time has been shown to stunt other, better, economic potentials of the area, and to render the community vulnerable to political manipulation. There is a need more than ever now to develop industries that contribute to the economic self-reliance and well-being of the communities around the base sites. In the end, these communities and the Philippines as a whole would have to build up an economy that moves beyond the fragile political environment on which the daily life of people seems to hang ever so precariously. It is deluded for anyone, particularly the Aquino government, to cling to the magical promises of the U.S. government of economic assistance as the path to economic recovery. After all, international politics is not premised on a big brother–small brother philosophy; only self-interests are permanent.

Bases and Prostitution: More than National Sovereignty

When Corazon Aquino took on the helm of the Philippine government in 1986, one of her most significant pronouncements had to do with the prostitution industry in the country: "I will do my best so that we will be able to provide jobs for our women . . . so they will not have to resort to [prostitution]." It was the activism of the feminists in the nationalist movement that had placed prostitution on the bases issue agenda.

The bases as an object of dispute between the national movement, on the one hand, and the Philippine and U.S. governments, on the other, has been premised on the question of sovereignty. But for the women's liberation movement now in full swing in the Philippines, the bases question is more than a question of sovereignty. It is in fact a question of national dignity, class inequalities, sexual politics, and racism.

The Pinatubo incident opened another venue for the entire nation to take a closer look at the bases issue. Media reports on the affected communities and the damage to the bases filled the airwaves and page after page of the dailies. Even the almost forgotten Aetas, the tribal group that anthropologists say are the forebears of Filipinos, received headline treatment. Everyone whose homes and property were destroyed merited at least a line in the news. There was, on the other hand, a too obvious silence on the plight of the prostituted women, marking once more this group's invisibility. Yet they constitute a large sector of the affected communities in the baselands, perhaps even larger than other workers in the labor sector. And undoubtedly they are in no better situation than anyone else. Patriarchy misses no opportunity.

The draft agreement between the Aquino and Bush administrations did not project any concern for the prostituted women. Yet any military agreement is implicitly premised on the host country's ability to provide the nonmilitary "needs" of the base personnel—sexual services, a need that patriarchy has always taken as a right unto itself. Militarism and sexism are the twins that have been created in the bowels of patriarchy, and through time, they have littered the histories of humankind in the name, ironically, of peace and progress.

In not having to consider, in even the minutest manner, the impact of the bases on the lives of prostituted women, the Philippine negotiating team sold the dignity of thousands of poor women who, in their desperation—and lacking in education, skills, and all other basics for a possible socioeconomic mobility—view prostitution as the only option for themselves and their families. The patriarchies of this country once more have acquiesced to the sale of their own daughters to the highest bidder.

Thus bars and nightclubs conspicuously marked the cities of Angeles and Olongapo (as well as other areas where facilities, foreign and local, are located) before Pinatubo leveled it to its present gray landscape of ash and lahar. These were "entertainment" centers where women are the prime commodity to be haggled for, and where the routine of sexual bargaining had become part of the community life. Because prostitution is illegal in the Philippines, the same lawmakers who proscribed it have concocted the euphemism "entertainment." Here we don't have prostitutes, only entertainers—or, to convey a supposed racial trait of Filipinos, "hospitality girls" who belong to the "service sector." Nothing, of course, is more hypocritical than these linguistic acrobatics, or what may be called an official penchant for cleaning up a stinking social reality and turning it into an antiseptic framework of economic categories.

In all the studies conducted in the past, prostitution was analyzed in the context of poverty. It was easy: simply look around and the answer stares straight into one's eyes, with one's senses drowning in the poverty of the poor. Through the years, however, as women activists and the growing number of feminist researchers look more closely, poverty is too simple an explanation: why then aren't all those *poor* Filipinos opting to be in prostitution? Morals? In poverty, morals are oftentimes a luxury. In fact, in this country the most blatant immorality lies in the too blatant chasms in the social order.

Yet, sadly, the analysis of patriarchy has only begun, and almost peripherally, in the consciousness of the nationalist movement. Even some of the staunchest political activists, those with a well-developed framework of social analysis of Philippine society, have yet to, at the very least, appreciate the notion of Philippine patriarchy, the male political privilege that underlies the institutionalized use of women's bodies.

Patriarchal culture in the Philippines, or anywhere else, has produced men who think it absolutely correct—even proper!—to exercise what they perceive and hold as their right to the full expression of the range of their sexual needs, both within and outside of marriage—marriage being the only church-sanctioned institution in which sex is considered legitimate, and only then for reproduction (and this is a complex issue itself). In military prostitution, one sees the heightened integration of classism, racism, sexism, and imperialism. A popular T-shirt sold in Olongapo bearing the message "Little Brown Fucking Machines Powered With Rice" is one of the most disgusting racist concoctions imaginable, and one that only the so-called entertainment business could have given rise to. Racism and sexism are now seen as a fulcrum in the issue of national sovereignty. The stories of the women in the following pages are the most eloquent statement of these dynamics.

A study, WEDPRO,[3] which drew up a comprehensive bases conversion plan for women in the "entertainment industry" summarizes these issues succinctly: "underlying the bases–flesh trade are the exaggerated notions of manliness embedded in the military thinking which encourages the control and use of women—whether as wives, reserve labor or as prostitutes—to serve military objectives and the needs of men in uniform." Prostitution is the grossest form of sexual enslavement of women, and its proliferation vis-à-vis militarism makes this especially evident. Wherever militarism goes in the world, so too goes prostitution. Philippine women's groups have observed the mushrooming of small-town brothels and nipa hut–style discos and nightclubs, even in remote barrios. Where the military establishment has set foot, young women are now being traded as sexual commodities. The concept of "entertainment" must have indeed perverted the minds of those who accept prostitution as a daily routine in the economics of poverty. Entertaining U.S. military and base personnel, and Filipino males as well, means a whole routine of leaving behind one's dignity, the very essence of life.

Faces and Shadows of Poverty

The bases have provided jobs for thousands of Filipinos. Jobs they are indeed. Jobs that render women vulnerable, much more than other sectors, to AIDS, sexually transmitted diseases (STDs), sexual and physical battering, alcoholism and drug abuse, unwanted pregnancies, and a host of other socially unacceptable and often life-threatening situations. One can indeed say that our women contribute a lot in the service of the R&R needs of the U.S. military personnel and of Filipino men for paid sex, which keeps the club's and casas' cash registers ringing. And, in some cases such as Olongapo, the women provide the main source of income for the city; in the end, this fact is used to rationalize the need for the continued presence of the U.S. bases in the Philippines.

Withdrawal from the bases undoubtedly will have socioeconomic consequences, both negative and positive. Among the negatives are: loss of jobs and income, rise in under- and unemployment, contraction of business activity, increased demand for government social services and support. In the prostitution industry, income is minimal and the women are always hovering between periods of unemployment and underemployment. On the positive side, the WEDPRO study projects the following: decline in the rate of prostitution, which is a form of female sexual slavery; new employment opportunities for women in the entertainment industry; improved women's self-esteem and general life situation; decline in drug and alcohol dependency; diminished rate of STDs and AIDS; diminished crime rate and illegal activities; decline in illegal abortions; and a more stable and secure socioeconomic environment for the women, their children, and the community.

Popular perception holds that women in the R&R industry derive a relatively good income from their jobs as entertainers. The WEDPRO survey shows otherwise. It must be said, however, that income of women in prostitution is usually difficult to ascertain, since the trade is unregulated and the individual circumstances of each woman play a central role. Being involved in an "underground" economic activity, prostituted women as a group are more likely to be subjected to harassment and other difficult experiences by police and other legal authorities. Another area of difficulty in establishing the income of prostituted women is the inaccuracy of official reporting by the owners of R&R establishments.

Indeed, the women aspire to a more comfortable life and more material things—as most of us do. But the depths of the grossness of that reality goes beyond the garish gloss of entertainment glamour: drugs, booze, and not too rarely violent sex. Women take these as part of the territory of "entertainment" work. Inevitably, stereotypes of prostituted women have been propagated: a lazy lot who do not want hard work and who love the "good time" of drugs, booze, and lots of sex. The stereotype does not do justice to the majority of women in this industry. A common lament is heard in this quote from a prostituted woman: "We have to take drugs so we can forget our situation, and we drink so we lose our inhibitions. But too much of these could debilitate us at work, even as we have to drink at the tables because that's how we get our commissions. What do we do?"

The stereotype, most importantly, makes it hard for women to leave the industry, as they know that the image of the "sinful" woman will continue to hound them even after they leave that work. Their invisibility in the industry and their later marginalization from the mainstream of society is a vicious cycle. Those who have left the industry reported that they felt alienated from their comrades who are left behind in bars and nightclubs. The latter tend to feel that the ex-prostitute is "someone who's finally made a break and moved up somewhere," a place and situation that seems unreachable to the rest.

To a certain degree, creeping urban poverty has changed the profile of the women in the industry. Contrary to the popular belief that the prostituted women come from the poorest and remotest areas of the country, the WEDPRO study revealed that the majority of the women, both in Angeles and Olongapo, come from Tagalog-speaking areas, including the National Capital Region, and semiurban or urbanizing areas in the Visayas. The survey shows that a significant number of women, in their youth, experienced sexual and physical abuse including incest and unplanned pregnancy. Not a few, in fact, were forced to leave their homes because of what had befallen them. Quite revealing in terms of analysis is the negative role of the family for those women who survived the psychologically paralyzing experience of sexual abuse committed against them by their kin: here, then, is patriarchy at work in what this culture views as the foundation of society. Ironically, the popular media and the church have stereotyped these prostitutes as women with loose morals, yet the collective stories point instead to a hypocritical society as the biggest recruiter of young (females and males) for prostitution.

Women's Bodies: The Last Colony

The disaster wrought by Mt. Pinatubo's activities has radically changed the physical and economic environment of the baselands. The impact of the disaster has rendered hundreds if not thousands of women in the entertainment industry jobless, with no foreseeable prospects of immediate reemployment in the industry. Sad but in all probability true, society in general may be lukewarm, if not hostile, to immediate support for prostituted women, due to the stigma of their trade. In the face of the massive physical and economic dislocations of the populations affected by the volcano's activities, prostituted women are one of the most marginalized sectors with respect to relief and rehabilitation efforts.

An interesting question that follows Pinatubo's activities, and the consequent reduction of the traditional clientele, is whether prostituted women will leave their jobs. The extent and degree of women's continuing involvement in the flesh trade following the eruptions and the withdrawal from the bases might add to the general understanding of prostitution and the factors drawing and coercing women into it.

The victory of Fidel V. Ramos as the new president of the Philippines took place in a faction-ridden electoral atmosphere replete with scandals, charges, and countercharges, during which he made clear his position on the bases question. He said that he wants to "erase the anti-American image of the country developed after last year's decision to close the U.S. military bases." Antibases parliamentarians did not do too badly in the elections; a few managed to get reelected. But in a country where personality and patronage politics is still the primary charm swaying the popular vote—despite the efforts of the social movement to move it beyond the guns, gold, and goons—the bases issue did not manage to catch the imagination of the electorate. Outside of the valiant efforts of a handful of media people who have managed to make news out of the conversion issue, the plight of the displaced communities in the baselands, and especially that of the prostituted women and their families, seem to be dinosaurlike in the consciousness of the general public. Pinatubo is luckier, in this regard.

U.S. Ambassador Frank Wisner, on the other hand, stated that despite the closing of the bases in the Philippines, the U.S. would adhere to the 1958 security treaty between the two countries. The treaty requires the U.S. to aid in the defense of the Philippines.[4]

As the final withdrawal from Subic takes place in September 1992, plans for conversion remain in the blueprint stage. The bases conversion study undertaken by the Legislative Executive Bases Council (LEBC) in 1990 seems to have been relegated to the background—perhaps lost amidst the bulky files of government-initiated research—despite the viability of the programs proposed by the LEBC, as affirmed by respected academic and economic groups in the country. Instead, there are reports of a Disneyland being built at the giant Subic Naval Base. The Disney Corporation has reportedly shown interest in leasing the 40,000-hectare base area. Other proposals include the construction of a studio complex by Universal Studios, a casino, a plastics company, and a shipyard.

Olongapo Mayor Richard Gordon, who also heads the Subic Base Metropolitan Authority (SBMA), has actively pursued grants and loans to finance the proposed infrastructural conversion. The World Bank has promised to release by September 1992 an initial grant of $450,000; other local financing institutions have been approached for loans as well. Indeed, such an enthusiasm could be worthwhile and appreciated—if only the women in the bars and nightclubs actually figure in the schema of the new development strategy in the baselands.

Prostituted women in this country have a long path of struggle. The women's liberation movement, moreover, in its current attempt to trace the particular roots of Philippine patriarchy, can perhaps begin to learn some lessons from the contemporary history of the bases—for in it can be seen the interweaving patterns of racism and sexism, as well as their perpetuation in the neocolonial order. Women's bodies around Subic and Clark, and everywhere else where militarism thrives, are ultimately, to paraphrase the feminist scholar Maria Mies, the last colony of patriarchy.

---

1. *Sunday Inquirer Magazine*, 19 May 1991.
2. The women's movement in the Philippines, particularly among those closest to the women working in the clubs around U.S. bases, has chosen to use the term "prostituted women" rather than "prostitutes." The latter term is laden with stigma and stereotypes, whereas the former implies that the women to some degree are not choosing this work. Researchers who have undertaken studies on prostitution and the R&R industry in these areas believe that the total number of women in the entertainment industry can be conservatively estimated by doubling the number of registered "hospitality girls" to account for those working outside government regulation.
3. WEDPRO stands for Women's Education, Development, Productivity and Research Organization. It is a feminist research organization. WEDPRO published a technical report: *Feasibility Studies on Alternative Employment, Economic Livelihood and Human Resource Development Needs for Women in the Entertainment Industry: Clark and Subic*, and a companion volume, *Women Entertainers in Angeles and Olongapo* authored by Virginia A. Miralao,

Celia O. Carlos, and Aida F. Santos (Manila, Philippines: June 1990). The report is part of a three-sector study on base workers, urban poor, and tribal groups, undertaken for the Legislative Executive Bases Council (LEBC), a body constituted under the Office of the President of the Republic to draw up a comprehensive bases conversion program in preparation for the termination of the U.S.-R.P. Military Bases Agreement. Mandated to premise the study on a complete withdrawal of the bases, the WEDPRO Report included a survey of women in Angeles and Olongapo.

Some of its findings, based on the most current data, shattered the myths around prostitution and have highlighted the role of patriarchy in the structurally generated factors that breed prostitution.

4. *Philippine Daily Inquirer*, 29 May 1992.

Aida Fulleros Santos is cofounder of the feminist group KALAYAAN. A writer by profession, Ms. Santos has published many articles on women and social issues—especially those involving development and society—in local and international publications. She has published a monograph under the sponsorship of Women's Research and Resource Center (WRRC) entitled, "Towards a Feminist Consciousness in the Socio-Historical Analysis of Women and Work in the Philippines," and another article called, "Feminism and Nationalism: Co-existence or Compromise?" Aida is also a poet; two of her anthologies have won national awards.

OLONGAPO: THE BAR SYSTEM

Saundra Sturdevant and Brenda Stoltzfus

Prostitution is illegal in the Philippines. Olongapo, however, and the two small neighboring towns of Barrio Barretto and Subic City, have an estimated 15,000 to 17,000 "hospitality women." The term "hospitality woman" is a euphemism for prostitute or the sale of women's sexual labor. Approximately 9,000[1] of these workers are registered at the Social Hygiene Clinic (SHC) and are therefore "legal." Those who are not registered are called streetwalkers and are illegal and therefore subject to arrest and imprisonment. There are also smaller numbers of men working in the "hospitality industry."

Olongapo has 330 bars, massage parlors, and entertainment establishments. If, in addition, one counted the tailor shops, where women also sell their sexual labor and are required to be registered, the number of establishments where sexual labor can be purchased would rise.

The SHC is a joint project of the Olongapo City Health Department and the U.S. Navy. The Navy provides medicine and technical assistance. The Olongapo City Government provides the salaries of employees and the clinic building. When a woman is hired for the first time, she must register at the clinic in order to obtain a Mayor's Permit, which allows her to work legally.[2] To complete the registration, she must have a chest X-ray, a VD smear, a blood test, and give a stool sample. She then receives a card indicating that she is clean and is required to report for a VD smear twice a month and a chest X-ray and AIDS test twice a year. If 25 percent or more of the employees of any establishment are unregistered, the establishment will be declared off-limits to U.S. servicemen until the employees register. Some clubs have their own in-house health testing provided by moonlighting Navy corpsmen.

The workers pay for the tests at the SHC themselves. If a smear is positive, the bar is contacted and the woman must report for treatment and stop working until she is cured. Customers may ask to see a woman's card to verify that she is clean, but the customer carries no corresponding card to show that he is disease free. If men are found to have a serious sexually transmitted disease (STD), they are not allowed to leave the base. Some get treatment in clinics outside the base in order to avoid such restrictions.

Abortion is illegal in the Philippines and, due to the Catholic influence, considered sinful. The women in Olongapo do have abortions, however—generally under poor health and sanitary conditions. Abortions are commonly done by massage. A *hilot*[3] massages the abdomen until the fetus is dislodged and aborts. The woman pays according to how many months pregnant she is. If she develops an infection as a result of the procedure and goes to the hospital, obtaining care may be difficult due to lack of money. Delay in receiving care may also result from the doctor's wanting to make sure that the fetus is not still living.

In a bar, a woman may work as a cashier, a waitress, an ago-go dancer, or an entertainer/hostess. Any of these positions may include going out with customers, but not all women who work in a club sell their sexual labor. In many bars, however, the sale of a woman's sexual labor is required. If a woman refuses, she risks losing her job.

According to Philippine law, hospitality women are registered workers and are therefore entitled to receive minimum wage and maternity benefits. These laws are largely ignored in the hospitality industry. Pay varies according to the type of work, the individual bar, and the number of customers a woman is willing to receive. A cashier may earn P 600 per month. An ago-go dancer may earn P 20–40 per night. Wages for waitresses and entertainers are low or nonexistent.

Women earn primarily by commission on ladies' drinks and bar fines. A ladies' drink is a mixed drink that the customer buys for a woman when he wants to talk with her. A bar fine is the amount that the customer pays to the bar to take her out for the night or a short time. In both cases, the woman receives a commission of less than half the cost. Ladies' drinks range from P 25 to P 40. Overnight bar fines vary widely among bars, ranging from P 250 to P 1,200. Most overnight bar fines are P 300 to P 600.

If a customer is not satisfied with a woman, he may ask for his money back from the bar fine. If the bar owner agrees, the bar fine is charged to the woman. Bars usually also have fines for being late to work by a few minutes, wearing slippers (thongs) while on duty, not wearing the prescribed uniform, or not attending a pro-bases rally. All fines are deducted from the woman's commission before she is paid.

Any Filipina walking with an American can be stopped and asked for her night-off pass, a paper given to her when her bar fine is paid. If she has no night-off pass, she can be arrested as a streetwalker, whether or not she is employed in a club. If she is employed in a club and has her ID passbook as proof, without a night-off pass she is considered to be operating independently of the club and therefore illegally. In such cases, the bar owner or manager is contacted and must come for her. She is then fined by the club. To avoid such a penalty, when she does not have the night-off pass, a woman usually gives the arresting officer a bribe. Policeman and *baranguay captains* are able to supplement their income through such bribes. If a streetwalker is arrested and put in jail, she will be fined and may have to perform sexual services for the policemen.

The bar owners are Filipinos, Chinese, and American ex-Navy men who either have married a Filipina or have a front in order to own a bar. They are community members active in the Lion's and Rotary Clubs. The Mayor also owns several clubs. The club owners have an association, which enables them to control what happens in the bar system.

The level of income of the women is difficult to determine, but it is a myth that they earn a lot of money. A woman might earn a decent income if she works in one of the few high-class bars or is willing regularly to take several customers in one night. These women, however, find that they need to use alcohol or other drugs in order to accommodate numerous customers.

More often than not, the women are very poor and barely able to make ends meet. Incomes through commission are dependent on the coming and going of aircraft carriers. A carrier usually visits once or twice a month, but there are times when a carrier doesn't dock for one to two months. During long stretches with no ships in port, a woman may have no income and be forced into debt to her landlord and/or bar owner. When a ship does come in, she works, pays her debts, and, if possible, sends money home to the province to support her family. The cycle of poverty continues.

A woman may live in a room above or behind the club or in a rented room or shared apartment with other women. If she lives at the club, as what is called a *stay-in*, her movements are more controlled. Depending on the club, however, she may not have to pay as much rent. The rooms are generally small and crowded, but the same is true of rented rooms elsewhere in the city.

Another type of arrangement is that of a kept woman. A serviceman may pay for an apartment and send money to a woman on a regular or semi-regular basis. When his ship is in, he then lives at the apartment with her; and the agreement is that she stops working in the club. She, of course, is only able to keep up the arrangement as long as the money continues to come from him.

A section of the bar area in Olongapo that African-American servicemen frequent is known as the Jungle. Clubs in the Jungle tend to be smaller, with a more homey atmosphere, and owned by ex-servicemen. There are also certain bars on the main drag that cater primarily to African-Americans. Although African-American servicemen go to bars outside of the Jungle, Euro-American servicemen rarely spend time in the Jungle.

---

1. At the time of this study, there were approximately 9,000 registered women. This figure does fluctuate and with the eruption of Pinatubo and consequent closing of Clark Air Base, the number of women, registered and unregistered, selling their sexual labor in Olongapo and the tourist area of Manila has probably risen considerably.

2. Of the workers, approximately 90 percent are women.

3. Traditionally, a *hilot* is a woman healer using massage and acupressure as well as herbs.

MADELIN

Province: Manila/Sapang-Palay

Age: 22

My older brothers and sisters and I were born here in Manila. After I was born, we returned to Samar. I remember Samar, but I didn't live there very long. I was ten years old when we returned again to Manila.

In the province, my father and mother farmed rice in the mountains. They had some land, but it belonged to my father's mother. When my grandmother died, the children divided the land between them. There are many brothers and sisters, each of whom has his or her own family. When the land was divided up, there was little left for each one. My father said his brothers and sisters should have the land.

We came to Manila because life was difficult in the province. We lived in a squatter area. My father worked as a photographer. He was an extra. If there were many people working, whoever got there first was able to have a camera. When he didn't have a camera, he didn't earn anything. Sometimes there was in-come, sometimes none. Nothing permanent. My mother worked doing laundry. When she started, her salary was P 50 for a whole day, or until she finished.

We were moved from that squatter area to Sapang-Palay.[1] The owner of the land said they needed to get rid of the squatters because they wanted to put up a large office building. They said they would give us the land in Sapang-Palay and we would pay by installment. The land is ours now. Marcos was still president then.

Some things are better in Sapang-Palay. The houses are farther apart from one another. In the squatter area, the land was not really ours, and the houses were almost on top of one another. There were always fights. However, it's far to travel from Sapang-Palay for work in Manila. [When we lived] in the squatter area [in Manila] we could gather bottles from the garbage to sell. We sold cardboard boxes, tin cans, bottles, and metal. We gathered them from the garbage the truck dumped. My

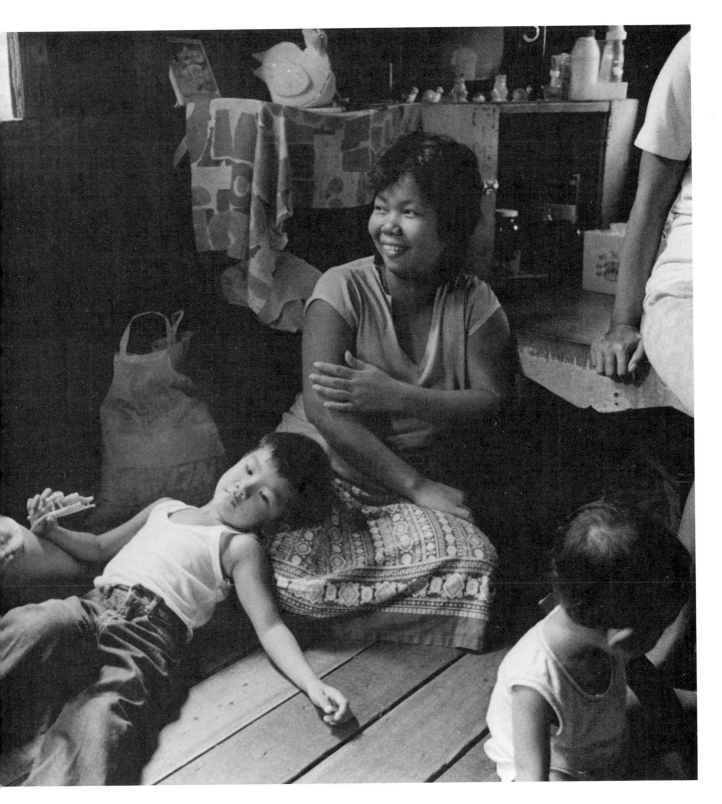

"Feeling great because we're together." Madelin with family in Sapang-Palay, a resettlement area about two hours from Manila. Under Ferdinand Marcos, an entire squatter community in Manila was relocated to this area in order to free the land for development.

California Jam: a large club on Magsaysay. Clubs vary from very large and quite posh to very small and run-down. The larger clubs often have live bands, whereas the smaller ones have jukeboxes and pool tables. Prices of bar fines vary accordingly: the posher the club, the higher the price.

older sister and I worked together. We would work all day and then buy rice and food for the house. The next day, back again. The most we made in one day was P 20.

I wasn't studying yet at that time. I studied when we moved to Sapang-Palay. I was eleven years old when I started grade one. I studied until grade three but did not finish. How could I? It was difficult. You go to school without food, and nothing the teacher says stays in your head because of the hunger. I also saw our poverty and decided I would not study anymore. I would work.

When I was about fourteen years old, I returned to Manila and worked as a maid. I had no experience yet. When I started, my salary was P 150 a month and later went up to P 300. I seldom had a day off. Sometimes I would visit my parents but only once in a while. Sometimes

they also took me to the movies. My work was difficult. There were two children who were studying, one in nursery school and one in kinder-garten. There were also two cars. Two children, two cars, the house . . . I had to get up very early. I cleaned everything. The children had uniforms for school. Early in the morning I had to iron the uniforms. All of it was my work—cooking, cleaning, and picking the children up from school. I got tired, bored, and impatient with my life, and the salary wasn't even enough to be able to help my parents. I decided to leave that job.

I had a friend in Manila who told me about a friend of hers in Olon-gapo. I said, "What's Olongapo?"

She said, "There are many Americans there."

"Americans? I've never seen an American. What's her work there?"

"Waitress. Do you want to come along?"

"What would our work there be?"

"We could waitress."

"Okay." I made a decision.

I told my boss I was leaving, but they did not want to let me. I left without their knowing. I only took a few clothes, just what I was wearing, and a little money for transportation. When I arrived in Olongapo in 1985, I was about nineteen years old.

When I first arrived in Olongapo, I saw many Americans because there was a ship. It was a large ship, a carrier. I was innocent. I didn't know what a carrier was. When I saw all the Americans I said, "Where are we? In the States? We didn't ride in an airplane."

"Stupid! We aren't in the States. We are in Olongapo."

We rode a jeepney going to Magsaysay. The Americans all looked alike to me. They were looking and looking at me. I was embarrassed. My friend said, "Let's apply."

"What do you mean, apply?"

"Get a job."

The bar she took me to was on Magsaysay. It was very large. I tried it for one day. I didn't like it because it was very noisy. I was frightened by the coming and going of the Americans. Later, I didn't see my friend anymore. She had left me.

I got to know one woman at that bar. On the first evening, I went up to her and said, "What's your name?"

"Neneng."

"Neneng, would it be possible for me to sleep at your place?"

"Why?"

"Because I don't have any place to sleep."

"Why are you here?"

"My friend brought me. She's gone now. She left me. I don't know where she is."

Maybe she felt sorry for me. She took me to their house, and I slept there. She had a child by an American. She said, "You're still a virgin and you've arrived in Olongapo. So, you're going to work in a bar?"

"Yes, because I don't have any work. How can I go back home? I don't even have transportation money. And I want to work."

"You can go look for work on Magsaysay. There are some wanted signs there."

Before I got a job at Scotties, I worked for two months as a maid for Neneng's neighbors.[2] By then, I really did not want to be a maid. I was tired of it.

I looked for work on Magsaysay. I saw signs saying "Wanted Waitress." I was afraid. I should have gotten a job right away as a waitress, but I didn't know how to speak English. I thought the Americans wouldn't understand me. Neneng said, "If you really want a job, you'll learn, if only by listening. You'll understand what the Americans say by listening carefully. When they order beer, if you don't know what they want, just say 'Sir, one beer,' like that."

I tried to be strong. I applied to be a waitress at Scotties. I didn't know what the work really was. What I knew was that you serve drinks and food. I did not know that you go with them for something else.

Ago-go dancer. Traditional Philippine culture is extremely modest with respect to clothing. Very few women will even wear a sleeveless blouse. Bathing suits are not worn. Women who work as ago-go dancers usually wear shorts and a shirt with sleeves when swimming at the beach.

I was first given a job at the Penthouse.[3] I was still a virgin then. I didn't know English. My God! The uniform! I didn't want to wear the uniform because it was so skimpy. You could see everything. It was like a bathing suit. I was very embarrassed. I'm not used to wearing anything like that. The manager got angry with me because I wasn't wearing a uniform and there were many Americans. I started wearing it. I was fat then, and the Americans kept pinching my butt. I wasn't used to that. I said, "*Gago*" (stupid). The Americans couldn't understand what I said, and I didn't know English . . . but I was angry. I saw many things that are natural in the bars, such as kissing. I thought: "This is a different kind of place."

When I began working at Scotties, they knew I was a virgin, but no one explained what the work really was. One of the women at Scotties who became my friend said, "Whether you are a virgin or not, you have to go out with Americans." I didn't know that going out with an American meant he would have sex with you. I also didn't hear anything from the stories of other women. When I asked what they did, the answer was, "Eat in a restaurant, disco, walk around. . . ." I found out!

Someone wanted to pay my bar fine. My friend said I should go. I was afraid. My friend said, "Nothing will happen in your life if you don't go on a bar fine." I went. The American took me to a hotel. That's where I was afraid. I didn't want to go along. He got angry with me and fought with me inside the hotel.

I understood some English but not very much. He ordered me, "You just sleep."

I said, "Yes, sleep," but I did not take my clothes off.

He said, "Take off your clothes."

"Oh, no, no, no."

"Why? Just make love like that."

"Oh, no, no, no."

That's what I knew before— "No," "Yes," "What's your name?" I could speak a little English but could not pronounce it very well. The American swore at me. "Shit!"

I said, "Oh, yes, yes, yes."

I was really stupid then. He got angry because I didn't want to take off my clothes. I told the story to some of my friends. They said, "Stupid. An American swears at you and you say 'yes.'"

The American got angry. I left the hotel because he was trying to take my clothes off. I said, "I'm leaving. You just stay there." He got his money back because I did not want to have sex with him. I didn't know that the regulation at Scotties is that if an American gets his money back, the bar fine is charged to the woman. It's your debt. I couldn't do anything. The owner deducted it from my salary.

My salary then was P 150 a month, P 5 per day. The bar fine was P 410, and P 110 went to the woman. More went to the owner. It

Street sweeper in the early morning on Magsaysay. Olongapo is a city of domestic immigrants. A wide variety of the 100-some dialects spoken in the Philippines are found in Olongapo. This man's first language is not Tagalog, nor does he speak English. This is also true of many of the women when they first arrive in Olongapo.

would take more than two months of my salary to pay for the bar fine that was charged to me.[4] Before, even when I wasn't going on bar fines, customers sometimes would buy me a ladies' drink. I wouldn't know that I had a ladies' drink. The American would call me. I would go over, even though I didn't know English. He would say, "You drink that." I wanted to ask why he was buying me a ladies' drink when I didn't even know him. That's it. When an American likes you, he plays with you. I learned that late, after I had been at Scotties a long time.

The first time I went on a bar fine and had sex was with the father of Maria. At that time, I was very, very poor because there hadn't been any ships and I was in debt. I had also received news that my sister was sick and there was no food at our place. I decided to go along with that one more thing. Maria's

Mardi Gras, held every few months in Olongapo, is a "special event" designed to put on a show and earn money. The main street is blocked off to traffic and everyone, including the women who work inside the area, must pay to enter. *Above:* Street children are dressed up supposedly to represent the Aeta cultural minority, but the Aetas never dressed like this. *Right:* Sometimes Aeta men and women come to the bar areas to sell traditional weapons or to solicit money. Many consider the Aetas to be the original inhabitants of the Philippines. U.S. Subic Naval Base occupies traditional Aeta land. Ulo Ng Apo—Olongapo—refers to Aeta ancestral leaders.

father stayed for two weeks in Olongapo. I always went out with him but only with him. Then I discovered that my menstruation was delayed. I was pregnant.

I felt troubled when I found out I was pregnant . . . because when I left home, I was a virgin. If my family found out I was pregnant and was in Olongapo, in that kind of work, they would get angry. I was ashamed in front of the people at home. I did not tell them I worked in a bar. They didn't even know I was in Olongapo. I had gotten word that my sister was sick and they were having difficulty with expenses and food when I wrote to a friend in Manila. She told me my mother went to Manila looking for me. My friend said she didn't know where I was because I had told her not to tell anyone.

When I found out my sister was sick, I went with an American so that I would have something to give them. I did make some money. I gave the money to them. They asked where I work in Manila and I said, "Just over there." I lied. They asked for the address, but I said I would just come home. I went back to Olongapo when I left.

When I was pregnant, I was afraid my family would find out and be angry. Once my stomach was large, I could not visit without their knowing. I decided no one at home would find out. I would just stay in Olongapo. I lived in a room in the bar at the time until the owner kicked me out because my stomach was getting large. If an American sees you are pregnant, he gets dis-

couraged and won't pay your bar fine. When I left there, I had a little money which I used to rent a room and buy my food. When that was used up, I left and found work as a maid.

I knew it was bad, but I decided to have an abortion because I was very poor. I went to a friend and asked for help because I didn't have enough money for an abortion. My friend is the one who paid. I went to a *hilot* who massaged my stomach. She also gave me something to drink and had us buy some medicine. I don't remember what the medicine was, but it was expensive—more than P 100. The cost of the abortion was about P 400, but you paid in small amounts. The agreement was that until you abort, you don't have to pay it all. It took a long time before I bled. I bled some but only a little. I was massaged three times but didn't abort. She said to me, "Keep coming back. Just have patience. Don't lose hope. Talk to your child and tell it that it should come out because you are not able to raise it."

When she told me to keep coming back, I was having a hard time because the massage hurt. My conscience was also bothering me. It was as if my conscience were talking to me. I decided not to continue with the abortion. It is a sin against God. I was also afraid maybe there would be side effects to the baby. I went to a friend and told her I wanted to know if there had been any side effects. If not, I would not continue with the abortion. When I found out there were no side effects,

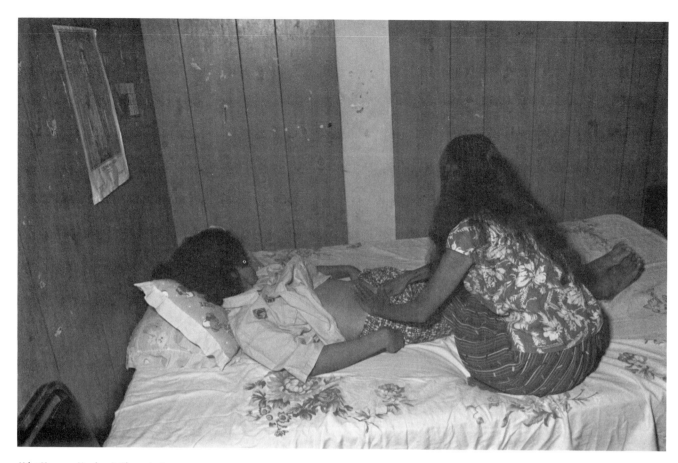

Hilot Massage Number 1. The majority of abortions in Olongapo are done by a *hilot*, the traditional woman healer. Several trips to the *hilot* are necessary, and fees depend on how advanced the pregnancy is. Abortion is illegal in the Philippines. If a woman has complications as a result of the abortion, she may have difficulty obtaining the necessary health care.

I didn't go back to the *hilot*. I continued working as a maid until I gave birth.

When I was in the hospital to give birth, I needed money for hospital expenses, but I had none. My friend—the one I worked for as a maid—spent money for the hospital, but they are also poor. I needed a cesarean because the baby was in the breech position. The cost for a cesarean was P 2,000. My friend did not have P 2,000. He said he was sorry he could not help me. He said I should talk to the top person in the hospital to see if they would give me a cesarean even if I had no money. They said it was not possible; you must have the money. I didn't have any relatives in Olongapo. My

friends also did not have any money. They work in bars and there had been no ship. The doctor said he would find a way so that even if I did not have a cesarean, the baby would come out naturally.

For a long time they didn't pay any attention to me in the hospital. My stomach was hurting terribly. They just kept saying it was not time yet; I should endure it first. I was on the bed with dextrose. My whole body hurt. The baby was moving around and kicking. Then, I really had to pee. The bed was high and the dextrose was also high. I couldn't get the dextrose. I couldn't get down from the bed. No one was there with me.[5] My friend had gone, saying he would come back right away. It was a long time before he came back. I really had to pee. Since I could not get down, I peed on the bed. When the nurse saw it she got angry with me. I ignored her.

There were many women giving birth. I arrived at the hospital before them, but they were taken care of first by the nurse. They probably had money. I had no money for payment, so they ignored me. My stomach hurt more and more. I cried and cried and screamed. The nurse just said it was not time yet. I felt the baby coming out and took off my panties. I cried out, "It's there, it's there!"

One nurse came over. She called the doctor and told him I might really be giving birth. The doctor said, "Okay, take her to the delivery room. I'll find a way." They took me to the delivery room. I could feel everything. I had no anesthesia. I felt it when they cut me. My baby did not come out. I was having a very difficult time. The nurses were holding me down. I screamed. Maybe the doctor realized I could not give birth naturally. I heard the doctor say, "Okay, get the things ready for a cesarean." Then I felt the doctor take hold of my baby and just pull it out. I lost consciousness. I did not hear any cry.

When I woke up, I was on a bed. There were other women who had just given birth. My friend arrived and said, "Okay, Lin, get ready. You're going to leave now."

"Where is my child?"

"You must be strong inside, because your child died."

"Why did it have to be like that?"

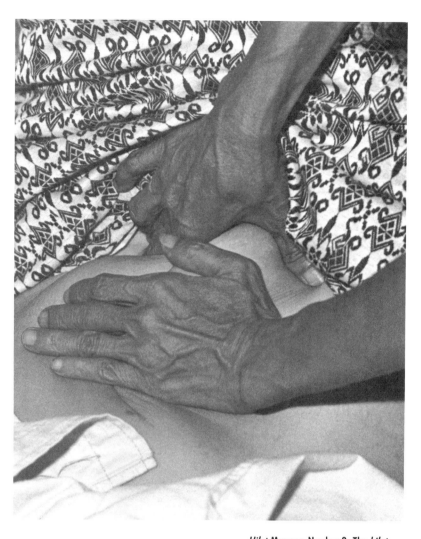

Hilot Massage Number 2. The *hilot* massages the abdomen to dislodge the fetus so that it will miscarry. No studies have been done regarding the safety and effectiveness of this method. However, if done during the first trimester, it appears to be successful.

The doctor came to see me. I was crying. The doctor said, "Mrs., life is just like that. You must be strong inside." He wasn't able to meet my eyes. I know he had done something that caused my child to die.

That very day, we left the hospital. There was still payment to be made. We had no money. They did not want to let my child out. I wanted to see her. I hadn't seen her right away. I was told to talk to the top person at the hospital about not paying if possible. Even though I was still feeling sick, I walked. We went to the top person. My friend

December 28, 1986, the birth and death date of Maria, Madelin's daughter. On All Saint's Day, the graves are cleaned, whitewashed, and the inscriptions repainted. The pile of brush on the left has just been removed from the grave site. Subic Naval Base and the Bataan mountains are in the background.

only had P 100. The payment was P 200. They said, "The father of your baby is American and you have no money?" They were insulting me.

I said, "Even if the father is American, he doesn't send any money."

We paid only P 100 and left.

They sent my child ahead to my friend's house. When we got home, she was there. I saw her. I felt very bad inside about what had happened. I did not see the burial of my child. My friend buried her. I was too weak to go along. I was not well. After some days we went back to the hospital. My whole body was trembling, and there was milk in my

breasts that didn't want to come out. I also had a constant fever. My friend thought it was because I felt so deeply inside about what had happened. We went back to the hospital for medicine. A friend helped. She paid for the medicine.

The father of my child knew I was pregnant. He said that since I work in a bar the child was not his. I was angry with him and felt hurt. By then I knew some English. I said to him, "The child is yours because you are the only one I went with during that time and the first one." He was the only man I had had sex with. From then on, he didn't write

to me. Before he used to write. I wrote and told him if he doesn't accept it, never mind. When his ship came, he also didn't come to see me. I was pregnant and wanted to see him. I wanted to show him I was pregnant. My stomach was large then. He knew where I was because I had left word with my friends at Scotties who know him. They said he never came. He does not know I gave birth. He is really stupid.

There are many children born to U.S. servicemen, but the Americans abandon the children. There are no possibilities for many of those children. They are to be pitied. I'm very angry with the U.S. servicemen because of what happened to me, but maybe not all of them are the same. The servicemen are afraid of their responsibility as fathers, so they turn their back on it. They say they are not their children. They have children all over the world that they don't know about. Or, maybe they know about but do not support. There are many such children in difficult situations. The servicemen are stupid. If I saw the father of my child, I don't know what I would do.

Madelin, two of her sisters, and her niece and nephew, in Sapang-Palay

After I gave birth in December 1986, I went home and told them I had had a child by an American and worked in a bar. At first, my parents did not seem to accept it. They could not say anything. They were just silent. I felt even worse. The pain of what happened and of them not accepting it got all mixed up inside. My brothers and sisters and mother were all crying. After some time they began to understand. My mother was okay. She talked to me some after I told them what had happened.

My father, however, just left. For three days he did not talk to me. I was very hurt. I said to my father, "I did it in order to help you. I didn't like what happened to me. I

hope you can understand me." Then he said it was his fault because he got married when he was not able to raise us, his children. I said to him, "That's okay. I understand. We are just poor." He said he was ashamed because of what happened to me. That is why, now, he really loves my daughter Michele.[6]

In March I went back to the bar again. My parents knew I was returning to Olongapo. They did not want me to go back, but I said I would be careful. It would not happen again. That's what I thought. I went back to Olongapo. My work in the bar continued. My father did not like it. He got angry. He said if I went back to Olongapo I should not come home again.

I did not want to return to Olongapo, but I saw our poverty. The house was in bad shape with the floor almost on the dirt. It was very ugly and small. We were crowded. There are so many of us, and some of my brothers and sisters have families. When we slept, we had to step over one another. I had not been able to finish school and could not find good work. I thought about how I would be able to help my parents, so I went back. My mother accepted it. She would go to Olongapo sometimes. I would give her money when she came. Then, I got pregnant again.

There was a center where you could get medicine so you don't get pregnant. I took pills, but it seemed I was allergic to them. I stopped taking them for one month and the first time I went on a bar fine, I was pregnant again. There was nothing I could do. It was there. In some ways, I wanted a baby in order to forget what had happened to the first one. The same thing happened with the father of this child. From the time he found out I was pregnant, he also stopped writing. I know he received my letters, but he did not answer. The servicemen are really afraid of the responsibility. They just want to be happy and have a good time. They do not think about the future of one child.

In my opinion, the U.S. Navy treats the women as a way to pass the time and do whatever they want. They have money, so they buy here and buy there. There are also sadists in the U.S. Navy. An American like that took me out once. I was preg-

Buntis—pregnant

nant with Maria. The owner had told me I had to stop working because my stomach was already large. One American wanted to pay my bar fine. I didn't want to because I was pregnant, but I thought: "I don't have any money. I'm pregnant. I'll be leaving work. I need the money." I went with him. He wanted to do things to me that I didn't like, such as three holes.[7] He said he would pay me for that. I was pregnant and thought maybe he had a disease. I was being careful. I didn't want to do it. I also thought he was high on marijuana, on a trip. He was giving me a trip. He did things to me. I fought. He swore at me.

He said, "Why don't you do that?"

I said, "*Naku*, I don't like that.

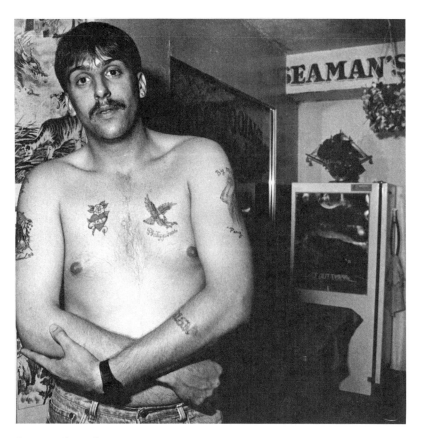

A tattoo parlor on the strip

You can make love to me, but I don't like that."

"Why? You bitch."

"You're a bitch, too. You bitch than me."

"Fuck you."

"Fuck you, too."

I fought him. I would not allow myself to lose. I thought we might both die. I was really fighting, but I was also shaking. I was afraid because his eyes looked different. We were in a hotel. He was choking me. I said, "Leave me alone. Be nice." He did not want to let me go. I was getting weak. I was having difficulty breathing. I cried. I thought I was dying.

The hotel employees heard. They knocked: "What's happening in there? Open the door."

The American said, "Okay, okay. All right. Keep quiet. Forgive me. Okay, I'm sorry." He was afraid he would get in trouble. He said to the hotel employees, "Don't get involved here."

I said, "I'm leaving."

"No, I need to talk to you." He said I should not tell the owner what happened. He had lots of things to say, and then he swore at me. He said he would get his money back.

I said, "Okay, you get your money back. I will report this to your ship."

"You know my ship?"

"Yeah, I know your ship." I told him what the name of the ship was.

He said, "Oh yeah, you know."

It's because most of the U.S. Navy [guys] are wild. They want to be wild in this one thing. I don't like that. What they want is that if they pay for you, you do what they like. They think that as long as they have paid, they can get whatever they want. I'm not like that.

There was one other American I went with who was somewhat stupid, but he didn't hurt me. He wanted to do the things he liked. It's embarrassing to tell. He turned me over and was entering my ass. I lost it then. I fought. No one had done that to me. I didn't like it. I had taken part in the wrestling in the bar before.[8] The American was strong, but I could handle him. I flipped him over on the bed. He fell. I grabbed an ashtray. I said, "Okay, you do that again . . . you be nice, *ha!*" But I was crying. I was crying out of fear. I said, "Okay, you do that again, I will do it. I will really hit you with the ashtray."

He said, "Oh, no, no, no, okay. I'm sorry." I ignored him, got dressed, and left. I was afraid he would get his money back, but he didn't. But with the other one, I would have reported him to his ship if he had gotten his money back. They say that is possible. You can get the Americans in trouble with the OPM or SP. I don't know what would have happened, if they would have believed me or not, but I know it is possible.

I also heard something when I worked in Barrio Barretto.9 I got to know a waitress there. She said a Marine killed two women in a hotel. She knew one of the women. They just saw the corpses but didn't catch the American. They said he stabbed the women and put them under the bed. That's why the hotel has ghosts. They said the bodies smelled by the time they found them.

For me, I can't say my work [in the club] is bad. It is life in Olongapo. But Olongapo is where the events began which led to the most painful thing that has happened in my whole life [the birth and death of Maria]. So, I can't say my work is bad, but it was bad. What I mean to say is that in other people's eyes, people who are not understanding, this work is bad. But they don't understand the reasons why the women do this. There is a saying, "When a person is poor, they will hang on, even to a sharp instrument." That's what happened to me. That's what happens to the women working in the bars of Olongapo. All

Ago-go dancers. With the approach of the renegotiations affecting the bases and the consequent media attention focused on Olongapo and the plight of the women, Mayor Gordon began "cleaning up Olongapo." Part of the cleanup included requiring ago-go dancers to wear one piece suits instead of the skimpier bikinis that they had been wearing. This was well received by the women.

my companions at Scotties had their own difficulties. Almost everyone had a problem.

There are many different reasons. Some have problems with their husbands. Their husbands abandon them, are drunkards, have no work, beat them. I have one friend. She has some children. She is married, but she was always being beaten by her husband. The man would get drunk. He had no work. She decided to work herself and ended up in Olongapo. Some are also rebelling against their parents. They are angry with their parents and fed up with life. They come to Olongapo to work. For many the reason is also

poverty. They want to help their families. I also have a friend who came because she despaired over love. That is a bad-smelling reason.

I have one friend from the province. She wanted to work as a maid in Manila. There was a woman from her province. She would take women from the province in order to get them work as maids in Manila. But they were imprisoned in a room. Men would come and do all kinds of things to them. The women could not get out. One customer took pity on my friend. He paid for her to leave. It was a lot of money. She was able to leave and run away. But she is really in despair. She wants to

ruin her life. She came to Olongapo. She is working. She is no longer imprisoned. She is supporting herself. But she is messed up and doesn't know what she's doing. She takes a lot of drugs. She is an Ago-go dancer. In my opinion, she is hurting herself because of what happened to her in the *casa*.[10] When we talked, she said, "I don't have a future anymore. I'll just ruin my life."

I tried to make her pull herself together. I said, "It's still possible for you to change. You didn't want that to happen." She said no, she would just kill herself but that would be even more of a sin. She is still young. I heard that she is helping her parents, but only occasionally.

There are also women who want to marry Americans. That is their dream. From the start I really didn't have a dream like that. What I really wanted was just to help my parents because our life was so very difficult and my sister was sick. I had no dream of marrying an American. I would like to marry, of course; I have a child. I don't want a Filipino. There are Filipinos who are married and then they abandon their wives. They have children. They do not work. In the U.S. Navy, on the other hand, they have money and work. But now, maybe because I have learned some things, I don't

This kind of wedding, with all the trimmings, is extremely rare for women working in the bars, who may not necessarily desire marriage to a serviceman in any case. The bride in this wedding does not come from the bars.

Buklod beach party: Trying to create bonds among women bar workers. Launched in 1987, Buklod is a center in Olongapo for women who work in the bars. Four of Buklod's seven staff members are women who used to work in the bars. Here, women present a "drama-drama," which they've written about life and survival in the clubs.

like the U.S. Navy. If I married a Filipino, in my opinion, they would not accept me because of my past work. Perhaps it would also be like that with the Americans. But not everyone thinks alike. If there were someone who was able to understand my situation, love me, and accept what I have been through . . .

It is difficult to make friends with the women in the clubs—difficult and easy. But if I look carefully, I have only a few friends at Scotties. Most of the women at Scotties are

my friends, but not close friends. It's easy to make friends if they're in good shape, if they're not drunk. It's difficult to make friends with the women who use a lot of drugs. For example, you might be friends in the morning but when evening arrives and she is drunk, she'll fight you.

When the women fight, it's funny because even with so many Americans, they'll fight over one. It's because the Americans are butterflies. For example, a guy will pay the bar fine of one woman. The next day,

he'll come back and pay the bar fine of a different woman. So, the one who was bar-fined the first evening is hurt. She's jealous. She'll fight the other woman. But the one who is to blame is the American. So it's funny. When the woman fight about that, I just laugh. I say to them, "Don't fight. There are lots of Americans."

They say, "But, I like him. I have a crush on him. I'm in love with him."

"Stupid."

I fell in love with an American, the father of Maria, but from the time he did not accept his child, it was easy to lose my love for Americans. It was like I got angry with the Americans. But they are still there. For me, if you are there in that kind of work, you don't need to fall in love because you will just get hurt. And, the Americans, wherever they are, they have wives, women. Can you expect one of them to become your husband?

1. Sapang-Palay is an area outside of Manila. An entire squatter community from Manila was moved there. (See also Glenda's story, p. 114). The main problem is work: it is a two-hour commute to Manila by public transportation. This is very difficult for women with children to care for, many of whom have always taken in laundry as a means of livelihood.

2. Scotties is owned by an American. Although it is illegal for a foreigner to own property or business in the Philippines, many retired military men circumvent the law by marrying a Filipina or by having a front.

3. The Penthouse was a bar across the street from Scotties owned by the same man. It has been closed. Women were often moved back and forth between the two bars. If a woman said she worked at Scotties, it might mean she worked at either place.

4. She was charged the full amount of the bar fine, P 410.

5. In Philippine hospitals, a patient must have a companion or, literally translated, "guard," who buys food and medicine for, and looks after, the patient. Nothing is provided by the hospital. Prescriptions are given by a doctor but must be purchased at a drugstore outside the hospital and given to a nurse to administer.

6. Madelin has a second daughter by a U.S. serviceman.

7. "Three holes" and "three-holer" refers to vaginal, oral, and anal sex. Many of the women in Olongapo do not want to provide anal or oral sex.

8. In some bars, women used to be forced to take part in boxing and wrestling matches with one another while the Americans watched and placed bets. (See also Lita's story, p. 83). Madelin's training in wrestling, however, gave her the strength and confidence to "handle him." This is perhaps the only positive effect of the wrestling and boxing.

9. Barrio Barretto is a small bar area along the bay just outside Olongapo. The bars here are smaller, the women usually younger, and the atmosphere considered wilder.

10. *Casa* is the name of a place where women are kept prisoner. This practice is not uncommon but is well hidden and well guarded, and therefore difficult to research. Young women are recruited directly from the province or as they leave the boat upon arrival in Manila. In the former case, recruiters go to the provinces and find young women eager for work in Manila. Both the woman and her family are told she will have a good job as a maid or a clerk in a store. The family is often given money as an advance against the young woman's future salary. Upon arrival in Manila, she is placed in a *casa*, where she is kept prisoner and required to provide sexual labor. Although there are no studies or statistics available, stories from women who have escaped indicate a great deal of abuse of the women by the *casa* owner and customers. Women may be required to take up to ten or twenty customers in one evening. Customers may be foreign tourists or Filipinos. Women who have worked in these *casas* and manage to escape often end up working in bars in Manila or Olongapo. In comparison, the bars are a far better situation for the woman. Besides, she is already "ruined," so marriage is no longer an option. The *casas* as described here appear to bear a similarity to the brothel in Pusan described by Nanhee (pp. 192–94).

Lita returning to Samar to visit her family. Women returning to the provinces after working in Olongapo may face malicious gossip, or more benign curiosity, and expectations of gifts beyond her financial means. Many women choose to send money but not to visit.

LITA

Province: Samar

Age: 18

Almost all the young women from my barrio work in Olongapo. Not only in our barrio, but in many of the barrios in our area, almost all the young women are here in Olongapo. Some want to marry an American or make money. There are a lot like me who return to their barrio. A friend says, "I want to go along with you there." So of course, she comes along. I would bring her here and she would stay at my house first. After some months, when she knows how life is in Olongapo, she would start working in a club.

Before, when no one in our province knew much about Manila, when people were still ignorant, recruiters came there. My cousin was recruited. She was a victim. She was loaned a large amount of money and then given work in Manila as a maid. She is lost. She worked there for about one year, but was treated badly so she ran away. Something seemed to go wrong in her mind as a

Some of the children in Lita's barrio.
Almost all the young women from
Lita's barrio are working in the clubs
of Olongapo.

result of what happened to her. We don't know where she went. We haven't seen her. No one recruits in our barrio now because the people are no longer ignorant.

Many of my cousins are here in Olongapo. Some of us are friends, but not all of us. Some of them seem to think they are better than you because they have an American. They don't remember that we are the same: we are all hostesses.

When I returned home for a visit, I felt good because I was with my parents. One of the women there said that when others come back,

they are stuck-up, but I'm not. I have no reason to be proud. I'm a hostess.

They know I'm a hostess here. They know that I am being supported. When I arrive, they ask for things . . . cigarettes or *tuba*.[1] When we had a dance, there was one older man who liked me. He was being sort of rude at the dance; but he couldn't do much because all our relatives were there. He said he really liked me. I told him that I've been a hostess. He said that didn't matter, but when I said no, he got angry.

Lita with a sister and cousins in
the barrio

There was another young man at
the dance who is an old friend. He
said he wanted to marry me. I said,
"I don't want to. I've been a hostess." He said that didn't matter. I
thought maybe what he wanted was
money, because he knows I'm being
supported. I don't think I'd like to
get married in the province now
because I might be blamed for
being a hostess and I have a child.
If we fought, he would say I am
responsible.[2]

My mother voted for this young
man. She said, "It would be better.
Don't go back there. Get married
here. Say yes to him." But I only
think of him as a brother.

My older sister said if I didn't go

to the States, we could go into business together. I'd like that because I
don't want to go back to work in the
clubs. I want to have a different life.
I'm tired now of having so many different Americans. However, my sister is married again and pregnant.

I have seven brothers and sisters.
There were twelve of us. The others
died, probably because of the poverty of our life before. They were ill,
and my mother had no doctor. We
are close. Sometimes my older sister
and I fight, but now, since I am far
away from them, that is over. I miss
all of them. I would like all of us to
be together.

Before, when I gave birth and my
mother came [to Olongapo], she

Guys partying in a small bar in Olongapo. Guys sometimes go to smaller clubs where they can party without the pressure to buy "ladies' drinks" and to live up to the expectations of being a customer.

found out what my work was. She got angry with me, but that was all. It was as if her bad feelings kept pouring out because her child was a hostess here. She was hurt. That's as far as it went. She said, "I hope that the father of your child will be true to you." However, she was also happy to see her grandchild, who is an American.[3]

My older brothers were also hurt because I am the youngest, the end of the family, and I am the one who became a hostess. My family said, "We would have been able to pay our debt even if you did not do this kind of work."

I said, "It's already too late. There is nothing we can do now. I already have a child. Maybe that's the way life is." I also cried because of the difficulties.

Two of my siblings are still in the province. They are farmers. The land is my father's but is mortgaged. My mother mortgaged it when there was a typhoon and they had no money.

On the land that is mortgaged, we get part of the harvest. For example, we make copra from coconuts. When it is sold, we receive only a little. The owners receive a larger amount. All the other plants are ours. The coconut is theirs. We have other plants like pineapple, *kamoting-kahoy*,[4] corn, and the material to make *benigs*;[5] but the land is mostly coconut.

A woman at work in the barrio

Our life was difficult because there wasn't much food, only whatever you could plant to stay alive. When I was ten years old, my mother said we were going to go to Manila. We went to stay with my older sister in Manila because we had nowhere else to go. She lived in Bulacan.[6] She worked as a maid and later married someone from Manila. I think he lived next to her boss. They work as fisherfolk. We helped them sell the crabs and fish . . . whatever *kuya* (her husband) caught from fishing. I think we stayed there about two years. I took care of her children. She had an abnormal child.

My mother went to work as a maid. She talked to her boss about my staying with her because we were ashamed to be depending on my sister so much.[7] I helped with the work at the house . . . everything my mother did . . . even though I wasn't good at it yet.

They reduced the salary P 25 because I was with her. Our boss was kind. He said, "Bring your husband here from the province—I'll build

a small house for you." My mother didn't bring my father because she was shamed by the kindness of her boss.

Mother said, "We'll look for a small house to rent for the two of us."

After we had been there for a long time, I was nearly raped by our boss's son. He pushed me into his room and closed the door. But he wasn't able to rape me because I yelled. It was a good thing that his father woke up. He helped me. Afterward, the son hid. My mother was not there. She was out looking for a house. I was very frightened. I cried. When my mother arrived I said, "Ma, I want to go along with you wherever you go."

We left there. The woman of the house asked, "Why? Why are you leaving?" I didn't tell them. My mother also didn't know what had been done to me. I didn't tell her because I thought if I told her, she might get into a fight with them. Our bosses were kind; I didn't want that to happen.

Scavenging at Smokey Mountain. Smokey Mountain is the huge garbage dump for Metro Manila. A community of people live on top of Smokey Mountain and survive by scavenging.

My mother was able to buy a house in Tondo for P 250.[8] We earned a living there by scavenging bottles and plastic and selling them. We cooked side dishes, such as root crops, and sold them. We sold whatever we could. At first, we were not used to the smell of the garbage. When we got used to the garbage, I also scavenged there. My mother did not. When we had scavenged, she sold the plastic to large factories.

I was also studying at the time. After studying, I would go to the garbage dump. I was in grade one but I was already big. I had been in grade one in Samar but wasn't able to finish, so I had to repeat. When I left the school, I sold kalamay.[9] When it was all sold, I climbed up to the garbage dump and scavenged for bottles. Our earnings for one day were very small. Sometimes we made P 15, sometimes P 10, because what we were selling, plastic and bottles, was very cheap.

My father also came to Tondo. There were four of us living there— an older sister, my mother, my father, and myself. My sister sold coffee and bread. Our life was good. Even though we were living as we were, we were able to survive.

Once I was almost run over by the bulldozer that pushes the garbage. My foot accidentally got

because the garbage was heavy and hot. A man pulled me out. I could no longer hear. I fainted. They carried me. I had many cuts.

I went home. I was covered with blood. My mother said, "What happened to you?" She said, "Let's get out of here." My father had also almost died. He was also nearly run over by the truck at the garbage dump.

Just at that time, the squatters from Tondo were being moved to Cavite.[10] We were all moved. I think it was the president [Marcos] who moved us. All the houses were demolished and taken away in a truck. They helped in order, they said, to give land to those who needed it. We were able to have a lot in Cavite.

Life was also difficult in Cavite because there were not many ways to earn a living. The people there were also poor. I studied in grade two in Cavite for about five months, but I was already big.

We had no way to earn a living, so we moved to Laguna.[11] I had a brother who lived and worked in Laguna. The work was good, so they brought us to live with them. My parents got work in the fish pens. My father was a guard. He would shine a flashlight into the pens to prevent theft. We earned a good living there. We had someone watch our house in Cavite because it was far from Laguna.

We had been in Laguna a long time when my older sister suddenly got married. We also no longer had a house because of a typhoon. My mother said we should go home to the province. We had no other

caught in the garbage. I couldn't get it out. The bulldozer was coming closer and closer. I was caught in the moving garbage up to my stomach. No one saw me because the roaring sound was loud and the mound of garbage was large. It kept coming and coming. I didn't know what would happen to me. I thought I was dead.

I saw a child. I called out, "Child, help me." The child heard and yelled. Someone saw. They climbed up to the driver to get him to stop. He ran away. He thought I was dead.

I was buried in the garbage up to my chest. My eyesight was blurred

Journey to Lita's barrio. Lita's barrio is on a small island off the island of Samar. The journey is a long one. The bus ride, on a non-air-conditioned bus, from Olongapo to Manila, takes three to four hours. From the Manila bus station to the pier is about one hour by jeepney. The trip by boat from Manila to Catbalogan, Samar, is twenty-four hours. A ride on a smaller boat from Catbalogan to Lita's barrio takes another four hours. This photo is taken on the final leg of this journey. Transportation costs for this one-way trip would be approximately P 400. Food is an additional expense. People aboard this boat are bringing back items purchased in Catbalogan to sell in their barrios.

house, and the house in Cavite was too far away. We sold the house in Cavite for P 3,000 in order to be able to go back to the province.

My cousin came to the province, too. She had pictures of Olongapo. I saw the ago-go dancers who had Americans with them. I said, "What's that?" She said one could earn a lot there. I thought about what my mother had said—that we needed money to pay off the land. We had a large debt.

I said to my cousin, "Is there work as a maid in Olongapo?"

She said, "Yes, the salary for maids is high, P 400 [per month]."

I said, "I'll go along."

She said, "Okay, I'll pay for your transportation."

My mother didn't want to agree because Olongapo is so far away. I was the one who insisted. I said, "We need the money. We have no-where else to go now." My mother, however, didn't realize what was going on; she thought I was going to work as a maid here in Olongapo.

I knew what my work would be in Olongapo because I had seen the pictures. My mother also saw the pictures. She said, "Don't get to be like that. I'll let you go there, but only as a maid." For several months after we arrived in Olongapo, I stayed with my cousin. I couldn't find other work, so I was her maid. She paid me P 200 [per month]. I sent the money home. She worked in a bar. Some of my other cousins

Men at play; women at work

who came from the province went to work in bars, too. One cousin was engaged to a *kano*.[12]

One of our friends said, "If I were you, I would work in a bar because you can make a lot of money."

I wanted to earn a lot of money so I said, "Okay, I'll work in a bar."

I applied at the Penthouse. My friend said, "You might not be accepted because you're still so young." I was fourteen then. She made me up with lots of makeup and dressed me in high sandals and nice clothes so I would be accepted.

The owner of the club asked, "Is she still a virgin?"

My friend said, "Not anymore," so that I would be accepted. If he thought I was still a virgin, I wouldn't have been accepted.

About the third day, someone paid my bar fine. I didn't know how to speak English yet. My cousin said, "Okay, go on that bar fine." I knew what a bar fine was . . . that you would lose your cherry. They said, "It should be a lot of money."[13]

I said, "What will I do? I don't know how to ask for money. I don't know how to speak English."

"Just say to him, 'give me money.' Just say that to him."

I thought about our debt in the province. I said, "Okay, I'll go with him."

I went with him. We went to a hotel. He was small and already old. I felt like I wasn't able to go through with it. I cried. I tried to make him

A very young woman on her way to work, with a *kano* seated behind her. Legally, a woman must be eighteen to work in a club. However, one often finds women as young as fourteen working in the clubs, especially in the larger discos. The youngest one the authors knew of was eleven. She was pregnant. Younger children, boys and girls, sell their sexual labor on the streets.

feel sorry for me so he wouldn't have sex with me.[14] I cried. I said, "Don't have sex with me."

He said, "Come on, I'll pay you a lot of money."

I thought about out situation. I agreed because he gave me money. I didn't know how much it was because it was dollars. What I saw looked like a lot in my eyes. Of course, I came from the province. I didn't know the value of dollars. I only knew dollars are supposed to be worth a lot. It was only $30 plus P 500 that he laid out.

I really didn't want to, but he forced me. It was very painful. I bled. He tried to undress me but I wouldn't get undressed. There was a lot of blood on my clothes. I walked down Magsaysay. I went to my cousin's house. I knocked. It was raining. I was holding on to the money tightly.

She said, "What happened to you?"

I cried. I said, "*Ate* Grace, the *kano* had sex with me." He paid my bar fine. She knew he was the one who broke my cherry because I was crying and holding my money tightly.

I sent the money to my mother. Maybe my mother thought it was my salary as a maid. She didn't know I was now working in a club. She said we were able to pay off some of the debt.

Vendors selling hats and shirts with this kind of logo are omnipresent in the bar areas of the Philippines, Okinawa, and Korea.

Afterward, I seemed to lose something. What else could I do? A *kano* said, "Come to work for me as a maid." He was married to a Filipina. "I will pay you P 300 (a month)."

I said, "Why should I work as a maid again? I've already lost my cherry." I didn't agree. I continued working in the club. I went on bar fines all the time then.

The third man to pay my bar fine was old. He was black. He said, "Come here, I'll pay your bar fine." I agreed. I thought it would only be sex. He wanted me to give him a blow job and do different positions. I had just recently lost my cherry. I couldn't do what he wanted. He had already had sex with me. His penis couldn't enter because it was too large. I cried. He said, "Why are you crying?" He was a sadist. He pushed my head into the pillow so I wouldn't be able to yell. He pressed the pillow down hard on my chest. He took my clothes off. He did all kinds of things to me. I cried.

I said, "I'll call the OPM. I'll have you arrested." I didn't know how to do that yet, but I only wanted to frighten him.

He said, "Okay, I'll go back to the Penthouse. I'll get my money back."

He said to the club owner, "Give me back the bar fine of P 400." He said I didn't let him have sex, but

Late-afternoon Shore Patrol briefing. Shore Patrol is staffed by CMO (Civilian Military Operations), whose job it is to function as military police in the bar areas, along with men from ships in port designated by their unit to pull twenty-four-hour Shore Patrol duty. Their role is to prevent and mediate conflict between local people and U.S. military personnel.

he had already finished on me.

The owner said, "What did he say? Why didn't you let him have sex?" He got angry with me.

I said, "He already did."

They wouldn't believe me. They believed the customer. I cried and cried. The owner said, "Don't cry. We're giving him the money. You will have to pay it back." I cried even harder because I would have to pay the money and he had already had sex. I paid the amount in one month. Of course, they subtracted it before giving me my commission.

The second time this happened, we had already moved to Scotties.[15] An old black man paid my bar fine. I went with him. I didn't think the same thing would happen. I didn't like what he wanted me to do. He

wanted a blow job. I said, "I can't do it." I cried.

He said, "If you can't do it, I'll go back. I'll get my money back."

I said, "Why? You already had sex with me." I fought with him. I was upset. He was doing the same thing to me. I said, "I'll call the OPM." I knew a little more by then. My friend had taught me. This was the second time a man got money back for me, and he had already had sex. We had already been at the hotel for about four hours, and still he was going to get his money back.

The *kano* went back to the club. The owner said, "Where are your night-off papers?" I gave them to him.

I said, "Sir, don't give the money back because he already finished

having sex." The *kano* also seemed kind of wild. The owner got angry with him because he was answering the owner nastily. Maybe the owner also felt sorry for me because this was the second time. He said he would not give the money back.

The *kano* got angry, "Why won't you give me the money?" He was fighting the owner. The owner had a boy call the OPM.[16] They talked to me. They said, "What's going on here?"

I said, "He wants his money back, but he's already had sex with me."

The OPM said, "This one is drunk. We'll take him in." They took him back inside the base in their jeep. The owner didn't give the money back.

The club had boxing and other kinds of games. I didn't want to participate because I was small then. I didn't want to join in on the boxing or wrestling. The owner said, "Come here." He took hold of my face: "Don't answer back." I didn't know there were other bars that were different. If I had only known there were bars with good regulations, I would have moved then.

I said, okay, I'll take part in the boxing. I didn't know how to box. The woman who was my competition was very good. She was bigger than I was. I lost. If you lose, you are paid P 50; if you win, P 100. A lot of Americans watch. They say they like to watch the Filipinas boxing, and they make bets on who will win.

Guy undergoing an initiation rite in a mud pit formerly used for women's wrestling in the courtyard of a club. The city council banned women's wrestling and boxing in 1988 after a strike at one club. During the strike, an organizer was shot in the head and killed on Palm Sunday by a gunman hired by the American bar owner.

A wall in Lita's room above T's Tavern

Stay-in rooms above T's Tavern. Two or three women share each of these nine-by-ten rooms.

When I wrestled, I won because my competitor and I were both small. However, I sprained my foot because the *kano* pushed us down hard. At the end of the game, there is one round where six women wrestle one *kano*. If the women lose, the *kano* has two free bar fines. If the *kano* loses, there is no bar fine. He loses if the women get his shorts off. If that happens, the lights are turned on. The women have won. If it goes on for a long time and they can't get his shorts off, the women lose. He can choose two women and they must go with him. The woman has no choice. Sometimes the *kano* is given a T-shirt if he doesn't want to bar-fine a woman.

The regulations are very strict at that bar. We were *stay-in*. The room was free but not the food. There were many of us in one small room. There were beds all over the room. When a ship came in, the women had to get up early. If you didn't get up, you were fined P 25. Sometimes, by 8:00 A.M., you were already working because there were so many Americans. Some of the other women would get up early and have a *kano* right away. Sometimes I would have an attack of laziness. I did not want to become sweet smelling. If I was lazy, I just slept.

When I became engaged to an American, he said I should move. I got a small house. My cousins lived there with me. There were three of us. Each person paid P 80. But all my clothes were stolen from that house—another problem—we moved again.

I got pregnant. The father said,

"I'll send you money." I didn't know if he really would send money. He might just have been lying. After a month, I received money from him. I continued the pregnancy because I was afraid to have an abortion. It is a sin. They say it [the fetus] will become a ghost. I didn't want to do it. In addition to doing this kind of work I would have an abortion. I kept working though I was three months pregnant. Sometimes the father sent me $50 or $20.

When my stomach got large, I didn't go to work anymore. I stayed with my cousin. When I was seven months pregnant, the father came to Olongapo. He took leave for two weeks in order to visit me. When he left again, he said he would send me money for the birth; but he didn't. I was very angry. I said, "These Americans are really liars."

My mother was here when I gave birth. We borrowed money. About a month after I survived the birth, he sent money—whenever he felt like it. He only sent a small amount, only $50, but I was able to pay a lot of debts. My mother took the child, Mike, to Manila when he was three months old. I went back to work in the bar—at Scotties again. What happened there was the same. It already seemed natural to me. It wasn't like before when the Americans got their money back. They were able to have sex with me in the ways they wanted to because I had already had a child.

After some months, I moved to another bar. I thought: "Now that I've had some experience I'll probably be able to work elsewhere. They

Inside T's Tavern

say the customers in the larger bars are wild. You have to get drunk in order to be wild with them. I can do that now." I went to work at T's Tavern. I worked there as an ago-go dancer. If you went to work at 4:00 P.M. and worked until 2:00 A.M., you were paid P 40 a night. It was only P 20 at Scotties and you only got paid monthly. At T's Tavern, if you worked from 4:00 A.M. until 12:00 noon, you got paid P 50. I was able to give my parents money, if only a little. I was surviving. I didn't have any more debts.

The father of my child sent me a letter. He said he would bring us to the States. I didn't believe him, be-

cause I thought it would also be like before when he said he would send money and only sent a little. He sent me $600. He said it was for my papers. After that, I believed him. I kept working because I didn't want to spend the money since it was for my papers; and I wanted to continue sending money to my mother.[17]

I had money at that time. I earned money because I was always going on bar fines. I was able to do that by getting drunk and taking drugs like cough syrup. My *barkada* took me along when they did things like that.[18] And when there were many Americans, I was embarrassed about dancing. I didn't think alcohol was bad any longer. I earned

DJ at work in a club

enough money so that I didn't have to touch the $600.

I also had an American who was a steady customer. He was stationed here for three years and always paid my bar fine. He knew I had a fiancé. I didn't want to continue with him because he also had a girlfriend. He said his girlfriend was coming to the Philippines if they worked it out. If not, he would come back to me. I didn't like that. I told him we just shouldn't see each other anymore.

I made another mistake. I met a Filipino. There were two DJ's [at T's Tavern]. They took care of the bar and did the cleaning. [He was one of the DJ's.] When I was having the relationship with the Filipino, I didn't go to work. I hadn't had a Fil-

ipino boyfriend before; and I liked him. Maybe what I really liked was being entertained and amused by hanging out with my *barkada*.

My cousin thought I was still working. My aunt was taking care of Mike in Barretto.[19] She thought I was working, but I wasn't. The four of us—my cousin Baby, her Filipino boyfriend, my Filipino boyfriend, and myself—were together all the time. We always went to the movies.

Eventually, I didn't have any more money. I took some of the money I had put in the bank, the money sent to me by Mike's father. I rented a house for P 1,300. My cousin Baby was still with me. The four of us were living together. I took

Terri, Lita's cousin, is from the same barrio. She and Lita came to Olongapo at about the same time.

care of Mike myself and no longer went to work. Mike's father continued to send money, but only a little. He didn't know I had a Filipino boyfriend now.

I got pregnant by the Filipino. He said, "Don't have an abortion." I had fallen for him because he was kind. I also loved him. I didn't think about my fiancé, that we would get together again. I didn't think about anything.

When I ran out of money, he said we would live at his house with his parents. We were there for about three weeks when he went to Manila. I was the only one there, myself and Mike. Mike was very sick. I didn't know where to get money. I didn't have any more of my own.

I went to my cousin Terri. She said, "Okay, leave your Filipino and stay here."

I thought: "Maybe what I'm doing is wrong." *Ate* Terri helped me. She loaned me money to take Mike to the doctor, and he recovered.

Now I have a debt of gratitude. I told my cousin, "I'll leave the Filipino and when my money arrives I'll have an abortion." I was already three months pregnant.

The Filipino, Eugene, looked for me. He said, "Why did you leave the house without telling me?"

I said, "My child was sick. You can't support him. You don't have any money." I used words to hurt him so that he would be able to forget me.

T-shirt shop on Magsaysay: one of the jobs available to young Filipinos in Olongapo

He said, "What is it, really?"

I said, "I have a fiancé. You knew that before we met. You said to me, 'That's okay.' Now you're chasing me. What are you chasing me for? Money?" He cried. He said he loved me. He didn't see me like that. I said, "I am a hostess. I have a child by an American. You aren't good for me, and I don't like you anymore."

Another reason was that I had learned what life is like with a husband. It was as if we were married when we were living together at the house. Housework is difficult. You wash, you get up early, and then you have to take care of your child. I experienced everything—all the work at the house plus my child and no money and debts. It reminded me of being in Manila and working as a maid. It was too difficult. I also had

to put up with his parents. It seemed as if we couldn't get along.

It wasn't good together for us because of my child and because I've been a hostess. I thought: "Even if I love him, I'll leave him. I have a child. I need to give him a good future. If I marry a Filipino, we would be poor. He wouldn't be able to support my child." His salary was P 800 [a month]. And he had been fired from his job because of me. It's prohibited to have a relationship with another employee. They say it's embarrassing in front of the customers.

In my mind it's not the same if you are married to an American because the American has work. I'm not certain he would always give me money, but he has work. The Filipino has no work. I like the Filipino

Early-morning garbage collection on Magsaysay: another job available to Filipinos

more, but I have a child by an American. When the two children got older, they would fight.

I said to my cousin, "I'm going to have an abortion." She took me to a friend for the abortion. It cost P 400. My cousin said I should think about it first. I didn't want to think about it anymore because my stomach was already large. I didn't want anymore time to go by. I said it was up to God now what happened to me.

They put a small, long catheter in my vagina. It didn't abort the first day. The third day I was having difficulty. I said, "Take me to the hospital. I can't take it anymore." On the first day I was here at the house. On the second day I was at the place where the abortion was done. On the third day they send me to the hospital. I borrowed P 2,000 from *Ate* Terri.

I was bleeding a lot. They had to lie me down and the doctor felt me with her finger. She said, "Your uterus is still closed. It isn't possible to do a D and C yet." I endured the pain. The next morning the nurse said I should urinate. I urinated in a bottle, and they examined it. From testing my urine they said the fetus was still inside and alive. It wasn't possible yet to do a D and C.

I couldn't take it any longer. I was in a lot of pain. I was given an injection. I don't know what it was or what it was for. My stomach hurt more. I couldn't stand it. I went to the bathroom. I pushed and pushed. It was like giving birth. Afterward, a lot of tissue came out. I carried it out to them. It was the fetus. They

The women's work is integral to the economy in the working class neighborhoods that make up most of Olongapo: they pay rent, they buy food and other necessities, they hire tricycles, and they bring their customers home.

said they had to take me for a D and C. The next day I could leave.

Ate Terri took care of me in the hospital and was my guard.[20] No one else came to see me except *Ate* Terri. I have a debt of gratitude to her. After we left the hospital, I stayed at her house. Eugene kept coming back. He was there almost every day.

He said he wanted to talk to me. I said, "I don't want to see you anymore. Just leave."

He was carrying a knife. He said, "If you won't talk to me, it's better if I kill myself."

I said, "Okay, kill yourself but don't do it here."

He slit his wrists. I couldn't look because of the blood. It was dripping. Just at that time *Ate* Terri arrived from work. She was angry. We made him leave. He sat out in front of the store.[21] We closed and locked the gate. We lay down. A little later he was there again.

He said, "Please, open up—talk to me. I want to talk to you."

Ate Terri got angry. She went over to him and said, "You—if you don't leave, I'll yell. I'll say you are stealing." He was opening the window. He still didn't leave. *Ate* Terri yelled, "Thief! Thief!" The neighbors woke up. He ran away. The next morning we went to the *baranguay captain* and gave him Eugene's picture so that he could be picked up. We said he was a thief.

Maybe I would like it if Mike's father and I continued our relationship. I don't know very well yet what he's like because we haven't spent much time together. We were only together for two weeks, and I was pregnant then. I don't know if I would be treated differently there [in the United States]. Maybe when I arrive there he'll have another woman. I might just be a maid for her. Sometimes I don't want to go there. I might have a hard time

Marines

because I don't have any education, and I still don't know how to
speak English very well. I might be
treated differently because I'm a
Filipina. If we break up, I'll go back
to the province.

Even if I don't want to, I would
go to the States because of my child.
He said, "Don't worry, when you arrive here [in the U.S.], we'll send
money to your parents." But when I
arrive, he might not give me money.
Maybe he'll just take Mike and send
me back here again. He might tell
me the only thing he needs from me
is my child.

If that's what God is giving me,
I'll accept it because I've worked
here a long time. I'm tired now from
what I've experienced and from
having different Americans. I've had
enough of it.

I would like Mike to be able to
complete his studies and not see
anything bad about me. If we are
there [in the States] when he's
grown, he'll have some money in the
bank. If he grows up here and I'm
still like this, I won't be able to
send him to school. And he might
ask why I do this work. I don't want
him to blame me. I know many

Entrance to Porky's bar

women here who have male children. The boys become drug addicts. They don't stay with their mothers. They say their mothers are bad. I don't want that to happen to me. Since Mike is an American, I want my husband to be an American.

What I don't like about the Americans is that they make you do things you don't like. They make you do blow jobs and get in different positions that they like. I've had enough. I'm choosy now. From the time I had some experience, I no longer went with older wild men because I thought I might get sick.

In my eyes, Americans treat Filipinas like toys. They take one woman for a day or maybe two

Retired men hanging out at a bar, without their Filipina wives

nights and then they take a different woman. It's really like playing a game. The women, like myself, need the money so they go along with it. The Americans say they like Filipinas because they are out at sea a long time and afterward want to have a good time. Others say they want to marry Filipinas because they have small bodies and are black. I say to them, "I like American women better because they are beautiful and white. They go well together, American men and women."

Americans like Filipinas because the women here are cheap. Maybe there are women in the States, too; but they are probably expensive.

Some Americans say to me they don't like American women because some of them are butterflies and some of them only want money. I said, "Probably not all of them. I like the American women when they come off the base. I talk to them."

I go to church. I pray to God because I have committed many sins. I had an abortion—I killed a person. Plus, I am a hostess. I go out with different men. That is a sin. It's because I need the money. We sell our bodies. That's a sin. I decided in order to lessen my sin I would go to church. I think God understands why I am here.

I'm guilty of other sins because I had a lot of money and didn't send

Women working in a tailor shop on Rizal Avenue in the Jungle. Women who work in tailor shops may also sell their sexual labor. Like women employed in the clubs, they are required to register at the Social Hygiene Clinic and must carry an ID passbook.

any to my parents and siblings. I ask God to give me another opportunity. I ask for forgiveness. I ask that when we arrive in the States it won't be too difficult. Maybe when we get there they will say I only want money. I pray that our relationship will be good.

1. *Tuba* is an alcoholic drink made mostly in the provinces. It is made in the morning, sold cheaply during the day, and does not need refrigeration.

2. Lita is referring here to something women in Olongapo often comment on. They say that if they marry a Filipino and there are fights or problems in the marriage, he will blame her for the problems because of her history of selling her sexual labor.

3. The child, Mike, is technically not an American. Lita, however, calls him an American because he has an American father. It is common for Amerasian children to be called American or *kano*.

4. *Kamoting-kahoy* is a type of root crop.

5. A *benig* is a straw mat used for various things, especially for sleeping.

6. Bulacan is an area just north of Manila.

7. Maids are often live-in.

8. Tondo is a poor urban area of Manila where Smokey Mountain, the large metropolitan garbage dump where people live and scavenge, is located. The cost of a house in Tondo is relatively speaking, very low, compared for example with the house purchased later in Cavite after the squatter community was relocated. The range in housing costs in Manila is extremely wide, with housing in poor urban areas at several hundred pesos to housing in the elite areas costing several million pesos. Housing in Cavite would cost more than in Tondo and making a living would be more difficult.

9. *Kalamay* is sweet rice cooked with coconut and sugar.

10. Cavite is a town about an hour and a half outside of Manila.

11. Laguna is another town about an hour outside of Manila. It is beside the largest lake in the Philippines, Laguna de Bay, which has been a large fishing area and now has immense fish pens. It is also very polluted.

12. *Kano* is the term used by the women in Olongapo to refer primarily to their customers. It is also, however, sometimes used to refer to anyone from a Western country, Australia, or New Zealand.

13. The price for a virgin is higher. However, in this case it was up to the woman and her friends to ask for more money from the American because the bar owners were under the assumption that she was not a virgin.

14. The term used here is *galawin*, which the women use for sex, but it can also mean rape. It is used for sexual intercourse with or without the consent of the woman. Literally, it means "to move." In its usage by the women, it is clearly something being done to them by someone else. They do not use the term for more mutually participative sexual intercourse, *nakikipagpalik*.

15. A bar across the street, owned by the same American.

16. Young Filipino male employees who do the cleaning and odd jobs are called "boys."

17. Lita is referring to the bureaucratic procedure that she must go through in order to marry a serviceman and go to the U.S. This takes a great deal of time and money. Part of the procedure includes a grueling interview at the U.S. Embassy in Manila. Women who have been through the interview say they are belittled and put through something more like an interrogation than an interview.

18. Women often talk about taking drugs in order to overcome their embarrassment and shame in front of Americans. This is especially true for ago-go dancers. Drugs also serve to overcome the shyness resulting from embarrassment, enabling a woman to approach men and get customers.

19. Another smaller bar area along the bay outside of Olongapo.

20. See p. 67, note 5.

21. The Philippines has many small stores with benches in front where people hang out. Men often gather there to drink beer.

MANANG, MOTHER OF LITA

Province: Samar

Age: 56

When I was still a young woman I wanted to study first. I didn't want to get married right away. But my father said, "We don't have any money." Whatever our dreams are, they fail. My children work, but I am already old. I have difficulties with my body.

I was born in Leyte.[1] I had seven brothers and sisters. I was the fifth child. I'm told I was there until I was two years old. My parents moved to Samar. They said it was better in Samar, because there were more opportunities to earn a living. That was true. We didn't return to Leyte.

My parents were able to buy some land. We worked very hard. We planted bananas, coconut, root crops—everything. Bananas were very cheap then, only fifteen centavos per bunch. Not like now with high prices. Clothes were also cheap. My father was able to earn a little bit from farming to send us to school.

Manang

Manang's barrio is on a small island off the island of Samar. There are no roads and no electricity. Like most of the Philippines, Samar was originally covered with rain forest. Extensive logging has destroyed 90 percent of Philippine rain forests, and the remaining 10 percent is fast disappearing.

I was only able to study for about three months because the Japanese came . . . the fighting. I stopped studying because my parents were afraid to go to the mountains [to farm]. It was common knowledge that if the Japanese saw a Filipino, they would shoot. There were children in the mountains who got stabbed with bayonets. My parents were afraid.

We had a hard time finding food. We couldn't go to our land because of the Japanese guards. Whenever Filipino soldiers saw Japanese soldiers, of course, there was fighting. We stayed in our house in the barrio. We earned a living from the sea. If there were fish, we sold them. If we earned a little money, we bought some food.

Because four of the children were girls, my parents said, "Don't go to the mountains. It's dangerous. The Japanese or the soldiers might see you. We heard they pick up young women." Everyone knew that the Japanese would rape young women and then marry them. That was true—it did happen.

My mother had no food. She cried. There were so many of us . . . how would we eat? My father went out fishing in the sea. When he came home, we didn't have any rice to cook. I said to my older sister, "*Ate*, let's go get some of our food. We'll be careful. We'll check to be sure there are no soldiers or Japanese around. If we see any, we'll hide in the grass."

My sister said, "Okay, Di."[2]

Manang and her sister toasting with *tuba*

We ran very fast. We got some root crops and put them in a sack. We ran together. When we arrived back at the house, my mother was very happy because we had some food. She said, "You weren't seen by any soldiers?"

"No, Mother."

However, someone said to us, "Don't go back to the mountains because there are soldiers on the other side." We were frightened and did not go again.

My father returned in the evening with some fish. He said, "Where did you get the food?"

My mother said, "Our children were determined. They ran to the mountain. They were able to bring back some food. How are we going to make it? We don't have any food here."

My father said, "You might be seen."

The next day, Japanese soldiers arrived. There was fighting in our barrio. The soldiers were looking for the *barrio captain*.[3] My father was the *barrio captain*. We entertained them at our house and fed them eggs. The Japanese really like eggs.

The next day, some Filipino soldiers came through. We thought we were done for. The soldiers and the Japanese met at the place where we had gone in the mountains. They shot at each other there. We heard the guns. We stayed far away.

After the war, my father's work was the same . . . in the mountains. I made *benigs*. We would exchange the *benigs* for rice. One *benig* would

Mangingisda—the fisherman

be exchanged for three liters of rice. If we were able to make five *benigs*, we would have one sack of rice. That's how we earned our living. I also made sombreros and bags. We sold them in our barrio. A lot of people bought them. One sombrero cost five pesos. The bags cost six pesos.

We were not able to study. How could we return to school? There were bad storms. One year, there were three typhoons. Money was hard to come by. We had no clothes. During that time, we made clothes out of bark from large trees because we had no money. It was a problem if the clothes got wet because they were so thick. I was about twelve or thirteen then.

When I became a *dalaga*,[4] my husband was courting me. We were from the same barrio. My parents really liked him. My father said, "He's industrious. He knows how to work, to plant all kinds of plants." We got married with my parents' blessing.

I was sixteen. The priest advanced the age to eighteen, and we got married. Our work was the same as my parents . . . farming. We had our own land that we got from his parents. They had divided it up among the children, and my husband had one portion. We grew coconut and other plants. That's how we raised our children.

When we were married, whatever happened, we worked hard and ate

together. I took care of my children and raised chickens and pigs. When the pigs were large, I sold them and bought small ones.

I had twelve children. Eight of them are still alive. I only wanted to have three children. But how? We didn't have anything to prevent pregnancy. I kept on having babies—on and on. When I was in my forties, I stopped having children. I was thirty-nine when I had Lita. Lita is the youngest. When I stopped having my period, I stopped having babies.

I'm the one who took care of myself during childbirth. I was alone at the house. We were in the mountains. Our house was the only one around and there was no midwife. I knew how to give birth. I was not afraid. I lay down on the floor. My stomach would hurt, and then suddenly the child would cry. After giving birth, I cut the umbilical cord. There was no light. My only fear was that evil spirits might come to me.

When my oldest child was two years old. I had the second child. When the second child was two, she died. I don't know why. They say there are little people who live in the ground who took her.

When the second child was two years old, I was already pregnant again with the third. He also died. He was already big when he died, three years old. It happened suddenly. At about four in the afternoon, I was sweeping in the back. The child was not sick. At around six o'clock, he suddenly threw up. He died right away. I had had three children, and two of them died. Only one was alive. The fourth is Gina.

The death of the third child was very sudden. At two in the afternoon, she was running around in the back. I didn't think anything would happen to her. She was already big. I fell asleep. While I was sleeping, the child lay down. Suddenly she threw up, but she had not eaten anything. When she threw up, there was a lot of blood. I ran and called my husband immediately, "Hurry up! Come home!"

When we arrived at the house, the child was weak. After about two minutes, she died. I don't know what had happened to the child— she was vomiting. We were in the

A woman in the barrio

mountains, far from the barrio.

The other one only had a cough. He was four years old. The cough was not serious. I don't know what happened. He died right away.

There is no nurse or midwife in our barrio. Another barrio has someone, but it's far away. You can take a *bangka* boat, but it is far to walk. There are a lot of people with the flu right now. When I left last time, three people had died.

I wasn't able to send the children to school through the higher grades because my husband's only source of income was farming. When they were growing up, a typhoon came. The plants were destroyed in the typhoon, and we had no more root crops.[5] The typhoons were contin-uous. When the land was destroyed by a typhoon, we had to plant again. Right after planting again, we had nothing. I already had six children.

There was nowhere else for my husband to look for work. He went out to sea. If he brought back some fish, I exchanged it for corn or ba-nanas or coconut and sold that. I kept having children. It's good the oldest was able to study up through grade six because I worked hard making *benigs* and other things.

It was the same with Gina. I said, "Okay, work hard and endure so that you have some education even if it's only a little—so that you know how to write." I went to a friend of mine who has a store and borrowed

Naglalaba—Doing the wash. In the Philippines, clothes are usually washed by hand. In the barrio, water for house-hold use is carried from the community pump. Laundry and bathing are done in a river, waterfall, or spring.

Riverside transportation center and bathing and washing area. Manang's house in the mountains was a day's walk from a place like this where she could take a bangka boat to a larger barrio or urban center for health care.

In the barrio, health care, western and traditional, is limited or nonexistent. The old and the young are especially vulnerable. Some barrios have a health clinic with a part-time nurse and/or midwife. Many barrios have a *hilot* who does massage and acupressure. Traditional medicine using herbs is experiencing a revival throughout the country. An additional difficulty is the militarization of the countryside. Doctors and nurses who go to the countryside to treat people are frequently harassed by the military as communist sympathizers.

Mangingisda—Fishermen—in bangka boats repairing nets. Extensive logging leaves the land vulnerable. Heavy rains and typhoons wash the loose soil down onto the reefs and mangrove swamps, suffocating them, and the availability and variety of fish are drastically reduced. Fisherfolk are forced to travel to deeper waters and resort to dynamite and cyanide fishing. Today, 25 percent of the reefs are alive.

Bangka boats are the primary form of transportation in many rural areas. In Manang's barrio, they are the only form of transportation and are necessary for fishing. Here, bangka boats are constructed by men in the barrio.

Labandera—women who earn their living by washing clothes. This is one way for women to earn a living when they are no longer able to work in the clubs.

work with an agency.[8] I thought about it. I didn't want to because they said they were afraid to go to Manila. They didn't know Manila. All of them got married except Lita. She only studied until grade four. She was moved around all the time. She studied here but didn't finish. She studied in Manila but didn't finish. She studied in Cavite but didn't finish. Then we moved back to the province.

Lita and I went to Manila. I worked there as a maid. My boss deducted P 25 for the food Lita ate. I couldn't leave her with my husband in the province because she was still small. I brought her along so that I wouldn't be sad and homesick. My boss said he would send her to school. It would have been good for me even if my salary was smaller as along as she'd be able to study.

We moved. I got work washing clothes. I rented a room for P 70 per month. My husband was still in the province. I wrote and said, "If you come here to Manila, we won't have a hard time because I have a room." They came. We lived in Manila. Lita was already growing up. She said, "Ma, I'll go to work."

I said, "You study first. Even if you don't get through the higher grades, study first."

She studied. She didn't finish, because they moved us to Cavite. They said we would be given a lot in Cavite, but there was a charge of P 6,000.[9] They said after two years we would be asked to pay. That is also very difficult. Where would we be able to get the money to pay? We

some money to buy paper [for her schooling]. My husband worked as a laborer on the land and earned only thirty centavos in one day.[6] Rice cost fifteen centavos for one *salop*.[7] We could buy two *salop* in one day and not eat all of it. He worked as a laborer on the land and I had children. Our life was difficult.

There were those who said I should send the young women to

would be even poorer.

While we were in Cavite, I bought vegetables in the market and went around to houses to sell them. I cooked root crops and side dishes and sold them from house to house. When I came home, I would have one kilo of rice.

My husband said, "It's better if we go back to the province. It's difficult here. We have no way to earn money and nowhere to borrow or buy on credit." We sold the house and used all the money for transportation. We didn't sell the lot because it wasn't ours. We went to the province.

When we arrived in the province, this one [Lita] decided she wanted to go to Manila and get work. She ended up in Olongapo, in this work. Never mind. I'm not ashamed. It's up to her. We didn't say, "You work there." She thought about our poverty—that's why. She really wanted to go to Manila, and we agreed. She couldn't stand it in the province. She earns money if there is a ship. If not, nothing. We still love each other, even if we are there in the province. We are old now. Our crops were destroyed again in the typhoon.

When Lita first came to Olongapo, we were in debt. We had mortgaged our land because we were sick and there was a bad typhoon. We had nowhere to go for food. We were still the ones to farm it. When there was money from selling the copra, the rent was taken out, and the workers were paid first. What was left we split with the owner. We mortgaged the land to our cousin in the barrio. He is the *barrio captain.* He said, "Don't worry because our agreement is that when there's a harvest, we'll divide it."

For two years there wasn't any harvest because the typhoons were bad. The next year there was a drought. The crops and trees died. We were even poorer. Sometimes we would not be able to buy rice because we had no money. One salop

Women salt vendors. This is another way for women to earn a living when they are no longer able to work in the clubs.

Women and children in the barrio

of rice cost twenty pesos. Corn was fifteen pesos. How could we manage? We couldn't fish in the sea because the wind was strong and the waves high. If we had some clothes, we sold them to other people. Then we got money from Lita.

Before, our dream was to earn a living and buy good land so that whatever happened to our family would be good. How could we do that? After two years, you have a baby. After three years something suddenly happens to your family. Whenever we had money, our children got sick. How could I do everything? My husband only worked as a farmer. When the corn was high, the wind was strong. Nothing. If the typhoons had not come, we would have had many crops. Even our house was destroyed. If it hadn't been for our children, we would not have survived. No matter what we thought of to do, nothing worked. We had a carabao but had to sell it because of the poverty. Now we're old.

When Lita came to Olongapo, I didn't know what would happen. I agreed to let her come because I thought she would be working as a maid. My niece is the one who brought her here. They didn't say right away what the work was. She was still young. I said, "Okay, so that you will be able to reach your dreams of what you want to be." Later, she wrote and said she had a steady boyfriend, American.

I am ashamed, but I leave her alone if she wants to do this work. She said that she could earn a living. I'm the one who took care of this child who left me. Of course, you remember that you are a mother. You have many tears because of what went wrong. But we can't prevent them from doing what they want to do. I don't like it because she is still young; but what can I do? She wants to be here. I said, "Be kind. It's good if you stay with your husband.[10] Just be kind. I can't stop you, because you have your own mind."

If she goes to the States, she will be far away from us. If something happens to us, she won't know. If something happens to her, we won't know. We have no money. We would not be able to visit. I wept thinking about my child being so far away. It would be better if she had more education, but she only has a little. What will happen there? Of course, you worry. She will be alone there. I cannot stop her. I said, "Just be kind there."

If she has some [money] to give to us, that's good. If not, how will we make it? If my children give me support, that's good. If not, that's also fine. As long as they take care of themselves.

Ago-go dancers in a bar in Olongapo. An ago-go dancer earns from P 25 to P 40 per night, depending on the bar and the shift hours. Waitresses rely entirely upon tips and commissions. Some women, therefore, choose to work as ago-go dancers for the additional money. They generally dance for three songs and sit out one. The hours are long and exhausting.

Manang, being hugged by Lita in Lita and Terri's room in Olongapo. Manang's grandson, Michael, is in front of them. The young woman to the right is a relative from the same barrio. The child in front of her is the son of Terri, who is Manang's niece. The natural fathers of both boys are U.S. servicemen. The day this photo was taken Manang, Lita, and Michael left Olongapo for Manila to complete the paperwork for Lita and Michael's move to the United States.

1. Leyte is the island southwest of Samar in the Visayas. It is usually counted, with Samar, as one of the poorest islands.

2. A term used for younger sister, common with Cebuano-speaking people. People in Samar speak Wari-Wari and/or Cebuano.

3. *Barrio captain* is the rural version of *baranguay captain*. The *barrio captain* in the rural areas is an elected official with a similar role to that of a mayor of a city.

4. *Dalaga* is the Tagalog term for young woman and/or virgin. See glossary.

5. Rice is a staple in the Philippines; but when their poverty precludes even rice, people live on root crops. The loss of these root crops was therefore the loss of the only food left.

6. At the present exchange rate, this would be less than a penny.

7. A measurement equal to three liters.

8. There are agencies that go to the province to recruit young women to work as maids in Manila and/or to work in the clubs selling their sexual labor. A woman may be told that she will have a job as a maid and end up in debt, working in a club.

9. This was part of a resettlement program for people living on Smokey Mountain, the garbage dump. It was common under Marcos, and continues to be common, for squatter communities to be moved from Manila to the outlying areas. This was often done to make room for large buildings. Cavite is several hours south of Manila.

10. The American whom Lita planned to marry.

GLENDA

Province: Manila/Sapang-Palay

Age: 30

Glenda, her daughter Angela, and
her companion, Inday, at home

I want other people to know that the
life working in the clubs is difficult,
especially for the women they call
prostitutes . . . the loss of sleep . . . if
you don't earn anything, there is no
money for food . . . they get sick and
have to spend money on medicine. If
you really look at it, they have great
difficulties. It is ugly. All different
men have sex with you. It should be
that only your husband has sex with
you but in the bar, it's all different
men. If it were possible, I wouldn't
do it. But there is nothing the wo-

Team Spirit troops partying in Olongapo. Team Spirit is an annual military exercise conducted by U.S. military forces with the military forces of various other countries in the region.

men can do to earn a living. The work in the club is dirty because you're not respected by the Americans. They really look at you as pigs. If I were in the Americans' position, would I respect you if you were just bought?

I think that, if possible, it would be better to get rid of the base and give better work to the women. Maybe they would accept that. Their situation is very bad. They don't want the base to shut down because that's where they earn their living. I understand. But I would like the women to be able to change so that they wouldn't be in the bars all their lives.

My dream was to finish my studies, but I was not able to. I was an athlete in school. I played volleyball, and ran track and field. I would have won a trophy, but I couldn't continue because I didn't have a uniform. You have to have money for uniforms. I wanted to be a singer because I have a good voice, but my sisters said nothing would come of that. Now, my hope is that [my daughter] Angela will finish school.

We are twelve siblings, five girls and seven boys. I'm the third youngest. All the girls have worked in clubs.

My parents are from Bicol, but I never lived there. They went to Manila to look for work because it was hard to earn a living in Bicol, even though we had land there. My father used to plant corn and root crops, but he only had a small piece of land and my mother didn't have any. That's why I was born in Manila.

Water sellers: Smokey Mountain urban poor area of Manila

My parents didn't have regular work. Even so, my father managed to build a small house and we were able to study. My mother washed clothes, and my father worked as a carpenter. There were a lot of people. It was really a squatter area. The houses were very close together. There were also thieves and killers. It was frightening.

We stayed there until someone high up in Manila decided to force the squatters to leave. They said it was because someone was building a high building. There was nothing we could do. Everyone who lived there had to leave. Everyone was moved to Sapang-Palay.[1] I was about thirteen when we moved.

It was difficult in Sapang-Palay. In Manila, if we didn't have any work, we were still able to eat because we lived near my mother's boss. They gave us food and supported us. But in Sapang-Palay, if you have no money, you go hungry. You won't be able to study. You'll die if you have no work.

It was better in Sapang-Palay than Manila because, in Manila, the place was very small. In Sapang-Palay, you had your own land and could build a house. We were grateful to be given land in Sapang-Palay but getting work was difficult, especially if you had not finished high school. Sometimes my father's friends invited him to help build a house. In Manila, he would work in different places when his friends called on him. In Sapang-Palay, he was only called occasionally. My father planted rice. Four of us children cultivated the land. Before, there were not many houses. There was still a lot of grass. We are the ones who cleared the land. We planted root crops, bananas, rice, and corn—just food for ourselves. Sometimes when it was too hot, our crops died.

I sold water. We lived near the well. I would take water to those people who had no well. One container cost two pesos. I only earned a little bit every day because there were a lot of us selling water.

Neighborhood near the bar area

I finished grade six in Sapang-Palay. I also studied through the third year of high school, but I didn't finish. I had a Filipino lover in Sapang-Palay. He was older than I. He was married and had children who were already young women. I was about fifteen or sixteen then.

My friend introduced me to him. I didn't realize he liked me. He said, "Come to my house . . . I have some money to give to you." I should have known that he planned to do something to me, but I just wasn't thinking. I was happy about going to his house. I thought he would give me money. But what he gave me was [my son] Edwin.

He asked me if I would like some coke. I said I would. I didn't expect the coke to have something in it that would make me go to sleep. While we were talking and talking, he had me drink the coke. I couldn't go home for two days. I stayed there lying down. On the third day, I woke up. He had gotten my virginity. I was able to go home after the third day.

At first my father was very angry. He said, "If you have thrown yourself away on someone older than you, even older than I, that's ugly to see." Edwin's father was fifty-eight. My father beat me and tied my feet to the ceiling of the house. My head

was hanging down. I got very dizzy. He said it was because the man was old. If he hadn't been old, it would have been okay for them. I accepted it because I had done wrong. My mistake was going to his house when my parents didn't know. He got my virginity. I blame him for taking my virginity, but he was very kind.

If I got money from the father of my child, I gave it to my parents. I thought: "This is what is being given to me, so I will do it." Also, if I did not act on my own, I would die.

Then I gave birth to Edwin. I went [to his father's house] regularly. He would give me food to take to school. He said he would support us, that he would not abandon us. But in the end, when Edwin was two or three, he died. He had a heart attack. I have only had a relationship with one Filipino, Edwin's father.

My father said I should stop studying because he couldn't support us. He said, "You can work for your sister as a maid." My sister was already here in Olongapo. I thought it would be good to study here. I thought my sister would support me. I moved here to Olongapo and worked for my sister. But my sister did not send me to school. My father said, "If you aren't able to finish studying, just go to work in a bar."

Women with their children. Most women working in the clubs have one or more children.

Three of my sisters were already working in bars. They had run away from home. My parents knew that my sisters worked in bars. There was nothing my parents could do. They said that if my sisters did not work in a bar, who would support them? My parents have also been here in Olongapo. They come to stay with my sister. Sometimes they stay for one or two months. They say the work is good. You can earn a lot of money.

In Olongapo, my sister said, "Don't worry—I'll give you a boy-friend." I didn't expect that my older sister would give me an American. He was at my nephew's birth-day party. He courted me, and we were married at the Aglipayan church. He is the father of Angela.

My husband was kind. He also took my Filipino child, Edwin, to his heart. He was never strict with Edwin. He really cared for Edwin and loved him. My child called him Papa. Edwin and Angela, they did not even tease each other or say things like, "You, your father is dif-ferent, my father is different." They were really brother and sister. They helped each other. That's what I really liked about the two of them.

There are some Americans who are really kind. They are open to your whole family. My husband was different. He wanted his support to only be for myself and my children. That didn't happen. My family al-ways came to me. My mother would ask for money and then, the next day, my sister would ask for money. How could I save? How could I stand on my own feet if they were al-ways at my house? Maybe my hus-band noticed and wondered why it was like that.

He didn't support us every month. His mother in the States is the one who sent us money. The letters and packages were addressed to my sis-ter. My sister took the money and the packages. She only gave me a lit-tle bit of what was there. She also took the most beautiful clothes. If it weren't for my family, I would be in the States now.

A lot of people say it is also diffi-cult in the States. You have to work. I think: "I have not been able to fin-ish my studies. What would happen to me? I would just be a maid to my husband in his house." I think it's good I wasn't able to go. I like it here in the Philippines. Even if you haven't finished your studies, you can find some kind of work—whatever kind—and be able to eat. In the States, things are very expen-sive. How would you be able to earn a living if you don't know English?

I started working in a bar in 1980. The support from my husband wasn't enough. It's because of my family that I started working in a bar. I started working in Subic City at the Continental Bar.² My mother was with me when I applied because I said, "I don't know how to work in a bar."

She said, "I'll talk to the owner of the bar because I know him." She talked to him. I got a job.

I didn't have any girlfriends then, not until Inday arrived in our bar. Her uncle was the owner of the Continental Club. He was a womanizer. He wanted to have sex with Inday. I told her, "If I'm gone on a bar fine, lock your room so that nothing will happen to you. You know your uncle is a womanizer—be careful." We became close. She also loved Edwin and Angela.

My children didn't know I worked in a bar, but they knew I lived there because I was *stay-in*. I didn't have my two children sleep in the bar, but I supported them. Angela and Edwin would come to our bar at about five or six in the evening and the person caring for them would come for them. Sometimes Angela said, "Aunti [Inday], where does my mother go? Why does she have an American with her?"

Indy said, "They're just bar-hopping. She'll come back here."

Edwin was studying. My nephew took him along when he ran away. My nephew often ran away. I don't know why he took my child. He was only eight. My nephew was ten.

We looked for them here in Olongapo. We had a radio announcement to look for him and we went to our friends to see if he was there. I went

Bernadette with her mother and brother, visiting her mother's bar on her night off

around to the street children, but he wasn't there. They had gone to Manila. My older brother in Bulacan saw them selling ice.³ He took them to his house, but they ran away again. Maybe they thought I would beat them. We still haven't seen him. It's difficult. I love my child.

Filipinos working and hanging out in a bar on a slow night. Young men in Olongapo work in the clubs as bartenders, janitors, waiters, or DJs. In the smaller clubs, male Filipino friends may also come and hang out, particularly on slow nights.

I think the truth about my nephew is that his mother didn't love him. She loved her youngest more than her oldest because the oldest was ugly. The youngest was good-looking. Maybe the oldest rebelled. He thought he wasn't loved by his mother, so why should he stay there? But I never got angry with my child. I never hit him.

Even now, Angela asks if her brother will come back. Sometimes she cries. I say that I don't know. If he comes back, we will accept him, even if he's married or sick, because he is my child. He is my blood and part of me. I told Angela, with the grace of God, maybe her brother will come back.

My sister had a Filipino husband [live-in]. She loved the Filipino until she lost all her belongings. She didn't think about the fact that she already had an American husband. She only thought about love. She didn't realize that the Filipino was living off of her. All her money in the bank was used up. Now her Filipino is also gone. He has another woman. He ran away from her.

When I see hostesses who have Filipinos, I don't like to look. The money they earn, they give to their Filipinos. They say they love the Filipinos more than the Americans— they just earn money from the Americans. Their Filipinos don't work. They depend on the women.

It's very difficult to work in a bar, especially if you are *stay-in*. You can't easily leave the bar. You have to ask permission even to go to church. Before 3:00 P.M. you must be back in the bar. You constantly lose sleep, and then a ship comes in. You have to get up at two o'clock to take customers. Sometimes when there are no customers, you have no food. You have no money. Whom could you borrow from? Sometimes there weren't very many customers in Subic and Barretto. Not like in Olongapo, where there are many.

I was afraid with the first bar fine. I didn't know about blow jobs and three holes. I thought: "I already have children . . ." But they say that if you go for three months after you give birth without having sex, it hurts. It was anal sex that made me cry.

An American said, "I like you."

I had a friend. I said to my friend, "What's that: 'I like you'?"

She said, "It means he wants to pay for a short-time. Do you agree to do a short-time with him?"

I said, "Yes." I didn't expect that with the short-time, there is a three hole. I really didn't expect it.

He said, "I will put my penis there in your ass."

I said, "What do you mean, put your penis in my ass?"

He said, "The position is like this."

He put me in position and suddenly pierced me with his penis in my ass. That's what three hole meant. I thought he was just going to put it in the bottom [vagina]. When he was finished, he gave me P 2. I really cried then. I thought: "So that's what it is like here if you

Waiting for customers in Barrio Barretto. Women working in Barrio Barretto tend to be younger and cheaper. As in Olongapo, they are integrated into the community.

Bakla waiting for customers. Young men also sell their sexual labor in Olongapo, but there are far fewer of them than women. Bakla is the Tagalog term for gay and/or effeminate men.

don't know English. The Americans take advantage of you."

My friend said, "That's right . . . you have to be wise."

The first time I gave a blow job, I threw up outside. I didn't know that throwing up outside is banned. I carried a small towel with me after that.

I worked there for a month and didn't make very much money. One of my friends said, "Why don't you try doing floor shows. You might make a lot of money."

I really needed the money because Angela was very sick. I said, "I'll try. Take me along when you do a floor show."

We did them at Baloy Beach.4 There were a lot of Filipinos watching. I cried. There were only three of us doing the floor show. We were completely nude. I put an egg in my vagina. I broke the egg and pushed

it out of my vagina. I didn't know that some of the shell was left inside.

After a week I had pain in my vagina. I smelled the eggshell inside. I went to the bathroom. There was a piece of shell the size of a fingertip. My friend said, "Go to the doctor and have a checkup. You might have an infection." I would have developed an infection soon if I hadn't gone to the doctor.

I got used to that bar. I began earning more money by giving blow jobs under the table. I would give blow jobs to five men at the same time under the table, one right after the other. I would finish them all. I would get P 40 from each American. I divided what I earned with the manager and the owner. I thought: "If I don't earn this way, my children and I will go hungry. If I am not like this, we will die." So I just made my face thicker.

A woman with her work rag. Women who regularly do blow jobs carry rags to throw up in afterward and to wipe their mouths or hide their faces.

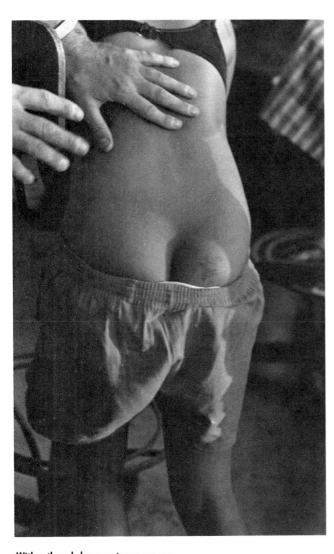

With a three holer, a customer can use a woman's vagina, mouth, and anus to have sex. A customer shows others what a three holer is.

Seeking customers

I got used to doing blow jobs and floor shows in different places in Subic. All the women there did the same thing, not only me.

What I felt about the Americans when I did floor shows is that they seemed brutal. It seemed they didn't respect Filipinos—like they saw us as pigs. My friend said, "That's what they think of us, the Americans, that we really are pigs because we do this."

I said, "There is nothing we can do. We do this in order to earn money."

The truth is, I have experienced everything. The things that my sisters did not experience here, I have experienced.

Once, an American paid my bar fine. He was drunk. We were in a hotel. Our room was far from the counter. I didn't think he was a bad man who would beat me. I thought

he looked kind. But he put a pillow over my mouth and hurt my vagina. He did not want me to stop what he was doing. He put the pillow over my mouth and then gave me many hickies on my neck. I couldn't breathe because my mouth and nose were covered. He kicked me and hit me. I tried to avoid the blows.

I kicked him and then kicked the door of our room. That's how I called for help. If I hadn't been able to kick the door, I might be dead now. I was crying. The boys came.[5] They helped me. They said, "Miss, sorry, but we didn't hear anything. All we heard was the air conditioner. We didn't know your customer was like that. Don't blame us. Blame yourself because you don't choose your customers carefully." The boys beat him up and put him in a jeep going back to Olongapo. He had been taking drugs, injecting himself.

City police at the Magsaysay Police Station. Like the majority of the Filipinos, the police are underpaid. Some women report that police solicit bribes from streetwalkers and women in the clubs. These women may provide sexual labor as an alternative to paying the bribe. Women also report that some police are involved in drug trafficking.

That's what I can't forget. I only had one customer like that.

He was a sadist. My friend said he had killed someone. He wasn't caught. His friends look for him if he is drunk because he is a sadist. When he isn't drunk, they say he's kind. I thought he was going to put the Pepsi bottle in my vagina, but he used it to put his cigarettes in. He also burned his skin with his cigarettes. He was a sadist.

Inday went home to Tarlac. I went to Tarlac, and Inday and her sister, Fely, came along back to Olongapo. When I brought Inday and Fely back to Olongapo, my brothers and sisters wouldn't talk to Inday. They ignored her. It was as if she were dead. My sister said, "Do

you have to have a companion? Do you have to feed her and provide a place for her to sleep?" My sister wouldn't let us sleep at her house. We slept wherever we could. Our situation then was very difficult. We had only five pesos. We just brought cheap bread. Inday got angry with my sisters. Sometimes my mother is also like that. If you have money, my mother is nice. If you don't have money, she treats you differently.

Angela doesn't love my mother because my mother hits her. My mother wants Angela to come immediately when she calls. But Angela is still a child. She needs to play. My mother doesn't want her to play. She wants Angela to always be by her side. Once, Angela was downstairs playing and did not use "ma'am" when she answered. She beat my child with a wire and was going to push her out the window. I saw her. Inday saw her. Inday cried. I cried.

It's like what she did to me when I was partly grown. That's what she is doing to my child. We all had many experiences like that—all us children. My parents treated me better when I was still young because they loved me. They were affectionate with me, and I was affectionate with them. I didn't taste beatings. But by the time I was thirteen or fourteen, I was already being beaten by my father and mother.

My father would say, "You have to work now. You must return the food we gave you—everything." None of my siblings stayed with my parents very long. I know my youngest sister resented them. She ran away, and we haven't seen her since. She was nineteen. She worked in a club first and then ran away. It was my parents' fault.

Once my mother wrote to my husband. She said to him, "Your child, Angela, we're going to have her adopted." My mother thought she could frighten my husband.

I said, "Why did you do that? If he's going to support us, he'll support us. If we try to frighten him, he really won't give us anything."

Angela received a letter. He said, "How are you, Angela?" But, my name was not there. It was for Angela. He said, "Finish your studies. Maybe when you're fourteen, I'll bring you here. Say hello to your mama. I have a wife now, I hope you won't be too shocked." That was all. No money.

Street children may live on the streets, or may live at home and work on the streets to help earn the money necessary for their family's survival. Beginning with selling chewing gum and cigarettes, the children often first sell their sexual labor when a serviceman asks and they discover they can earn more money. Only about 10 percent of the street children have mothers who work in the bars.

There haven't been any more letters. Angela thinks her father will return. I said, "You can think what you want to." I don't want to interfere with my child's mind, with her thoughts. I don't want to crush them. She's big now. She can understand, and she knows what is right and wrong.

I loved my husband. It hurt when we separated. He also can't blame me for falling in love with a woman. Before, I had a tendency toward being a "T-bird."[6] Before I had the Filipino, when I saw a beautiful women, I couldn't. . . . But, even if I have a woman companion, I don't abandon my child.

Sometimes Angela's friends tease her and say, "Your mother is *tayma*."[7] They call it *tayma* or father 'n' mother. But she does not believe that Inday and I are lovers. She doesn't know it's considered bad. Maybe in the end I'll tell her, when she's older. Maybe she'll say that it's ugly.

She knows her aunt really loves her. She really loves Inday. Before, when Inday went to Tarlac, Angela said, "Auntie, why don't you and Mama get married?"

Inday said, "How could she marry me? She has breasts."

Angela said, "Oh, I guess I made a mistake—it's not possible."

Women with women is not good because there are so many obstacles. Inday and I have many stumbling blocks, like my mother and my other friends.

Angela knows I work in a bar. Once she said, "Mama, don't go with Americans, because sometimes they don't give you money and some-times they also hit you."

I said to Angela, "What do you think about my work?"

She said, "Ma, it's ugly because there are many men having sex with you. There are many different men. Many men kiss you. That's why I don't kiss you because many men kiss you. Mama, it's ugly because there are many mothers and daughters who work together in the bar."

I said to her, "Do you also want to work in a bar?"

"Mama, if possible, I don't want to be like you there. I want my life to be good."

Angela is smart, but she watches too much TV and gets low marks on her report card.

I took care of Inday and Fely [in the bar]. If they had a customer, I was the one who talked with their customer. I said they were both still cherry. The regulations at Scotties are also difficult. They are strict. Even if you are a cherry, you still have to go on bar fines.

I told Inday, "If you go on a bar fine, tell him to bring you back home, that you are still a virgin. Before you have sex, you must get a lot of money." She said she would be careful. But Inday was not careful and now she's pregnant. It hurt me inside that she got pregnant, that she lost her cherry, and I didn't know. I was the last one to know. It was as if she had put shit on my head. I said, "If you had been care-ful, you wouldn't have had sex."

To tell the truth, I was really an-gry because it was as if she had eaten her words. She said that before she went with an American, she

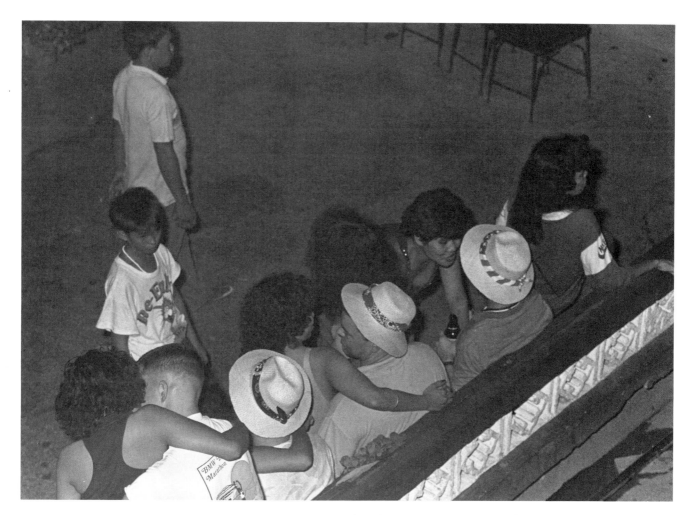

Four in a row: women at work

would ask for a lot of money. Thank goodness she stole $40. If she hadn't done that, where would she have gotten money? He would have had sex with her and she wouldn't have gotten any money from it.

The American doesn't know. She didn't talk to him, and now her stomach is large. He used to be on the *Midway*. He's old. He didn't come back to her. He has another woman. I said, "If he arrives, if you see him on the street, whether or not he's drunk, tell him. Even if he has a woman, open your clothes, show him your stomach is large because of him only." She doesn't want to. There is nothing I can do. I don't

want to say any more. I don't want to fight.

It's our problem. It's also my problem, but it's more her problem. Even if it is the father's problem, he doesn't make it his problem. We are the ones who have the problem, not the father. It hurts me, but I don't always say that to her. We don't blame each other. We would only fight. I know she made a mistake, and we must both accept it.

Now she's thinking of having an abortion by catheter. She's already five months pregnant. I think: "Can Inday survive if she hemorrhages? If her body loses a lot of blood? It would be good if she were heavier

A woman

and her body had more substance to it, but she's thin. She might die." When she talks about having the abortion by catheter, I ignore her because I know it's bad. It's already a child.

I have not thought of having an abortion, but I've had a tubal ligation. I don't want any more children because life is already difficult. I wish other woman would also do the same so that they don't keep having children and having abortions.

I go to church occasionally. If I have a big problem I say, "God, help me with my problem. How can I solve it?" Sometimes I think: "I work in a bar and then I go to church, maybe the Lord won't accept me." But, maybe God understands my situation.

When I go to church, I notice that when there is a ship, no one goes to church. When there is no ship, there are many at church. But does the priest have to say that when there is a ship, no one comes to church? The priests do not help the women in the bars. What help can they give the women in the bars? Just sermons. They shouldn't preach to the women because maybe they understand why the women are in this situation.

What I feel about myself is that I am ashamed. It's as if I'm not needed in the world. Maybe now that I'm like this, the One above will understand.

1. Sapang-Palay is a resettlement area about two-hours outside of Manila. Whole squatter communities from Manila were moved there. (See also Madelin's story, p. 48).
2. Subic City and Barrio Barretto are two bar areas along the bay outside of Olongapo. The bars are smaller, the women younger, and the atmosphere considered wilder.
3. Bulacan is an area on the outskirts of Manila.
4. Baloy Beach is a beach resort just outside of Olongapo.
5. The term "boy" is used for young males who work in hotels or clubs doing janitorial work and running errands. Sometimes they also work as waiters.
6. "T-bird" is the term used for women loving women.
7. *Tayma* is a combination of the Tagalog word for father, *tatay* or *'tay*, and *ma*. It is used in reference to someone who is both a father and mother to her child.

LINDA

Province: Iloilo

Age: 37

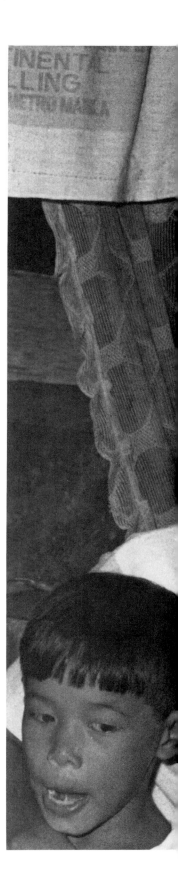

I studied at the elementary school in Iloilo. I was sickly. I used to have sudden attacks of stomach pain several times a year. Some people said if you lit a cigarette, it fought the illness. My father bought me cigarettes. I smoked. The illness did not go away. The doctor said it was an ulcer, but I always ate well. Some people said when I started to menstruate the illness would go away. I seldom got ill after I started to menstruate.

They said I inherited it from my mother, who also used to be sickly. Sometimes she would go to the hospital for a week, but she did not get well. Since she decided to go to the witch doctor, she hasn't gotten sick.[1] Every year, she makes an offering of food and gives it to the people of the earth—the people we can't see.[2] She also now knows how to treat people who are victims of witchcraft. If someone has a fever, she knows if they should see a doctor or if it is from the invisible people.

My father was just a farmer. We had about fifteen carabao, and many pigs, goats, and chickens. My mother was industrious, working in the house and taking care of the animals. When we didn't have any money, she would catch a chicken and take it to the market to sell. We had plenty of rice because we had our own rice field. Sometimes if we really had nothing, we would sell the rice. My mother was also industrious about fishing. We weren't poor because both my mother and father worked very hard.

However, my father got sick with cancer [after I left home]. We sold the land, the carabao and goats. He stayed in Manila for three months in two different hospitals, but he did not get well.

When I was still small, my father was my inspiration. He's the one who took care of me when I got sick. Even if he was tired from work, he would come and hold me. I was already in sixth grade, already big, but he would still hold me. I would sit on his lap and he would play with my hair. Even my mother didn't do that. That's why we loved our father.

We also loved our mother, but she didn't seem to have time for us. It seemed as if she was always sick and always angry. If we did something wrong, just something small—of course, children get in trouble—

Linda at home in Olongapo with
Marlon, Michael, and Maricel,
her three youngest children

Drying fish on the road

tuba. She said, "You love your work on the school more than your children, more than us. When tomorrow comes, we won't be able to buy any food because you don't have any time for farming or for your family."

My father said he was taking care of the farm and, of course, there was the opportunity for this school so he gave it priority. It was important for the students. He said, "Why don't you kill me? Get it over with."

My mother left. My brother took the knife and returned it to its place. We were all crying. I was about seven then. My father gathered up his clothes and said he was leaving. He said, "You are grown now. If we don't see each other, you will be able to earn a living yourselves. Help your mother. There is a lot of rice, and you can sell the chickens and goats and pigs and carabao. I'll go somewhere else."

He wasn't able to leave because one child was hanging on to one leg, another the other leg, one on his arm—there were a lot of us then. We were all still at home. One of my sisters took his bag of clothes and put it in the firewood container so that he wouldn't see it. Afterward, my parents didn't speak for a week. My father continued to work on the school.

There are twelve of us. Two of the children died. The second oldest died giving birth to her fourth baby. The other one, a boy, was seven years old when he got sick with measles and died. Twelve are still living.

she'd yell. If we didn't listen, she'd hit us or pinch us.

When my father was the *barrio captain*[3] our parents fought. He was in charge of everything in the barrio. If there was trouble, he had to take care of it. Then, a new school was being built. My father had to supervise that. He no longer had time for our livelihood or home.

Once when they fought, my mother got the *sangol*.[4] She put it against my father's neck. We had about ten coconut trees, which we used this knife for. My father made

Our oldest is fifty years old now. She's still a virgin, an old virgin.[5] She was disappointed twice. She says that men just play around. When she was thirty-five, she said if she got married then she wouldn't be able to have children. It would be useless. She works as a maid in Manila. She lives with her bosses. She has been their maid for thirty-seven years. She is treated like a sister.

One of my sisters went to Manila because she was intelligent. She always got top honors. Some missionaries took her. They were Protestants, Baptists. She went to a Bible school. They paid for her studies.

When we were all studying, there were a lot of expenses. The second sister was smart at her studies. My father said he hoped she would help the rest of the children who were still studying because, "We are old now and all of you eat a lot." She said she did not plan to get married, that she would help my parents.

We killed a pig to celebrate her graduation from college and return. When she came home, she brought along a husband—a diploma and a husband.

My father was angry. He said, "We were counting on you, but you lied."

My mother cried and cried. All of us cried. My mother said, "You, the rest of you, you'll get married, too. Our money is wasted. We are defeated by our sweat and afterward you just get married. You don't help us."

My parents said, "Starting now,

Entrance to an elementary school in the province. It is difficult for families to keep children in school because they need the child's labor for the survival of the family. Women in the clubs often have three to six years of education.

Children watching a carpenter at work

none of you are going to study." I thought they were just angry.

I was ugly, but there were a lot of men courting me. My father said, "Especially you, Linda. You have all these men courting you. I'm sure you'll get married." I didn't answer, because I was hurt.

At that time, my aunt was there from Manila. She worked at Faith Academy.[6] She said, "Your parents are angry. There are still so many of you, and your father is only a farmer. I'll get you a job with the missionaries. The salary is good, and the room is free. You'll be able to help your parents."

I said, "I only have three months left to graduate. It seems like a waste." But I was also discouraged by what my parents said.

Before, my father was the one who cooked our breakfast. By 5:00 in the morning, he would be awake. He would cook the rice, there would be water for coffee, and our lunch would be prepared—wrapped in banana leaves. We would just eat

and bathe. That morning when I woke up, there was nothing on the table. At 6:00, no one was moving around, I thought: "They really don't want me to go to school, because my father has not cooked. I'll go with my aunt."

I said to my parents, "I'm going with Aunt to Manila. She'll get me a job with the Americans." My mother said, "Okay. It's good if you work. If you want to finish your studies, it's better if you are self-supporting so you know how difficult it is."

I went to Manila. I was sixteen or seventeen. I started working at Faith Academy as a maid. Some of the high school students boarded there. They had lots of clothes. It wasn't difficult because they had washing machines.

After a few months, some house parents decided that they liked me. They said I was industrious. I agreed to work for them. They didn't treat me like a maid. They were kind to me. I had a day off on Sunday. They would escort me to wherever I was going, because it was a long walk to public transportation. I didn't know how to cook. They said, "Just watch so you can learn." I learned how to cook their food. At first I wasn't used to their food. At lunchtime they didn't eat—they would just have bread.[7] But I got used to it.

The woman wondered if I wanted to continue my education. I was happy, of course. She said, "Take whatever course you want. We're only here for four years. After four years, we're going to leave. If you want, we'll take you with us." She said they would find me a job there.

Edward, the man who became my husband, also worked there as a gardener. I had a boyfriend. We planned to get married. Sometimes I would tell Edward about him. Edward was always putting my boyfriend down. When he saw a picture, he said my boyfriend was ugly. I didn't know that Edward liked me. When we talked, it was as if we were brother and sister.

One time, the women of our house said, "Linda, we are leaving for three days." It was just myself and the three children. One evening, after I put the children to bed, Edward said, "Come here. I have something to give you. I bought some *pansit* [a noodle dish] and *dalanghita* [a type of tangerine]."

I went into his room. I trusted him. I took a *dalanghita* and peeled it. He was standing by the door. He was nude except for his shorts. When I went to leave, he was there by the door, blocking it. I said, "Let me out." I thought he was just joking. He just kept looking at me and looking at me. I said, "Why won't you let me out?"

Then, he pushed me. He took a knife and pointed it at me. The knife was long. I wasn't nervous or afraid yet. I said, "Why are you pointing that knife at me? I'll slap you." His face was very red. It was as if he had a demon inside of him. I tried to take the knife away from him. We

fought over it. I didn't know that I'd been cut. Blood was dripping.

He tore my clothes. That's when I knew he was going to rape me. I ran. I yelled. No one heard me. I fought back. The room was a mess. The fan had fallen down, and lots of things were broken. I grew weak. He got all my clothes off. He was strong. He raped me. I cried and cried. I said, "Mother . . . Mother." I thought I was going to die.

When it was over, he said he was sorry. He said, "I did this to you because I had no other way. I know you don't like me. I know you're planning to get married. I like you. I couldn't speak because you treat me like a brother."

I said, "If you love me, why did you do this to me? Why did you rape me and hurt me?"

He said, "I don't know why I did this. Don't worry. I'll marry you. I did this because I want to marry you."

I said, "What kind of reason is that?"

In the Philippines, once a man has had sex with you, once you are raped by a man, you can't marry anyone else. You must marry him whether you want to or not. If you have a boyfriend and he finds out you are not a virgin, he won't want you. Those are the traditions of the older generation. There is a saying in the Philippines: "Wherever you fall down, that's where you get down. Or, whatever man has sex with you, he's the one who will marry you." At the time, I also

Beginning of Magsaysay Strip: jeepneys lining up across from the main gate to the base. The bridge over the canal at the left leads from the base to the strip. The canal, commonly called "Shit River" because it is so polluted, separates the base from the town.

thought like that. I was confused. I thought: "This is my life. All my dreams are gone." I didn't think that even though I was no longer a virgin, I could go on as usual. In my mind, that was not possible.

The next day, he took me to his mother and father in Pampanga.[8] When we arrived, I was crying. I told his family that he had raped me. His stepmother said, "You had sex. She is your wife now. Do you have money for the expenses of your wedding?" He said he had been putting his salary in the bank.

The next day we talked. Edward told me what I should do and say. I should tell my sister that I liked him so she wouldn't get angry. I should also say the same thing to the woman who was my boss. I just said yes. We went home to Manila.

When we arrived, the woman embraced me. She cried and cried. It was then I felt that even though she was not Filipino, she really cared for

me. We hugged each other. She noticed my skin. She said, "Why? How did that happen?" I told her about his raping me. She got angry. I said there was nothing they could do. It was over now.

She said, "We're here. If you plan to finish your studies, we'll take care of that. It's okay if you leave him. Think about it well. Don't get married to him if you don't like him." I explained to them the Philippine tradition and that I still held to the traditions of the older generation. I didn't know much about life yet. I followed the traditions because I was afraid.

We went to my sister's place. I told her everything. They didn't like my husband. They said he was too young. And they didn't like people from Pampanga. They said people there had dog's blood because they liked to eat dog. She said, "You can still leave him even if something has happened. You could go home to

our province." She said to Edward, "You can't marry our sister because you raped her. You haven't finished your studies. Can you give our sister a good future? Can you support a family?"

My husband said, "I'll be able to support her, and I will marry her. I won't abandon your sister. I have work. And I did what I did because I love her."

My one sister said I should call my boyfriend. "Maybe he'll have compassion on you." I thought: "I have been raped. Is that still possible?" Before, he had said, "I want you to be a virgin when we get married." He didn't have sex with me because he said we should get married first. We were together for two years, and he only kissed me. I thought: "Will he marry me? I've been raped." I cried and cried.

I talked to my aunt. She said, "You must get married now in order to fix up the trouble in your life; in order to be acceptable." I thought: "What happened in my life is fate. I'll get married even if I don't like him."

My sister sent money to my parents so they could come to Manila for my wedding. I told them everything. They said, "What can be done? It's finished. It's good if you get married."

I had my period one month and then no more. I was pregnant. We moved here to Olongapo. My husband worked as a jeepney driver for about five months. He rented a jeepney. Sometimes he earned P 50 in one day. It depended on whether or not he could get Americans to pay for a special trip to Subic.9

It also depended on whether or not there was a ship. If there was a ship, there were a lot of passengers and he could earn P 200 or P 300. If there was no ship, there were few passengers. It was also like the clubs. If there is a ship, they earn a lot. Everything in Olongapo is like that.

Liberty. When an aircraft carrier and its escorts pull into port, up to 10,000 servicemen may descend on the bars of Olongapo, Barrio Barretto, and Subic City for liberty. "First liberty" and "last liberty" are considered the best business days.

Banks, supermarkets, and large stores employ armed guards. Middle-class people use banks primarily for keeping cash safe, or for transferring cash from one city to another. Women working in the clubs seldom have enough cash to open an account; theirs is a boom-bust economy based on the coming and going of ships. They borrow from street money lenders, and are often in debt to landlords and sari-sari stores (neighborhood shops that sell a little bit of everything).

Most of his cousins worked inside the base. One cousin said, "Apply to be a driver inside the base. We'll help you." He was able to get a job driving a taxi. His earnings got better. Sometimes he would make P 200 or P 250 every day. Plus, they got a salary. He was able to save. I put the money in the bank. Whenever I have money, I put it in the bank immediately.

We had five children. Our lives were going well. He really loved me. He would do whatever he could to make me happy. He made me love him. He was affectionate. When we slept, he wanted to hold me even if it was hot. If I didn't like it, he would get angry and push me away. "You don't want me to hug you? Okay." He would turn his back. I'd be the

one to reach out to him.

He didn't like to arrive and not find me at the house or to arrive and find the children dirty. He wanted the children always to be clean. He also didn't like the house to be dirty. Sometimes I didn't clean very well because, with children, you sweep and it's dirty again right away. But if he was about to arrive, I would clean.

If we fought, it wasn't the kind of fight where we yelled. We talked when we went to bed without getting angry. If he knew he was wrong, he was the first to talk. If I realized I was wrong, I was the one who would approach him. The children grew up without hearing us fight. When we talked, we were sweet.

Other people said it was like we

Neighborhood children playing in Olongapo

Michael

and the children will be healthier in Pampanga because the air is fresh."

I didn't think he was cheating on me, because his salary was always all there when he gave it to me. And sometimes he gave me extra money. When he arrived, he would bring a lot of food. He always wanted to have good food. He bought all my clothes, even my bras, panties, and dusters. Some people said he was a little bit effeminate, but he wasn't gay. When I was still a virgin, I thought he was gay. You can see those mannerisms in Michael, too. Michael is like his father—even his looks.

Sometimes he said, "If I were like other men who cause trouble, would you still love me?"[10] He knew that I loved him.

I said, "I know a lot of husbands who have mistresses. Just so that there would be no trouble, so that the children's lives would continue the same, if you had another wo-man, it would be okay with me." When we talked about that, he was especially kind to me. He would hold me very tightly. I said, "You would think we saw each other for the first time today."

In December it happened. He didn't come home. My younger sister was with me in Pampanga then. I said, "Take care of your nieces and nephews. I'll go to Olongapo. I'll see why your *kuya* hasn't come home."

In Olongapo, I went to see my sister-in-law. She said, "Oh, Ni (they called me Ni), your husband is

were newly married. Some said, "Your relationship is so good. I wish my husband was like that. He always fights with me and always beats me." I said, "That's up to the two of you to talk about."

We moved to Pampanga because, in Olongapo, the children were always getting sick. We built a house in Pampanga because his family had land there. He said, "I'll come home every day. We'll save money cheating on you." I was shocked. She told me everything. "He's coming here. Talk to him later." His sister was kind to me. She was angry with her brother. I didn't speak. I was thinking.

I was very angry. [When I saw him], I said, "You motherfucker. You have no shame." I usually didn't swear, but I swore then. My husband was very large, like an American. He was fat. I was thin because I had had children. He grabbed me. He held my mouth shut because I was swearing. He didn't like that. He said, "Don't make a scene—it's embarrassing in front of other people."

"Ah, motherfucker, you're embarrassed? What you're doing, that isn't embarrassing? You have a wife. You have children. Then you do this. Ay, I'll shout this all over Olongapo—you prostitute! You animal! You womanizer!"

He carried me to his friend's house. While he was carrying me, he held his hand over my mouth. Whenever his hand came off my mouth, I'd shout. We arrived and went up the stairs.

He said, "Linda, don't shout anymore."

I looked for a knife. I said, "I'll kill you." But he was holding me. He was strong. I was small.

I cried and cried. He held me. He also cried. He said, "I'll explain now."

I said, "Don't explain. It's already happened. You made a fool of me. You made me into jewelry. Now, work hard so that you will be able to support your children. It's good that I planned to get a tubal ligation. You would have left me with small children."

He said he was sorry. He cried. We both cried. I said, "Why? Don't you love us anymore?"

He said, "I love you. I wouldn't trade you."

We patched things up. He did well. He came home on time, plus there was extra money with his paycheck. I only spent it on milk and rice and food for each day.

When about a month had gone by, he stopped going to work all the time. In his pay envelope, the days were listed. I saw that sometimes he only went three days or four days. Of course, his check was smaller. He still gave me the envelope. We fought. I was only concerned that the money be given to me, that his salary be for myself and the children. One of my friends found out what was happening and said, "You have to be wise about money. You must earn a living now, too."

I said, "Yes, we're selling watermelon and corn."[11]

The last time he came home was November first, All Saints' Day, to visit the dead.[12]

It was payday, and I expected him to come home on the twenty-ninth. He didn't come home. I went to Olongapo. I said to my brother-in-law, "*Kuya*, have you been paid yet?"

He said, "Yes. I was already paid." None of his brothers and sisters kept secrets from me. I said,

The cemetery on All Saints' Day. Filipinos spend most of the day and night at the cemetery on All Saints' Day. They bring food, drink, flowers, and candles to remember the dead and celebrate the living.

"He did not come home today."

He said, "There is a ship—the pay is good right now. I'll go and see if he went to work today and if he got his paycheck." If he had not picked up his paycheck, his brother could pick it up and give it to me. My brother-in-law came back. He said, "Ni, he already got his paycheck yesterday. Go home and wait for him." I wanted to cry, but I didn't. My tears would have been useless.

The next day I was shaking. Whatever I thought about him was bad. I washed two bins of clothes. I

wallet and I would hide it. I said, "Why don't you want to give me your wallet? I'll only take money for the children and myself. I know where your other money's going."

He got angry. He went upstairs. I went upstairs. I said, "Motherfucker, face me." I hit him and hit him. I was trembling with rage. I wanted to kill him that day. I wanted him to face me, to hit me because I had hit him. He didn't hit me.

He said, "This motherfucking life." He wasn't saying it about me but about life.

I said, "Who is a prostitute? Me?[13] You are a demon. If you hadn't raped me, how would you have known I wasn't a prostitute? If you hadn't raped me, would I be your wife?"

He went down the stairs. Our house had two floors. Our stairway was made of bamboo and had eight steps. I was very angry. I was shak-

Liberty: women at work; men at play

cooked rice. He arrived at 11:00. He was laughing. I was all wet. I hadn't taken a shower yet after washing all the clothes.

I said, "Let me see your wallet."

"Why do you want to see my wallet?"

Before, he would give me his

An older woman in the barrio

left. I thought and thought. I thought about my children and what would happen to their lives. I got sick from thinking about my problems. I didn't know of any work that I could do. I wished I had an education so I could get a job in a factory. I was sick for a month. Sometimes I didn't eat. I was very thin. It was as if I had already gotten old. I had to hold on to the wall in order to stand up. I said, "Maybe I will die." I cried.

I talked to my mother-in-law's aunt, an old woman. I said, "I want to die. I want to die. I'll drink poison."

She said, "You want to die? You have no compassion for your children. Yes, you can kill yourself. Your life will be peaceful. Where will you leave your children? They're still small. You can earn a living. You don't know, your life might be even better. If food is your only problem, I'll give you rice." She gave me rice every day. She said, "Show your husband that you can support yourself even if he's not here. Make yourself beautiful. You might get married again." She was making me strong inside.

I thought about becoming strong. My money went for medicine. I ate bananas and drank lots of milk. I imagined having a beautiful life— that I was rich. I thought about going to a different place that was happy. I imagined things like that so that I could forget. Then, my illness got better. After a week, I wasn't getting sick. I was getting stronger.

ing. I kicked him when he was going down. "Motherfucker, now you'll die." He fell down the stairs. There's cement at the bottom. I didn't say anything else. I saw that he was crying and crying. I saw that he had cuts. My anger was gone. I blamed myself for kicking him. I got some clothes. He changed.

He said, "I'm going to the cemetery." He left the next day. He didn't come home again. I cried and cried, but it was as if there were no tears

After about a month I was fine. The neighbors said, "Ah, Linda is beautiful." I laughed, but I didn't really laugh. I was always serious. Sometimes they saw me crying.

A neighbor who sold candy came from Bulacan.[14] I started wrapping and selling candy. I traveled to Angeles, San Fernando, all over. I sold a lot in Olongapo: at the school, in the market, and to sari sari stores.[15] I would finish about 7:00 P.M. and then go home.

Then, the prices of everything suddenly went up. The price of milk and transportation went up. The peso-to-dollar exchange rate went up. Making the candy got to be too expensive. The people in the market and sari sari stores did not buy as much. Before, two pieces had cost 25 centavos. The price went up to

one piece for 25 centavos. The last time I delivered candy, I couldn't sell all of it. I thought: "What will I do now?"

My neighbor said, "*Ate* Linda, why don't you get a job as a waitress in a club."

I said, "What? People might say I'm a hostess."

She said, "No, you would just waitress. There are a lot of waitresses on Magsaysay. I have a lot of friends there." Her mother-in-law rented out a house in Olongapo. A lot of women who rented from her worked at Pussycat.

I said, "I think it's difficult. I don't know how to do that."

She said, "Your children have to eat and go to school."

She helped me apply at Pussycat. She said to a friend, "Ida, help my

Selling *titseron* (fried pork skins), quail eggs, *puto* (rice cakes), and peanuts. Many women work as street vendors before or after working in the clubs. This is a large part of the informal economy.

On the strip: Pussycat Bar

cousin get a job as a waitress. Her husband left her, and she doesn't have any work. She has a lot of children." There was a ship in at that time. There were a lot of customers. Ida said to the manager, "My cousin is applying because her husband left her and she has five children."

Celso [the manager] said, "What? That's a lot of children. You probably don't know how to do this kind of work. You'll have to put on weight first. You're too thin."

Ida said, "That's why she's applying, *kuya*. She has to have work in order to make money. If she has money, she can eat well."

He said, "Okay, if she wants to, she can start today."

I stayed that day and began to waitress. Ida said, "*Ate* Linda, just serve drinks." She was also a waitress. A waitress can serve drinks or entertain. If Ida had a customer, she said, "Stay here by me." That evening I earned P 8.

The next day, I went to work again. I earned P 50 in tips. I thought: "This isn't bad." I saw the other waitresses earning a lot. They had a lot of customers since there was a ship. Ida said, "*Ate* Linda, if you work hard, you can earn P 100 especially if there is a ship, as long as you are not shy. If you are new here, the other women will put you down and take your customers. You have to be strong."

After about a week, I was earning

a lot. In 1984–85, it seemed as if the tips were very large from the Americans. I thought: "This is good. If you work hard, you can earn a lot." I got to be more experienced. I didn't go on bar fines, but I worked very hard. Pussycat was open twenty-four hours a day. If I saw people coming to the bar, I didn't go home. I slept at Pussycat. I was able to save money.

On Saturday and Sunday I went home [to Pampanga]. Marlon was only three years old. He was always getting sick, and there was no one to look after him. I felt sorry for him. Marriane was only in the fourth grade. At noon, she would come home and cook.

Then, I rented a house [in Olongapo]. A friend said, "Linda, I'll help you. I'll pay for the house. It is cheap, only P 300. I can manage that." She worked at Pussycat. She had been there for four or five months. Later she had a Filipino boyfriend and didn't go to work anymore. I was the one earning. I said, "We'll split the rent for the house so it isn't too much of a drain on you. I'm earning good money now." She agreed.

Then she left Pussycat and moved in with the Filipino. I was the only one paying the rent. Marlyn joined me. She had a steady boyfriend [American]. Another came to live there too, so there were three of us at the house.

In 1987, things got tougher. Tips were less, there were often no ships, and prices went up. Rent and elec-

Girls in the province

tricity also went up, and often we earned nothing.

Before, even if many Americans liked me, I didn't go out with them because I was afraid. The women said some of them were sadists or had VD. I didn't want to get sick. But sometimes I thought: "There is never any money, and the children get sick because I can't take care of them. If they have a fever and go

Women sharing a small living space in Olongapo

to the doctor, I don't have the money. There are expenses for food, payments at school, and their lunch. Four of them are studying." I was confused.

When I went home to Pampanga, Maricel said, "They say you're a hostess now."

I said, "Why? Of course not."

Maricel said, "Ma, don't be a hostess." Marriane also said that. They knew what a hostess was. I felt bad inside. Why did people say I was like that? I thought: "What business is it of theirs? They don't support us. They don't give my children food."

About 1987, I started going on bar fines with Americans. I had prepared myself, because I thought at least I would have some money and my children wouldn't know. Whatever happened would happen. The

first time, nothing did happen because the guy was drunk. I was afraid. He said, "Why are you afraid? I won't hurt you." We went by tricycle to his house. He was stationed in Olongapo. I knew what a bar fine was, but it was my first time with an American. I didn't know what to do. It's good he was drunk. He just went to sleep. For several hours, I didn't sleep. I thought: "He's drunk, I'll just leave." I went home.

It was a long time before I went out again. I got fatter. When I gained weight, it was Negroes who liked me because I had a large ass.[16] I also liked them because they were kind. Once, I went with a Negro. The Negro was a little drunk, but he still knew what he was doing. My roommate said, "Let's put msg in his drink, Linda. Don't say any-

Tricycles lined up for customers. Being a tricycle driver is a desirable job for male Filipinos in Olongapo. Like everyone else, tricycle drivers earn more money when a ship is in, ferrying women and customers from the bars to the women's houses.

thing. He'll sleep here. He has money. We'll steal it."

I said, "Ay, don't. I'm afraid."

She said, "I'll take care of it."

We put in the msg. He drank a lot. When he was drunk, he just lay down. My roommate got P 300 from him. She said, "Lin, you have money now."

I said, "That's not my money."

She said, "Don't worry. Tomorrow, we'll wake him up early, at 4:00 A.M."

We woke him up at 4:00. She said, "We're going to Manila for something important."

He left. He also had to go to work. He was grateful that we had woken him up. He didn't know she had taken P 300. She gave me P 200. She said, "Take it easy. That's the way life is in Olongapo. You have to learn. If they know how to trick us,

we also know how to trick them." I learned.

Then, I met a Marine on the USS *Anchorage*. I was being playful with him because he had a woman sitting with him. I said things to get him to buy drinks for her.

He said, "You're the one I like."

I said, "What? No. I don't like you." I sat down. He moved over beside me.

Ida said, "*Ate* Linda, he's generous with money. Money's hard to come by now. Their last liberty is tomorrow. He might have money."

I talked to him. Celso said, "Get him to buy you drinks, Linda. There you are talking to an American, and he hasn't bought you any drinks yet."

I said to him, "My *papasan* is angry because you haven't bought me any drinks."

The Olongapo city market, called Bagong Palengke (the New Market). Built with U.S. AID money, it was part of an ongoing effort to create positive sentiment toward the existence of Subic Base.

He said, "Bullshit. Why should I buy drinks. The money is just wasted."

I got irritated and I said, "Just stay there."

He said, "No, no, don't leave."

When he left, he gave me P 350. He said, "That's yours." I was thankful. He came back the next day because it was their last liberty. When he left, he gave me P 200. He said it was money for rent, "because I'll stay with you when we come back."

I said, "I'll see."

He came back. He didn't pay my bar fine, because he knew the system. He said it was useless. He said, "I'll just go to your place. You find a house, and I'll pay the rent." I found a place nearby for P 250. It had a room and a small kitchen. He bought things for the house, because I had nothing. He said, "How much do you need to buy things for the house?" I was stupid about the money. I said, "Whatever. It's cheap. Just a bed. I don't have a bed." He said, "I'll give you P 500. Go to the market. Buy what you need." He paid for the house in advance for three months.

I was happy. I thought: "Even three months' rent, that is a lot of help. Even if he gives me some money every day, that's good." He seemed kind to me. I agreed that we would be together.

He said, "We'll be here for two weeks."

I said, "I have to go to work. If I'm absent, the manager will get angry and might fire me. You have to pay my steady bar fine."

He said, "Steady bar fines are bullshit. How much is a steady bar fine? A thousand pesos. Why don't you just spend the thousand?"

No one knew someone was staying with me. I didn't want to tell anyone because I was ashamed. I said to my roommate, "Don't say anything. I am afraid Celso might find out." I would be fired if he found out. He would make me pay the steady bar fine and another fine. If I couldn't pay, I'd be kicked out. That's the penalty. He worked from 9:00 in the evening until 4:00 in the morning. At 4:00 in the morning, he came straight to the house. At 4:00 in the afternoon, we went to work together. When we arrived at the corner near the bar, we separated so that it wouldn't be noticeable.

He stayed for two weeks. He gave me money every day, P 150 or P 200 or sometimes dollars. I didn't have any ambition to be rich, just to have money for the children. My mistake then was not telling him I had children. The women had taught me, "If you have a customer, don't say that you have children because they'll get discouraged and won't give you money."

On the third day he was here, I said, "Stan, I'm going home to Pampanga to see my mother. I'll only be gone about forty-five minutes."

He said, "Okay, but come back right away. You must be here by noon."

He came home about 2:00. He was tired and went to sleep. I left at about 5:00 in the morning. I gave money to my sister for food and rice. At about 10:00, I came home again. I didn't notice my loss of sleep or

"Rules and Regulation for Employees Only." Each club has its own set of rules and regulations. They are enforced primarily though fines deducted before a woman is given her commission.

Before paying the bar fine and taking a woman out for the night, a customer usually spends time buying her "ladies' drinks" and talking or dancing with her in the club. Regulations in the club require him to buy her ladies' dinks in order to talk with her. The music is often so loud that they have to shout in each other's ears to be heard. This and language differences make for limited communication.

fatigue. I only thought about the children and felt sorry for them. I thought: "This is a chance to get some money. Even P 200 is good. I don't earn P 200 in one evening." When I arrived, he was still sleeping. I cooked and woke him up to eat. Then I went to work at 4:00 in the afternoon.

He was very kind. He would say, "Okay, you sleep now. I won't disturb you." Or, "How was your work? How do you feel?" It was like he cared for me. I liked him. I was able to save some money. I was able to buy clothes for the children.

When he had last liberty, I cried. I was sad because he was like a hus-band to me. He said, "Linda, eat well so that you don't get sick. Take care of your body. Don't lose too much sleep." I thought: "Why is he talking like that? He is not my husband." He said, "Don't worry if you write to me and I don't write back. I don't have time to write because I'm studying." He was getting a promotion and had to study for five months. When he left, I wrote. He didn't answer any of my letters, so I didn't write anymore. I haven't written since.

I met another sailor. His ship was an escort of the *Enterprise*. From the time I met him, he didn't leave me. He would come to the club early.

His friends would also come along.

He said to me, "Do you have a boyfriend?"

I said, "No. I don't have boyfriends."

He said, "What if I became your boyfriend?"

I said, "That would be good."

He said, "Do you like me?"

I said, "Naturally, I like you." But I was just joking.

The others said, "Lin, get him to buy you a drink."

I said, "No, I'm just fooling around."

Then, when I asked, he bought me a drink. He was okay when it came to buying drinks. My friends said, "Drink fast so you can earn more." I drank and drank. I didn't have to say anything. If I put the glass down, he would buy another one. I had maybe twenty drinks from him. I thought: "That's not bad." I thought he seemed generous with money. We talked about our lives. Then he bought me a flower, and we had our picture taken. He gave me the picture as a souvenir. I still have it. He put a dedication on the back. I thought: "He's kind."

I said, "Have you been in love?"

He said, "Of course. Why? Is that bad? She's a woman, and I'm a man. But I don't like this kind of thing because I love my two sisters and my mother." He said if he oppressed women here, it might be his mother whom he was oppressing. I thought: "This guy will be a priest someday."

I said, "The customers, the Amer-

Overshadowed

icans, don't treat the women well. The Americans are dogs. Sometimes they beat the women."

He said, "You can't stop that if they're drunk."

I said, "And you, you don't get drunk?"

He said, "No. I don't get drunk."

He didn't leave until closing time. He said, "You know, I really like you. I only met you today, but I really like you. I want to stay with you."

I said, "Your ship has been here a week already and you don't have a steady?"

He said, "No. If you like, I'll stay with you while my ship is still here. Don't worry, I'm kind. I'll give you money to spend."

On the strip: checking it out

Celso said, "Linda, I think you'll end up taking that guy home. Get him to pay your bar fine."

I said to the American, "He says it is closing time, and you haven't paid my bar fine yet."

He said, "Bullshit. I don't pay bar fines. I'll just give the money to you. How much do you want?" The bar fine then was P 400. He gave me P 500. Maybe it was payday. He had a lot of money. He said, "It's up to you if you pay it or not."

I thought: "It's closing time already, why should I pay it?" I said to my roommate, "Marlyn, he gave me P 500 and said it's up to me if I pay the bar fine or not."

She said, "Don't worry. I have a bar fine, I'll take him." Marlyn knew how to do things. She was wise.

She talked to him: "Wait fifteen minutes so that it isn't obvious to Celso. After fifteen minutes, go downstairs to the street. I'll be at the corner. When you see me, I'll get in a tricycle. You get in a tricycle, too."

I didn't sit with him anymore. I walked around so that it would not be obvious to Celso. Marlyn took him to the house. The women said. "Celso, it's time to go home, there are only a few more customers."

He said, "Whoever wants to go home can go." I left.

When I arrived, he was there at

the house. We talked. He said he would stay. I said, "If you stay, you have to pay for the house, because the truth is I don't go with Americans. I don't go on bar fines."

He was generous with money. He gave me his wallet. I was the one to hold it. In the morning, he would come home to the house and sleep. When we were at the house, we would talk with my companions and we were happy.

Marlyn asked him, "Why don't you and Linda get married? Linda is kind. You can see she treats you well."

He said, "Yeah, Linda is very kind. I love her." But he wanted to have a higher rank and a lot of money before getting married.

I said, "That's okay."

He left after a week. He gave me $100. I bought some clothes. He came back and stayed with me again. When he left, he didn't come back. It was a long time, maybe a year, before his ship came again, but he wasn't there. I said to his friends, "How is Stanley? He hasn't answered my letters." He had been writing to me.

They said, "He had an accident. The accident was bad, and he needed an operation. He said to tell you that if you have a boyfriend, it's okay, you should just get married. I don't know if he'll stay in the Navy."

Once I picked up an American. I thought he was just on the same jeepney with me because every evening when I go home, there are a lot of Negroes on the jeepney going home to their girlfriends. I walked very fast. I was alone.

He followed me. He was right behind me. I didn't look at him. I walked faster. He also walked fast and called to me, "Hey, wait!" I waited. I wasn't afraid because I was used to Negroes. "I want to sleep at your place."

"Why? You aren't my boyfriend."

He said, "I don't know—I like you. I don't have a girlfriend."

I said, "I don't have an electric fan. I don't have a bed. You'd have to sleep on the floor." I did have a bed and an electric fan.

He said, "That's okay, even on the floor." He was a Marine.

"I don't know you. If you sleep at my house, you pay."

"How much?"

"How much do you have?"

He said, "P 100."

"P 100, that's not possible."

"I really like you." He said he wanted to make love.

I said, "Ah, P 500, that's possible."

"You don't have an electric fan or a bed and you are asking P 500. That's stupid."

I thought: "This guy is too much."

I said, "If you don't like it, go away."

He followed me to the gate. He said, "Okay, okay, okay. P 300, but I won't do anything. If you don't have a bed, that's okay. We'll just talk."

He gave me P 300. Marlyn was there. She had a boyfriend, a bar fine. I went inside. Marlyn said, "Who's that, Lin? do you have a bar fine?"

I said, "No. I picked this one up, but it wasn't me who picked him up. He picked me up." I said, "If you

Some clubs require the women to work whether or not a ship is in port. Large ships may arrive once a month or once every two or three months. Consequently, during the many days and weeks when there are no ships, no customers, and no income, the women go into debt to pay for necessities. When a ship does come in, earnings are used to pay off the debts. Anything left over is sent to families in the provinces. After the ship leaves the cycle begins again; and if she is pregnant and decides to abort, she will have to go further into debt.

want to make love, it's P 500." It was then I realized that life is like this when you have no money— you agree to anything. In the end, I said yes.

In May, all the children were here for vacation. It was the rainy season. There was no ship, and I had no money. School enrollment was in June, the following week.

Then the Air Force arrived. Someone wanted to sleep at the house. He only had P 200 and a dollar for the taxi. He said, "I'll give you P 200 if I can sleep at your house. Don't worry—nothing will happen between us. I won't make love to you. I like you, but I respect you because I don't see you going after the Americans." Since he had met me, he had not seen me with a boyfriend or on a bar fine. That's what he liked, a woman who was not a butterfly.

I always talked to Marlyn about my problems with Americans. I said, "How can I manage? The children are there."

She said, "Okay, this is what you'll do. Go home. Tell them someone will be sleeping there so they have to sleep in Ophelia's room." We each had our own room, but they were all in one house. "Tell the American he should come back at closing time, about 12:00, so that I can take him home. I'll go home a little early because I have duty tomorrow."[17]

I went home at about 9:00. Maricel said, "Why are you early?"

"Someone is going to sleep here."

"An American?"

"Yes, a Negro."

She said, "I don't like it."

I said, "Just don't be noisy. You'll sleep with your *Ate* Fely so that he won't be disturbed."

Marriane seemed to be thinking, but she didn't say anything. Maricel cried. I said, "I don't want you to be crying. I'll hit whoever cries. He's only sleeping here. He'll give us money. When I arrive, you must be sleeping." I left and went to Pussycat.

At about 1:00 A.M. I came home with the American. Maricel was still awake. Her brothers and sisters were sleeping. When I opened the door, the dog barked and she knew we were home. I could see her looking through the curtain. I said, "Get out of there." My voice was quiet. The Negro thought I had no children and was the only one sleeping there.

He said, "Lie down. Don't worry, I won't have sex with you. We'll both sleep."

I said, "It's okay—I'll sleep on the floor."

He said, "No, this is your bed. I'll

sleep on the floor and you sleep here."

I said, "No, no, no. Okay, I'll lie down later. I'll change first. You lie down."

He took off his clothes. He was only wearing briefs. He lay down. I turned off the light because I didn't want the children to see. Marriane was awake, too, because Maricel was crying.

The American said, "Who's crying?"

I said, "Those are the neighbor's children."

"Why are they there?"

I said, "Their house is leaking, so they're sleeping here."

"Oh. Why is she crying?"

"Ignore them. Just go to sleep."

I talked to Maricel: "Don't cry." But I didn't speak very firmly because it might be obvious that they were my children.

The American went to sleep. When I heard he was sleeping, I got up. I said, "Why are you crying?"

"Because he's sleeping here. It isn't his house . . . it's our house. Send him away. I don't want someone sleeping in our bed."

I said, "Stupid. You know he'll give us money tomorrow. You'll be able to go home to Pampanga. You'll go to school and have some money to buy food."

She didn't respond.

"Stop now. Go to sleep."

I couldn't sleep. I thought: "This is bad. For only P 200, I'm willing to lie and say these are not my children." I felt bad. I cried, but I didn't let my crying be obvious. My tears just dropped quietly. I thought: "This is bad. This life is

Women with their passbooks waiting for VD smears at the Social Hygiene Clinic in Olongapo. Workers are required to report for a smear every other week and must pay for the tests themselves. *Bawal ang Tamad sa Olongapo* means "Laziness is prohibited in Olongapo."

hell. I got angry. This life is hell. There is not good work. It's always like this. How can you earn money?"

At about 5:00, I woke him up and said, "You have to go home now. It's 5:00." He held my face and kissed me on the cheek. I was carrying the pillow so that I could cover my face and the children wouldn't see, but Maricel saw it. She felt bad inside. Of course, she thought her mother is like that—having Americans sleep here and kiss her.

He gave me P 200. He said, "Next

Children and women in the neighborhood

payday, I'll give you money because maybe I'll sleep here again." I just said yes so he would leave. I thought: "It's like this when you have no money." Next payday he gave me P 300. I had money again.

About three months later, there were three Americans at the house. They were high. They were smoking marijuana and were drunk. Marlyn said, "Lin, they need women. You don't have enough money, and your children are going home tomorrow."

I said, "Stupid. They're still here." It was their vacation again.

She said, "I'll take care of your children. Don't worry . . . leave it to me. There's a lot of food here." Her boyfriend knew I had children but didn't tell the other two.

Marlyn went to my room. She woke up the children. She said, "Marriane, get your brothers and sisters and the pillows and blankets." She took them down the outside so that the American could go in the room and not see them. The American was high and drunk already. I was confused. Maricel was crying. Marlyn said to her, "You— you cry and cry. Your mother has a customer, and you just cry. She'll earn some money, and you are still crying. Don't you want to have money again? He has a lot of money. Your mother will be able to buy your clothes and your food."

I didn't like it. I felt sorry for Marriane because she was carrying Marlon. Michael was awake. They went around the back so the American wouldn't see them. I heard Maricel crying. She was dragging her feet because she really didn't want to go. I bit my lip so I wouldn't cry. The owner of the house woke up. She opened the window and said, "Why is Maricel crying?"

Marlyn said, "Because her mother has a customer." I heard.

Marlyn ran back to the house and said, "Okay, they're gone. Take him to your room."

I said, "I don't like it because of the children."

She said, "What? He has a lot of money. I'll take him to your room." She took the American to my room.

The American said, "*Mmmhhjrehnnn.*" Just mumbling. He said he wanted to make love. He took my clothes off. He hadn't taken off his clothes. He embraced me. I didn't like the smell of alcohol. And his mouth smelled bad from something—plus, cigarettes. I said, "Just a minute. I have something to do."

He said, "Hurry up."

"Yes."

But I was thinking about the children. I heard Marlyn saying, "Go on up." She was taking them up to her room. "There's a lot of food. You eat." I heard them eating because our wall is a curtain. Maricel was the only one not eating. I thought: "If it weren't for them, I wouldn't be doing this—going with Americans. But my children don't understand that it is for them, not for me."

The American said, "Come on, Linda. Come on."

I said, "Wait. Just a minute." He fell asleep. He was very drunk and high. I listened. He was sleeping soundly. Marlyn's boyfriend was also sleeping because he was drunk.

I said, "Marlyn, come here. He's sleeping."

She said, "Okay. He's sleeping soundly." She laughed. "Did he give you any money?"

I said, "No, I haven't asked."

"Take his money."

"I'm afraid."

"I'll do it."

She looked in his pockets. She got P 25. She said, "This is all he has. I don't think he has money." There was $5 in his wallet. "Oh, Linda, it's good he didn't have sex with you . . . he doesn't have money." She looked in all his pockets. There was $30 in one pocket. "Take everything."

I said, "That's too much. The poor man. He didn't have sex."

She said, "Why? Do you only make money if he has sex? Even if he didn't have sex, you have to have money. He's drunk. He doesn't know you took the money. We'll wake him up at 5:00 so he can go back to the ship because it's going to leave."

I said, "Just take the $25. We'll leave him $15."

She said, "Stupid. Their ship is leaving. When they find out you took the money, they'll be gone."

I said, "You do it. I don't want to."

She took $25. "We'll leave $10 for his transportation money. Tomorrow I'll give you this money so that if he looks for it, you won't have it."

I said, "Okay."

I said to Maricel, "Why are you crying and crying?"

"Because, Ma, you said you are not a hostess. Why did you bring an American here? You let him sleep in our bed. I wish you hadn't brought him here."

I said, "He's giving us money."

She said, "What do you mean giving? You stole it?"

I said, "I didn't steal it, Marlyn did."

"Even so, that's bad. Don't be a hostess. Don't be like *Ate* Marlyn."

I said, "Go to sleep now. We'll talk tomorrow." She didn't sleep.

Fely said, "It is 4:00 now. Let's send them home."

We woke up the Americans. We said it was 5:00 so that they would hurry. Marlyn said, "Let's take them to the tricycle." The three of us went with them. When we went down the stairs outside, he kissed me on the lips. My children saw it. I ignored them. I was ashamed. They saw that I am like that.

When I first started working in a bar and saw the women flirting with the Americans, I couldn't stand it. I thought: "Why is it like this? The women flirt." I thought it was easy to get money. I thought: "I won't do that." When I saw them kissing, I was ashamed for myself. I thought: "Why don't they only do that at home?"

Then, when I had been here a long time, I realized you can't blame the women. When you talk with them and hear about the experiences in their lives, like being separated from their husbands and no one supporting them—that's why they work as entertainers. I thought: "It is not bad after all."

Good times rolling: women at work;
guys at play

At the beach: Michael and Linda with a bar woman's baby

I told my mother-in-law that I was a hostess in Olongapo. They don't understand the life. They live in the province and eat well every day. They don't know that others are poor. Here in Pampanga there's a lot of rice. In other provinces, there's no way to earn a living. I said that you can't blame those who do that work. When they talk in Pampanga, I say, it isn't like that. I explain to them about hostesses not all being bad. But I don't tell my mother-in-law and sister-in-laws that I go with Americans. I don't want them to know. I'm also ashamed, especially for the children.

My mother-in-law said that whatever my work is in Olongapo, it's my body and up to me to decide. My sister said that once I became a hostess in Olongapo, she wouldn't help me. She is religious and says that it's a sin before God. You must be pure. That's okay if it's only you, but what about those you are feeding and putting through school. Never mind if I'm like this as long as my children can study. At least, if I work as a hostess, it's for them.

Recently, Marriane spoke to me. She had a classmate who said her mother was shameful. She said to me, "You know, Ma, some people say you're a hostess. Even if you are a hostess, even if you work in a club, I still love you." I cried. She said "I love you. We love you."

She said, "No matter what, Ma, I am not ashamed of you."

1. Linda uses the English term "witch doctor" here. Her use of the term is not pejorative, as it would be in English. This is an example of an English term being incorporated into Tagalog but without the negative baggage that it carries in English. The same is true of the term "witchcraft" used later in the same paragraph. There seems to be a great deal of ambivalence among Filipinos with respect to supernatural beliefs, and traditional healers. "Shaman" might be a more appropriate term, but it is not widely used in the Philippines.

2. The "people we can't see" are small people whom many Filipinos believe live in small hills or anthills. They can be evil and mischievous or they can be good and helpful.

3. *Barrio captain* is an elected official of the barrio. The *barrio captain*'s role is similar to that of a mayor.

4. *Sangol* is a large knife similar to a machete.

5. The Tagalog term used here is *dalaga* (see glossary). In this usage, "old maid" might be a more appropriate translation. She is old for being unmarried. Since women are not to have sexual intercourse outside of marriage, she must therefore, by assumption, be a virgin. The reality, of course, might be different.

6. A school for foreign missionary children located just outside of Manila.

7. For Filipinos, a meal without rice is not a meal.

8. The province just north of Manila.

9. One way a jeepney driver tries to earn a little extra money is to convince servicemen to rent his jeepney to go to Subic City, where there are more bars. There are jeepneys that go to Subic as a regular route for P 3, but the charge for a special trip is usually about P 50. U.S. servicemen who pay for a special trip must then find their way back to base again later in the evening or the next morning.

10. Causing trouble here means having another woman.

11. Watermelon and corn are often sold at roadside stands along the main road from Manila to Olongapo.

12. Filipinos spend most of the day and night at the cemetery on All Saints Day. They bring food and drink and flowers and candles. The atmosphere is a combination of remembering the dead and celebrating the living.

13. The word "fucker" used in "motherfucker" is the same as the word for "prostitute."

14. An area on the edge of Manila.

15. Small stores on the street that sell a little bit of everything.

16. The women use the English term "Negro." See glossary also.

17. The women all have to take a turn cleaning the bar during the day. "Duty" is their day to clean.

Tong Du Chun bar area. The main strip
is to the left and the Dark Man's
Zone (DMZ), where bars for African-
American servicemen are located,
is to the right.

The Southern Part of Korea

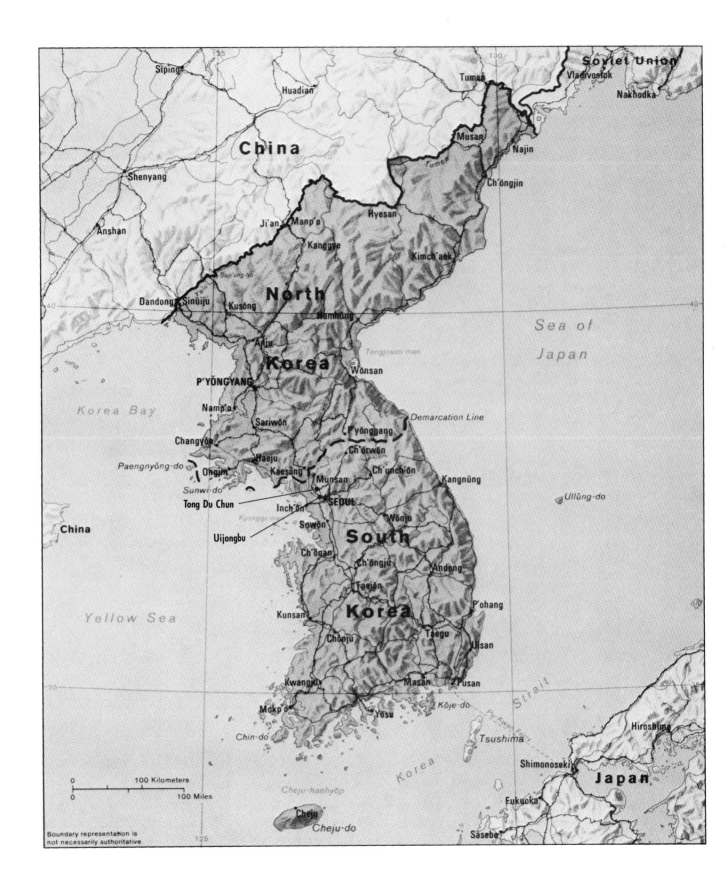

The 1989 exchange rate for the southern part of Korea was $1 = 660 won.

SILENT BUT DEADLY: SEXUAL SUBORDINATION IN THE U.S.– KOREAN RELATIONSHIP

Bruce Cumings

Over the past nearly half century the American position in Korea has changed from military occupant (1945–48) to midwife of the Republic of Korea (1948) to war maker (1950–53) to neo-colonial authority (1948–71) to the somewhat awed and apprehensive beholder of Korean industrial prowess that we see today, as the U.S. finally begins its first timid steps toward military disengagement. Through all these changes one element in the Korean-American relationship has been constant: the continuous subordination of one female generation after another to the sexual servicing of American males, to the requirements of a trade in female flesh that simply cannot be exaggerated. It's the most common form of Korean-American interaction, whether you're a private in the Army, a visiting Congressman (for whom special stables are maintained), or a Peace Corps teacher—which I was in 1967. It's also the most silent exchange, as if the trade were chaperoned by the deaf, dumb, and blind.

I had an inkling of the extent of the trade almost the first day I arrived in Seoul, when an upright Amherst graduate named David Greenlie and I were offered girls as we strolled near the American Embassy building, one sunny afternoon. "No! Get away from us!" David had bellowed. I got another hint when I rented a room in the Bando Hotel (then the premier hotel, and a former billet to the high officers of the American occupation) on the afternoon of New Year's Eve, so that we could have a Peace Corps party, and so various volunteers could have a much-needed hot bath before it started. As the bellboy left me in the room, the phone rang: "You want a girlfriend?" "No, I have a wife," I said. "But wife is in the States, no?" "Wife will be here in fifteen minutes." "Oh, sorry. Big mistake."

Although I have barely written about this aspect of Korean-American exchange before—partly because it is embarrassing to Korean pride, partly because I thought few were interested in a phenomenon simultaneously ubiquitous and unremarked upon, partly because of a male code that I will discuss shortly—it is the aspect that most struck me when I first lived in Korea, creating indelible impressions of a relationship that, because of the use made of Korean women, *could not be* what it was said to be: a free compact between two independent nations dedicated to democracy and anticommunism.

Why should sexual exploitation be so obvious and so soundless, making barely a cat's-paw imprint on the literature and lore of Asian-American relations? Among the reasons is surely a tacit male code to maintain silence, thus to keep wives, mothers, girlfriends, female reporters, and inquiring feminists in the dark. To remain silent because morally all this is unremarkable: boys will be boys, the oldest profession, war is hell, or—to use Spike Lee's metaphor—"It's a dick thing." If someone dares call attention to the ceaseless orgy, all the usual bromides pour forth to drown out the faint cries of peasant girls yanked off a train in Seoul and thrown into a brothel, a thousand little justifications for the abasement of a thousand little girls at American hands. Boys will be boys. To remain silent, that is, except among one's own kind, whereupon this becomes *the* subject of discourse, mulled over endlessly and needing no legitimation (it *is* a "dick thing"), the social construction of every Korean female as a potential object of pleasure for Americans. It is the most important aspect of the whole relationship and the primary memory of Korea for generations of young American men who have served there.

The male initiation rites begin immediately. When I told an older "Korea hand" that I was going to Seoul with spouse, he remarked, "Why take a sandwich to a banquet?" No sooner had our Peace Corps group (yes, the sexual fever is by no means limited to the military) arrived than lore began circulating about how many single male volunteers had frequented this whorehouse or that bathhouse, not once but twice and thrice, sometimes on the same evening. My experience with Greenlie was not unusual, nor was the Bando check-in. I was approached on the streets of Seoul time and again by pimps offering women, and any male checking into the major hotels got propositioned almost as soon as the ink was dry on the registration blotter. The average Korean surmised, since the evidence was so abundant, that American men seen out "on the economy" (American argot for the opaque, mysterious, unknown native territory otherwise known as Korea) were interested in "only one thing"—as usually they were.

Nearly all Americans in Seoul lived—and still live—behind fenced compounds in Itaewon next to the giant Yongsan military base (no Koreans allowed without a pass), up in the hills of what was in the 1960s a suburb but which now sits smack in the middle of this sprawling capital city, with American-style ranch houses, two-car garages, a golf course, and swimming pools—most of it catering to a lower-middle class of Americans who found rapid upward mobility through the military. One could be born to a down-and-out family in Norfolk (like John Paul Vann) and twenty years later live like the country-club set, albeit in Korea or Vietnam; one could be raised on an Arkansas farm and at eighteen rule a roost just outside the military gates, where a Felliniesque collection of shantytowns, bars, whorehouses, and small tradesmen catered to the American taste.

I don't need to rely on memory for vignettes of this milieu, because I kept a diary.

Herewith an account of a day spent touring Uijongbu, a military town north of Seoul, in early 1968:

The areas near the American military base are drastically deprived . . . here the local parasitic population lives . . . [in] filthy, backward, shameful "living establishments." The worst aspect, though, is the whoring district. There is no district—this aspect permeates that side of town. But there are clusters of "clubs," catering only to Americans. Rock-and-roll blares from them, they are raucously painted and titled, and ridiculous-looking painted Korean girls—often very young—peer from the doors. Nothing is more silly-looking . . . than these girls in minnyskirts [sic]. Several of them hooted at me as I walked by . . . but the most disconcerting of all was a middle-aged woman with two kids hanging on to her who, in the middle of the street, asked me to come and "hop on" in the chimdeh [bed].

The town is crawling with mixed-blood children. They seemed fairly well cared for—certainly not beggars. Several Negroes, playing with the other children. One small, sandy-haired, blue-eyed little boy ran by with Korean kids—and yelled "hello" at me—which is probably the ultimate irony in the effects of America here. These kids are probably well cared for because the whole town is in the dregs, removed from the prejudices of wealthy Koreans from which the terrible treatment of mixed kids results. There is no reason to shit on them—they'll bring in good money as whores or pimps when they're fourteen. Goofy-looking, stupid soldiers walk arm-in-arm with whores who are often only young girls—very, very young girls. How do these men (?) justify this to themselves?

. . . given Uijongbu as a whole, it is also apparent that America is leaving a legacy of hatred, a well of ill feeling that could be immediately exploited by any politician willing to do so. The town is different from others in Korea—the people are neither amazed by Americans, nor are they inured to them the way Seoul is. They simply hate them and exist by pandering to their ever-base desires . . . the adults avert their eyes when you look at them, and if they don't, they glare at you with a hatred that can be measured—an American who speaks Korean is the only thing that shocks them.

The account strikes me now as a bit self-righteous and superior, but otherwise I think it is the normal reaction of a young man to the squalor rimming and feeding off the American bases.

It may be, though, that things were even more squalid in the 1950s. A friend who served in the U.S. Army near Uijongbu just after the Korean War ended told me that on Friday nights half-ton trucks would careen onto the base, disgorging a few hundred women who would stay the night, or the weekend. These days Koreans have been making much of newly discovered World War II records of Korean women dragooned to the front by the Japanese, to serve as "comfort girls" for the troops in the field. Does it make much difference that American soldiers paid cash for the half-ton-truck girls, instead of giving them room and board as did the Japanese? Or perhaps the half-tonners "wanted" to do what they did and "freely chose" it in the marketplace of a Korea with a per-capita income of $100, as opposed to the evil Japanese who "kidnapped" the women? What, then, do you make of top-secret internal North Korean eyewitness reports, captured by the U.S. and recently declassified, that speak of some three hundred politically suspect Korean women (party members and people's committee leaders, mainly) confined to a warehouse and used at will by American forces in wartime Seoul in the fall of 1950?

Let me return to the 1960s. Once I spent an evening in Itaewon camp town with a male friend, who happened to be gay. We watched young peasant girls of sixteen with a smattering of English sashay forth from the bars named New York Club or Playboy or Cosmos; some of them catered to black soldiers, the girls speaking broken ghetto argot, and the blacks parading in lavender pants suits as if it were Harlem. Most were adolescents getting their first lay (although there were plenty of "lifers," too—paunchy middle-aged men in Hawaiian-shirt mufti). We went into a bar to have a drink, and a pretty teenager from South Cholla Province quickly sat down next to us: "I lose my cherry when I sixteen," she volunteered helpfully. Back out to the street we went. As we stood surveying the scene, a ten-year-old Korean boy pushed his bicycle past us laden with goods that he was ferrying somewhere, pointed his hand at us, and, in slow motion, pulled the trigger of an imaginary gun.

When the "boys will be boys" bromides seemed inadequate to capture the gerbil-like frequency of the thousand-and-one nights on the town, American men would justify their behavior by pointing to the equally fervent Korean male pursuit of the same thing. Perhaps this justification might be "When in Korea, do as the Koreans do," but in my experience the maxim was more like "When in Korea, do nothing as the Koreans do and hope like hell to get out as soon as possible, but meanwhile enjoy yourself." But that male Koreans have their own robust version of the sex trade cannot be doubted.

My job was to teach English in a local junior high school. One time a rich man, concerned about whether his son would pass the exams to go on to high school (at that time few children went past middle school), took me and a bunch of other teachers out to dinner, and, later, a beer hall. We went in his slick black jeep, its whitewall tires, full metal canopy, and plush interior masking its war-surplus origins.

The wealthy man's entourage of stiff-necked Confucian-rectitude teachers arrived at a *kisaeng* (kin to a *geisha*) house for dinner, and within minutes all were drunk and engaging in a kind of abandon I would have thought inconceivable, knowing them from the school—all except the teacher responsible for my well-being, that is, who sipped his beer and kept an eye on me. I kept an eye on the "hostess" who had sat down on my right, since she was massaging my thigh and going for my crotch but I had a strategic elbow blocking her. She fed me with chopsticks, and filled and refilled my beer glass if my friends neglected me, which they usually didn't.

Our stolid vice principal got up to dance with his hostess and immediately reached inside her brassiere, causing her to grab him hard between the legs and squeeze, whereupon they fell together in a giddy tumble and she crawled on her hands and knees out of the room, clutching her bodice around her. Some of the teachers did their best to stay on their feet and dance a few steps, while pawing the girls. I had been told that Korean men feel constrained by family relationships at home, so they let their hair down at *kisaeng* houses; I had no idea that the gap between Confucian formalism and raunchy substance was a chasm like this.

As the evening ended the house madam brought in a girl of about eighteen in silk traditional garments who threw coquettish looks my way. She was mine for the night if I wanted her, so I was told. I politely declined, and we were off for the beer hall. By this time the rich man had decided I was okay, so he sat next to me and poured out a few more gallons of beer. The hostesses here were less pleasant. In fact, they struck me as desperate. My newfound rich friend stuck his hand down the blouse of the woman sitting between us and pulled out a breast to fondle. Then he put it back in and grabbed my hand, plunging it into her blouse. I let it stay there in its clammy repose for a minute, "just to be polite," then withdrew it with a wan smile. I danced a couple of times, had some more beer, and the evening mercifully came to an end. As I walked out with the teachers, I was surrounded by several hostesses with cheerless faces, pawing pathetically at me and imploring me for "money," in a kind of literal low moan—"*mmmooaannny, mmmooaannny, mmmooaannny. . . .*"

In Seoul women were available on almost every block—in a bathhouse, massage room, restaurant, or in the ubiquitous tea houses all over the city. You could get them very young, probably around twelve; kids were shanghaied into a kind of slavery as they got off the train from the countryside, looking for work to support their peasant families. Kidnapped, gang-raped and beaten by pimps while learning their few necessary words of English, they were ready for the street in a week. And you could get them very old, according to American soldiers who frequented a place they called "turkey alley." I think I walked through it one hot, dusty afternoon, when a friend and I were trying to find a shortcut from the railroad station to a nearby hotel. We turned a corner in a maze of back alleys and all of a sudden from every door came a toothless old hag, a pockmarked middle-aged woman, a haggard and spiritless woman of thirty, to grab at our elbows, yank us toward a door, importune us for money. It was a gruesome, nightmarish specter in broad daylight.

I thought of this place a few days later when I was strolling in a back street with a Korean friend and a man heaved out of a bar, spied me, and spit full in my face—to the overwhelming mortification of my friend, who later patiently explained that not all Koreans liked Americans. (Indeed, packs of kids would trail after me yelling "monkey?" and it was typical for a Korean mother to try to get her baby to stop crying by saying "Look at the American!") Meanwhile the American embassy wrings its hands about growing "anti-Americanism" and blames critical scholarship (like my own) for this otherwise inexplicable phenomenon.

It may be possible to say that this is "their culture" (which of course fails to explain why American men take to it like fish to water). But I don't think so. It seems true that many Korean males are little despots at home and carousing nincompoops on the town, often staying out until midnight, and there will be little hope for women's equality or for democracy in the country as long as this persists. But then how can an American who has taken the night air around Itaewon talk about "carousing nincompoops" and keep a straight face?

Concubinage is a long-standing and still-widespread practice in Korea, with as many as four wives serving one husband in a careful hierarchy of status; put this abuse of women together with the *chador*-like public dress women used to wear and the ritualized confinement of female power to the inner sanctum of the home, and you have something akin to contemporary Middle Eastern social structure, even if changed much beyond that in postwar Seoul. But these practices are as old as the hills, imbedded in custom and ritual, and do not represent a perversion of Korean morality or dishonor to the women involved.

Prostitution, on the other hand, has no sanction in Korean morality. Nor is this the "culture" of North Korea, and that makes it hard to attribute the behavior to some unchanging Korean "way of life." Whatever else one may say about Kimilsungland, no such conditions exist. The regime outlawed prostitution and concubinage in 1946, at the same time that it established formal legal equality for women. (Upon returning from my first visit to North Korea, I lectured at a military graduate school about my experience. The students asked about this and that but waited until we sat down for a beer to put the most important, albeit alliterative, question for the accomplished Korean hand: "What's the price of pussy in P'yongyang?")

Furthermore, there is in South Korea the stark contrast between the unfortunate multitude of girls of the night and the dignified wives and stellar mothers that are the norm, plus the general Korean shame that such conditions exist in the first place. The wise and undaunted mother of the family with whom we lived, only a few years older than I, was the only upstanding Korean woman I knew who dared be seen on the streets of Seoul alone with me, lest she be taken for a prostitute. It is probably not kosher to quote George Blake, Seoul station chief for MI-6 in 1950 and infamous Russian spy, but he once said that in most countries he visited the women were far more admirable than the men, and this was particularly true of Korea.

The culture of camp towns, prostitution as a way of life, and sex tourism has nothing to do with Korean culture. It is an integral part of Korea's subordination to Japanese and American interests through most of this century; the military base in the Itaewon area, after all, was Japan's for four decades, and now it has been ours for four decades. In 1945 the camp towns just switched patrons. This patent subordination is obvious to anyone with eyes to see, or ears to hear. Furthermore from the horny adolescents out of Arkansas to the leaky old American ambassadorial residence, the web of subordination is seamless.

The compounds hold soldiers, generals, diplomats, CIA agents, and various hangers-on. Most are decent, humane, solid citizens of the American official diaspora, who wouldn't dream of exploiting anyone. Over time, however, a colonial culture and racist discourse developed apart from anyone's intentions. Full of idealist rhetoric in formal circumstances, in informal settings officialdom was a rule arrogant, racist, resentful, and colonial in the imperfect American way.

In the 1960s their arrogance expressed itself in limitless stories about the ineptitude of Koreans. Their racism led them to ask me, because I was living with Koreans and they rarely ventured out to "the economy," things like whether it was true that the Korean national dish, *kimchi*, was fermented in urine. Their resentfulness was aimed at their Korean counterparts, who were never quite willing to give up their last ounce of difference. Their colonialism consisted of accepting (with this or that degree of rationalization) and fattening off the structural circumstances of their privilege, where the highest Korean ultimately meant less than the lowest American in the entourage.

It was imperfect, of course, compared to the old Japanese style, because our imperial foundation was filled out and justified by its opposite, the doctrines of liberalism: we were there protecting freedom, our Koreans were good democrats or tending in that direction, their Koreans were evil dictators ("ferocious totalitarians," according to McGeorge Bundy recently[1]), Americans could never be imperialists, we were altruistically supporting Koreans until they could take wing on their own, so on and so forth—hardly any of it believed for the instant it took to leave someone's lips. Barely a one of them developed intrinsic interests in Korean culture and history for its own sake, took the time to learn the language, or had more than a possessive instinct toward the cultural treasures in which Korea abounds. It was ultimately this milieu, founded in neo-imperial hierarchy, that justified the sordid conditions of the camp towns and reinforced a general attitude disparaging of Koreans.

I haven't been to Seoul since 1985, but at that time the camp towns were still going strong, and the only difference in the downtown hotels was that Japanese men now competed with Americans for the available women . . . and probably paid better wages. Nowadays there is talk of giving Yongsan and the golf course back to Korea and beginning the withdrawal of American troops; the U.S. is even thinking of letting Korean generals command their own army (since 1950 it has been under U.S. overall command, with both armies squatting beneath the legitimacy of the blue flag of the United Nations). Breaking the nexus of subordination at the top may help it unravel at the vast, pullulating bottom.

If so, it won't be a day too soon. When the bases are gone, the camp towns will evaporate. Maybe then Americans and Koreans can regain their dignity and come to know each other as equals.

---

1. *New York Times* Op-Ed, June 25, 1990.

Bruce Cumings teaches East Asian and International History at the University of Chicago and is the author of a two-volume study entitled *The Origins of the Korean War* (Princeton: Princeton University Press, 1992).

TONG DU CHUN: THE BAR SYSTEM

Saundra Sturdevant and Brenda Stoltzfus

Altogether, there are about 18,000[1] registered women or "club women" working in the bar areas around U.S. bases in Korea. Perhaps an additional 9,000[2] women, who are not registered, work outside the clubs. Tong Du Chon (TDC), just outside of Camp Casey, has eighty-four clubs[3] and 700 to 800 registered women.[4]

All club women must carry a VD identification card. In fact, any Korean woman with a GI must have a VD identification card unless she is married and has a dependent's card. If she is married and still working in a club, she must have the VD identification card. The VD clinic issues the cards. Each bar area servicing the U.S. military has a VD clinic. The Korean Ministry of Health and Welfare operates these clinics with the help of the Korean police.[5]

Before receiving her card, the woman is given a medical checkup. Afterward, she is tested once a week for VD, gonorrhea, and syphilis. In addition, she is required to have a chest X-ray and blood test every six months and an AIDS blood test every three months. If a woman tests positive for a disease, she is taken to Soy San Hospital, the hospital serving the VD clinics. She must stay in the hospital until she is well. Treatment and food while she is in the hospital are free. The local Korean government also administers and finances Soy San Hospital.

Twice a month, base personnel, Korean authorities, and the Civilian Military Operations (CMO) go on VD spot checks. They stop women on the street and check their VD identification cards. The CMO are along because the guys sometimes get angry if the woman they are with gets stopped. If a woman does not have her card, she is taken to the hospital in a van for testing and issuing of a card. A woman can get twelve months in jail if she has no card.

Clubs are checked for their licenses and for sanitation, especially the ice used in the bars and the latrines. The women's rooms are also checked for sanitation and heating.[6] Clubs are allowed a certain number of women positive to a disease per month. If they are over that number, they are off-limits to the guys. A club is also off-limits if it fails the sanitation check three times. The Military Police monitor the clubs to make sure the guys are not going to a club that is off-limits. A club may present a protest to a disciplinary board of sergeants and officers on the base to reverse the off-limits designation.

If a guy gets a venereal disease, he must identify the woman or women, dates of contact, and name of the club(s). A sergeant goes with him to identify the woman, who then must report for a checkup at the hospital. The sergeant later calls the hospital to see if she has reported. She may also get treatment elsewhere and bring papers saying that she is well. There is a quarantine for guys. If they get sick, they are not to leave the base. But, according to base personnel, it doesn't work. There are quarterly VD classes for the guys and boxes of free condoms at the gate for them to pick up on their way out. It is too expensive for the base to give condoms to the clubs; but if a club is having a problem with VD, they might be able to get a free box.

A number of clubs have a salary system of payment. Usually there are one or two women in these clubs: one woman is the bartender, and one runs the cash register. Each is paid a straight salary of about US $80 per month. The women encourage the customer to buy high-priced drinks. They have a quota. If they exceed the quota, they receive a bonus.

An alternative method of payment is the piece-rate system.[7] Here, the women receive a percentage or commission on the drinks that they sell to the customer and on the money from the sale of their sexual labor. The amount of their commission varies from bar to bar. There are also quotas on drinks. The cost for sexual labor is $15 for short-time and $25 for an overnight. The women are paid their commission by the club owner at the end of the month, but deductions may be made toward their debts to the club.

The women usually have large debts to the club owner. When a woman enters the club, she must furnish her room, generally located at the back of the club. She borrows from the owner to buy the necessary items—bed, bureau, fan, sound system, TV. She may also have been introduced to the club through an agency. Agency fees range from $50 to $300.[8] She pays about $15 for her room and two meals a day.[9] When a woman's family is in need of money, she again borrows from the club owner, increasing the debt.

Debts may also be incurred when a woman has an abortion. Abortions on demand are legal and common in the southern part of Korea and obtainable for a "reasonable" fee. The woman often pays for the abortion by borrowing from the club owner.

Bar owners and procurers keep control over the women's movements to ensure that they do not moonlight. The degree of control varies. Women may live in the back of the club in a compound with access only through the club. In other situations, access to the woman's room may also be obtained by a narrow lane that runs beside the club. Here, an enforcer will monitor access. Other women live in a room in a brothel or in a hotel. Here procurement is done by a middle-aged *mamasan* on the streets who makes contact with the guy, negotiates a price, and then shows the guy to the woman's room.

Another situation is a kept or "key" woman. A guy will rent a room with a bath and kitchen, and the woman will live there during his tour of duty. When he is posted elsewhere, the woman will return to the bars for work—or, perhaps be turned over to another guy.

Finally, the three-mile-wide stretch of land separating the northern and southern parts of Korea is known as the Demilitarized Zone or DMZ. In the Tong Du Chun area, the DMZ takes on an additional meaning. Here, it is the Dark Man's Zone— the DMZ—the part of the club area where African-American servicemen hang out. As in the Philippines, the clubs in the DMZ are smaller and more homey. Some Euro-American servicemen go to clubs in the DMZ, and some African-American servicemen go to bars outside of the DMZ. However, the division is clear.

1. Young Mi Pak, Unpublished Manuscript for My Sister's Place, 12. My Sister's Place is a center in the Uijongbu area that works with women who are married to or living with American servicemen or are working in the clubs.
2. Ibid.
3. Interview with Sgt. Larry Lomax of the Civilian Military Operations, Camp Casey, July 1989.
4. Interview with Mr. Kim, VD Clinic in Tong Du Chun, July 1989.
5. Young Mi Pak, 12.
6. The traditional way of heating is *ondo*, which can give off fumes from coal block burning. The military alleges that some GIs have died as a result of inhaling these fumes while with a Korean woman.
7. My Sister's Place.
8. Ibid.
9. Young Mi Pak, 12.

NAN HEE

Uijongbu

Age: 33

The bar area lies just behind this row of buildings on the left. The entrance to Camp Casey is on the right at the end of the block.

My only wish is that the rich would help the poor. That kind of world would be great. People shouldn't be despised because they don't have anything. Wouldn't it be better to help each other than despise each other?

I am thirty-three years old. I have two brothers and one sister. I'm the youngest. My parents are no longer living. My father was a farmer. He had some rice fields and a plot of land. He grew peppers, soybeans, potatoes, yams, and corn. I worked on the farm until two years after graduating from elementary school. I missed many days of school because of the work. I helped with

These women pepper pickers range in age from twenty-five to sixty. They work in groups of four from 6:00 A.M. to 8:00 P.M. filling 40-kilogram bags with peppers. Each is paid half what a male pepper picker earns from the same work.

pumping water, picking up firewood from the forest, and with weeding.

My father also tilled other people's land. The owners were distant relatives. He would give half the crops to the owner. Then the owners wanted the land back because they wanted to farm it themselves.

We had to work hard because we didn't have much. If you have a lot of property, it doesn't mean you have to work hard. In rich families, you can buy labor to do work for you. But in poor families, you are busy trying to make ends meet every day. Life was difficult. We had to pay back the money we'd borrowed and share the produce from our little plot. After all that, we had nothing left to eat.

It wasn't too good between my mother and father. There were a lot of fights. I often heard him cussing Mother out. I didn't see Father beating Mother very much; but Mother told me that when she was younger, he used to beat her a lot.

There wasn't much interaction between Father and the children. He was there, and he wasn't there. Perhaps it would have been better if he had not been there.

I went to elementary school when I was ten years old and graduated when I was sixteen. It was a little late because I had the measles. I

Club woman studying English. Most women do not know English before working in the clubs.

At times, when I'm learning English, I wish I had studied more. But it doesn't mean I regret I didn't go to school. I want to live a normal life. I don't want to be despised by others for lack of education. Nor do I like it when educated people look down on others. I want to live on good terms with others.

My brothers left home to make a living, and my sister married early. We sold the little land we had, and I took care of my brothers in Seoul. I cooked for them.

One brother was in Anyang.[1] I went to live with this brother and commuted to work in a factory. We made light bulbs and parts. It was a small factory. I was there for a year, but it didn't amount to much. My pay was around 40 to 50,000 won per month.[2] We sometimes worked overnight, usually twelve-hour shifts. If we worked overtime, the pay went up just a little.

We had a labor union. If we couldn't get along with the supervisors, we'd quit working. They waited and waited. Finally, they couldn't find anyone to work so they asked us to return to work. The wage increases weren't much, only about 5,000 won. I couldn't make ends meet.

My brother worked at the Lotte department store.[3] My sister-in-law was also working there. The pay wasn't good, and no one could eat regularly. My brother got sick.

My mother came to take us home to the village. While I lived at home, I worked for other people in their homes as a day worker or maid. The pay was very little, 500 or 1,000 won

went to learn to read Korean and Chinese characters. I didn't study. I didn't want to. Our homeroom teacher would treat the kids from rich families well. But the kids from poor families, you know—I guess that added to my dislike.

per day. At that time my father was working as a houseworker and was paid with rice—five or six sacks per year.[4] He would live and sleep at other people's houses.

After that, a friend told me about a job in Taegu. I earned 80,000 won per month. We wove *kalkalee* (a type of rough cloth). Clothes are made out of *kalkalee*. I worked there about two years and earned about 200,000 won. I gave it to my mother.

In that factory, we lived in a dormitory. We had about seven or eight in one room that was not very large. The bathroom was outside. There were about 100 women in the dormitory. A factory usually has a dormitory on the premises. There was a

cafeteria. We paid for our food. We usually ate *kimchi* [spicy pickled cabbage]. They served beef soup once a week. Not too much food. We had two shifts and sometimes worked twenty-four hours straight. We would doze off while at work. Because of the work, I didn't get to go home for two years.

The people live in the dorms because they come up from the rural areas to work in the city. Also, people who are in a hard situation come to the dorm to live. Most of the women in the factories come from the country, although there are also some from the city.

Factories with dormitories contiguous to the work place are common. This allows maximum use of labor, with workers available for long shifts and overtime on demand. Korean workers have the longest work week in Asia, with an average of fifty-six hours per week.

The bar area is full of shops specializing in custom-made clothes and shoes for the guys, and fashionable factory-made clothes for the women to wear while working in the clubs. Many shops also have artifacts of U.S. military history for sale.

When *Chusok*[5] came, I quit and returned home to help Mother. At that time, my brothers had returned from the army. My oldest brother went to Vietnam on a battleship. Also the younger brother. They returned without any injuries. Both of them went out to look for a job.

A friend's mother told me about a job in a garment factory in Ulchiro. I started out as an apprentice and then became a sewing-machine op-

erator. I had an eye for sewing, so I learned fast. After one year I became an operator, but the owner wouldn't pay us during that time—only spending money. We were patient and waited. He wouldn't pay us so I said, "What the hell. I can live better as a maid." I left.

I had nowhere to go. I was twenty-two years old. I had to eat. As I was walking toward Tong De Moon,[6] I saw a sign: "Woman employee wanted." What the heck. I went in. They said they wanted me.

In the restaurant, I worked as a delivery girl. I slept in the restaurant. Including the cook, there were five or six of us. We got up at 7:00 A.M. and started working at 8:00. We finished around 12:00 P.M. While I was working there, I met a Korean man. Two months later, I started living with him. I lived with him half because I loved him and half because he raped me and I had no choice.

We registered as a married couple after we had begun living together. I left the restaurant in 1982. Our marriage is recorded as 1983. We started living together in 1979. We didn't have a wedding ceremony because we didn't have anything. Even the mother-in-law was unemployed. She was always drunk and acting crazy. My own family was not well-off either. How could we get married?[7]

When I moved in with the man, there was a brother-in-law and a mother-in-law. I lived with them in Samyangdong, at the top of the hill. It was their own home, but they had a lot of debts. It was about to be taken from them.

A sweat shop in the Tong De Moon area of Seoul

Poor people come to the city to live in areas like the one where we lived. People pay a fee to the owner for using the land and build their homes—in reality, shacks—there. The house, although illegal, is theirs. If the land is sold to another owner, the owner pays the people for the cost of the homes and everything is given to the new owner.

If you have some money, you put up some shingles. Otherwise, you put up wood paneling or slate for a roof. When I was there, some homes had running water, but most people carried water from a well. In the hills, there was no water service. The pipes didn't reach. People had to pump it and carry it home. There were no rich people living in this area.

The house was an illegal building with seven rooms. All seven were rented. My mother-in-law, brother-in-law, husband, and I lived in one room. Also, some of my husband's friends and brother-in-law's friends. We just slept somehow. My mother-in-law was always drunk.

My husband had no clear job. I didn't know he was two years younger than I. I was deceived. I thought I might as well take care of him since he was not mature yet and I had already moved in. I began working in a restaurant [again] to help make ends meet, but that guy wasn't worth it. When he got angry, he would beat me up. He was healthy and normal, so he should have thought about earning money. He was in bad shape. The creditors

A view from a sweat shop window

were always at the door. It was our house, but we even rented out the room we were living in and put up a tent on the rooftop.

We couldn't enter the tent standing. We squeezed in and out. My mother-in-law went to work in a restaurant, and the brother-in-law also left to look for a job. He and I were the only ones living in the tent. It was no honeymoon. A newlywed's home? It was already winter. There was no heat. I almost froze to death.

It was time for my husband to report for military duty. The conscription letter came for him to serve his term. Since he was on military duty, he could live and sleep at the base, so I began living by myself. The winter was cold and there was a lot of snow. When it snowed, the slabs [of tin] got too heavy and broke. The tent was useless. I called him asking what he could do. I said I couldn't live like this, that we should go our separate ways. I would go to a restaurant and live. Since he was living and eating on the base, he could survive. We separated.

I said, "Let's meet on Christmas Eve." But on the promised day, that guy didn't show up. I went to the base and found that he had gone AWOL two days before we were to have met. He probably didn't like working inside the base and wanted to hang out with his friends. I wasn't there, and it was probably

Rooftop housing

hard waiting for our date. He couldn't do what he wanted to, so he went AWOL. I went to the base and found that the idiot was serving a sentence. It was a military prison, and they wouldn't let me see him. The duty is for one year. Because he had gone AWOL, he ended up serving almost two years.

I worked, waiting for the day he would be released. He served some time, came out on a reduced sentence, and then returned to the base. His head had been shaved clean. If I had thought about it and run away at that time, I wouldn't be in such a mess today. I must have loved him since I stayed. I thought I could change him. I thought I would wait until he became a human being. But I also wanted to run away. When he came out, he thought I had run away. I said, "True, it was stupid of me to stay. I don't know why I live with you when you just beat me up."

We lived in the attic. This guy wouldn't think of working. If the day was hot, he would say it's too hot to go to work. If it was cold, he said it was too cold to work. If it rained, he couldn't work. Everyone was coming and demanding payment. He was becoming dependent. When I didn't give him money, he would beat me up. The mother and brother-in-law were with us again. They didn't think of earning any money. They just came back.

The corner store: a working-class area of Seoul

If the other family members tried to stop him from beating me, he would shout, "Who do you think you are, my mother?" and would beat up his mother. Even his friends wouldn't interfere when we fought. If they did interfere, he would go to their houses and beat them up for trying to stop us from fighting. He would break everything. No one even thought of stopping him. Everybody was afraid.

Then I noticed that I had gotten pregnant. People were telling me, "How did you get pregnant when so many people were sleeping in that small room?" I couldn't get an abortion because I had no money. I tried to lose it naturally. I also thought perhaps he would change with a baby. But it didn't work. You can't teach an old dog new tricks.

I really had nothing, nothing to eat. As my stomach grew, I was feeling weaker and weaker without any food. I slept all the time. We were living on top of a store. I would be busy every morning, trying to eat the discarded apples that rats had taken bites out of. The ones the rats had touched, the owner left outside the store. I was so hungry and weak, I ate these apples. It gave me strength but not enough.

That guy, he was bad, bad. I was waiting for him to straighten out as a human being. Even though I was pregnant, he would threaten to plunge a knife into my stomach. I dared him to cut me up. I shouted at him, "It's okay if I die, but what did the baby do?" He couldn't do it. I said to myself, "Just wait till the baby comes, then it's good-bye."

I had my baby in December. A son. After I had the baby, I had nothing to eat. I was so hungry. An elderly woman living nearby brought me a special chicken soup with rice. She said it would help with my nursing the baby. I ate like I was crazy. I was so hungry. But, other people also ate it. What could I do? They ate it all. A woman next door brought rice for us to eat. The brother-in-law brought us some heating coal. He was working then. But he wouldn't give me any money, since his brother would take the money away.

Then one of his friends came. During dinner, the guy [the husband] said that today they were to go and eat some dog meat, each person paying 5,000 won. I said, "Are you a human being?" He called me a "fuckin' bitch," saying that I had talked back to him in front of the others. We had a fight. His friend didn't even try to stop him, saying that my attitude needed to be corrected.

I got so beaten up, I blacked out. He was afraid for the baby. He gave it to his friend's wife, telling them to take care of it for a while, and continued to beat me.

At first, I didn't talk back to my husband. I just let him beat me. Later, I got pissed off, so I fought back. I said, "Where is the baby?" He left the house quickly. I thought, "Good—now is the time." I quickly changed my clothes. By then the guy came back with the baby.

The neighborhood people didn't like the guy. They would tell me to run away from him. I'd say,

"Where?" I couldn't make up my mind. I decided to run away. The baby was sleeping. The guy had been at the neighbor's drinking all night. He returned and demanded that I bring another bottle of liquor, shouting, "Fuckin' bitch, I'm your husband. Do as I say." I told him, "This is it. I've had it. I've been patient, but no more. It's finished. It's finished."

I told a student who was living in the back room to take good care of the baby. He would always say, "Sister, why don't you run? Why do you have to live this way, getting beaten up all the time?" I told him that I was running away for good. "If the baby wakes up, say you don't know where I am."

I ran over the hills behind the house. The shortcut would have been faster, but I was afraid of being caught by his friends if I took the shortcut. As I was walking, I saw a 100-won coin on the sidewalk. I changed it into 10-won coins in a pharmacy and called a hometown friend. I almost went crazy then. I told her that I didn't want to live.

At that time, there were five women living with my friend. There was also a housekeeper. I told them to pay me W 50,000, and I would do the housekeeper's work. So the housekeeper was fired, and I started work.

These friends worked in the clubs. We had known one another from the factory. Wages were low in the factories. The women whose boyfriends left them went into that kind of world. They would fall in love with a Korean man. The affair would end,

Video-game rooms are popular among women and servicemen in the bar areas of Korea and Okinawa.

I actually worked in four places. I worked at a restaurant as the housekeeper. I also worked for a man as a housekeeper. I would do cleaning jobs at different (dancing/drinking) halls and hotels. And I sold my body. It's not easy to sacrifice your body. I was earning quite a bit. I sent the money to my mother. I worked even though I had the flu. I thought: "What the hell, what is life if I live it one way or another way. I might as well help my mom. How long would she live if I didn't?" When she needed money, she would call.

Then I told the other women, "I want out." I went to an employment agency. They got me a job in an inn with thirty rooms—thirty rooms, mind you—all by myself. The owner gives you a salary of W 50,000. When you work in an inn, you don't share the wages but you share the tips. So even though it was hard work, I did it by myself. There was a woman who did the wash. I cleaned and played hostess to guests. When they asked for a lady, I called for a lady. I could earn 400 to 500,000 won per month. I'd buy cola at 200 won a bottle and sell it for 500 won. I even had a savings account.

I was twenty-seven or twenty-eight then. I lived there for a year. I didn't waste anything and must have had 1,000,000 won in the bank. Then the owner said the inn had been sold and I had to look for another place. Where could I go? But I had to go. I returned to the employment agency. I sent all the money in the bank to my mother.

and they thought their bodies were wasted. When you date, you go to beer halls, so you get to know those places. They could ask the women working in those places, or they could go to the employment agencies and be introduced. These are illegal agencies, of course. They were also introduced to it by other friends. Or they had to get abortions, but they had no money, so they ended up going to a pimp.

Women rent small rooms behind the club or, in this case, a few doors from the bar where they work. The women will go into debt to buy a bed, fan, chest of drawers, TV, and sound system, which are necessary to entertain customers.

At that time, my father was sick and laid up at home. He had epileptic seizures, so he couldn't move too much. As they got older, their relationship improved. There wasn't much farming in the rural areas then. He couldn't do any tenant farming. And we had sold the small piece of land we owned to cover the hospital bill that my father's sickness incurred. My parents lived on what their children sent them from their jobs.

My mother didn't say much about my working in the clubs. They thought it was their fault for being unable to educate us. She told me to do what I wanted to do. They didn't have any power to fight me or force me. Mother didn't think that everyone working in the clubs was bad. What could she say? I was helping the family out, after all. Of course, Mother would lie and tell the neighbors that I was working in a factory.

When I went to the agency, they said to go to an American bar. I told them that I had no schooling and didn't know any English. They said I could use my hands and feet to make gestures and it would pass. I said I didn't want to go there and asked them for an inn. But they were persuasive, and in the end, I said I would go.

Then, there was a man at the employment agency who said he had started a business in Uijongbu but had no women. I asked what they did there. He said there were American GIs but that they didn't drink. They only had juice and things like that. I said, "Okay, let's go." I asked for advance pay of 100,000 won. That was part of the total 200,000-won debt that I piled up at the beginning. I had to buy a bed and things like that.[8]

I didn't know a word of English. They told me just to say "yes." If they asked my name, I just said "yes." They would laugh and make fun of me. I was so embarrassed.

When the customers came in, if they drank a $3 or $5 juice, the $3 would get me 100 won and the $5 would get me 150 won. If I wanted to provide personal services, I could. That money would be held by the owner, who would give it to us at the end of the month. Overnight sleep was $20, and the hourly rate was $10. The room and board were 80,000 won. It included room, food, electricity, plus 5 percent interest monthly. If I had a 100,000-won debt, there would be 5,000 won interest. You have to be twenty to work in a club. I was a little old. I was twenty-nine when I got to know this kind of world.

One or two months later, I saw Mom in a dream. She had on a traditional Korean dress. It was strange. I went to my brother's home in Dobong-dong. I learned that Mom had passed away. Oh, my God. I had not been in touch with my brother. After I entered this kind of world, I had broken off all com-munication. I had kept up with Mom, but after I came here, I broke even with her. I returned to Uijungbu, borrowed 200,000 won from the owner, and went home.

I gave Father some spending money. Dad said that Mom had died waiting for me. He was crying. After the funeral, I returned. But I was upset and couldn't work. The owner was saying things to me about not working. So I said, "Fuck it" and went out with an American GI and stayed out for a couple of days. When I returned, they thought I had run off, so they turned me over to a Korean club.

They sold me for about 500,000 to 600,000 won. I said I didn't want to go. I said I had learned some English and could use it in some other club. But they sent me to a Korean club. I couldn't stand to work there. How could I do it with a traditional Korean dress on? So the owner sold me to a house in Pusan.

The new owner paid maybe 1,000,000 won along with an airplane ticket. I went with the man on the plane to Pusan. There were about twenty women in the house. The men would come to the place and choose. We would be wearing traditional Korean dresses and sitting pretty. They had one pimp for every two women. They were always watching us, so we couldn't escape. If I jumped out, I would break my leg. I decided to wait.

When I thought about the club in Uijungbu, I kept thinking about the American GIs. Korean clubs have better pay, but Korean men are mean and so disgusting. In the

Women at work; men at play

Taxis lined up late at night. Lacking even a rudimentary knowledge of Korean, U.S. servicemen find it difficult to use public transportation. The guys use taxis to go to bar areas and hotels.

American clubs, if you're new, it's okay. GIs try you out, and that's the end of that. But in the Korean clubs, if you're new, you have to go through an initiation. You have to do a striptease with five or six people in the hall. You do this whenever there is a new customer or especially valued clients of the club. They'd say, "She's new. She's got to show her stuff." [If you are chosen] you go to another room. It's not bright in there, so you can do it. In the American clubs, there isn't any such thing.

I told the owner that I wanted out. I calculated that I had worked enough to pay for all my debts and had three months of income coming to me. But even after three months, she would not settle my account. She just said, "Keep earning." I thought I'd die if I stayed any longer.

Then one client asked if I wanted to escape. I told him there was no way to escape even if I wanted to. He said that he would take me out of the house and give me a chance to run off. I added up the tips that the clients had left and it came to 40,000 won. I had it stashed away for transportation fare.

The client called and asked that I be sent out. The owner let me go since the client was a frequent customer. I got in a taxi. The customer paid the taxi driver a lot of money and told him to take me where I wanted to go. I told the driver to let me off in the middle of the road. After getting out, I ran into the alley and into an inn.

Early the next morning, I took the train and returned to Uijongbu. I

went back to the place where I used to work. I was about to give them a piece of my mind. I demanded to know why I had been sold off like that. The owner was glad to see me. She said she was sorry and asked me back. I said, "No way. I don't need you." But she begged me to work. I said, "Okay." I had a plan in mind to return her the favor. I told them, "If you complain that I'm not working hard, I'm going to report you for employing minors." They said they were sorry.

The guy [the ex-husband] caught me one day. He begged me to come back, saying he would change. He said, "Don't you want to see your child?"

"Don't you think I want to see my own child?" I said, "Okay, I'll stay

since you say it will not be like the
past." The baby didn't know me. He
kept calling me "Auntie, Auntie."
But in less than ten days, the guy
was back to his old self. When I
think about it, I start shaking all
over. I called my brother in Anyang.
I told him the trouble I was in and
asked him to resolve the situation.
My brother asked whether I wanted
to live there. I said I wanted to
make a clean break.

My brothers didn't believe me before. But when they saw with their
own eyes how the guy was behaving,
they told me, "Take the baby and
go." The guy was waving a knife
around. He stuck the knife into his
arms saying he would change. My
brother told me to escape. He said
he would take care of it. I took the

baby and ran. I returned to Uijungbu. I called him up and told
him that if he gave me a divorce, I
would return the baby. I told him to
meet me with the documents at my
brother's place. When I met him, he
had not prepared the documents.
What could I do? I told him to take
the baby and go.

I was pregnant. I returned to my
former roommate. She was living
with an American and working in
another club. I asked whether I
could work there. She said, "You've
got to give up the baby." They don't
let pregnant women in because it's
bad luck. I asked my friend to ask
the owner to advance me 200,000
won. With that I went to the hospital and had it aborted. The housekeeper made seaweed soup for me.

A number of *mamasans* and other older women who work in the clubs provide child care for the women.

In Korea, we can have abortions if we want them. They ask our name, the name of the husband, and then give us the abortion. You can give any man's name; they would still give you an abortion. I understand that overseas that you can't do that. I heard it takes a lot of money. In Korea, you can have an abortion for 40 to 50,000 won if it's before three months. There really isn't much inconvenience. The club owners usually help their women get abortions if they get pregnant. But you have to use your own money— you have to look out for yourself.

Those with weak vaginas can have easy abortions. Those with strong vaginas have a hard time. I've had three abortions. After the first baby, I put in the loop, but it must have come loose.

We get a weekly checkup and blood test, but there is no sex education. I don't know too much about AIDS. I've just heard about it. I've heard that there are several people with AIDS in other clubs. Since American GIs have more than one sex partner in many countries, we have to be careful about AIDS.

The women who live with GIs don't have too many babies. [In Korea] we get married and then have babies. A lot of the women believe in the men and so have babies. But a lot of them get a raw deal. Even those who have babies after marriage have a hard time going to the U.S.

If a woman has a baby without marrying the man and the baby is white, it is put up for adoption. If the baby is dark, that's harder to

do. There are people who will adopt white Amerasians, but there are very few Koreans who want to adopt. Many Americans who can't have children come and take them.

Within two months of working at this club, I met an American, but he was suspicious of me. He had been divorced twice. He was always beating me up. He was just like a Korean. He would break the table legs and other things. It was driving me crazy.

I lived with him for about three months. Then he said he was leaving. I asked why. I don't know what he said. At that time, I didn't know any English. My friends said even though I couldn't speak English I should still be aggressive. I said, "How can I be aggressive when I don't know any English?" But they said try anyway. Then after Team Spirit[9] was finished, someone jumped over the back fence. It was him. At that time, I was living by myself and was very satisfied. He came in and tore my clothes off and was trying to suffocate me. I told him that we weren't living together anymore and he should stop bothering me. Koreans and Americans, they're all alike.

I decided to go to a black club. I thought maybe blacks would be better. They weren't any better. I

It is difficult for a woman to keep a child with her in the small room where she lives and works. If the child's natural father is African-American, the stigma attached to the woman and the racism visited on the darker-skinned child in Korean society may make it wiser to send the child to live with relatives in the village. Children fathered by Euro-American men do not have this problem.

Outside of drinking and purchasing wo-men's sexual labor, recreational oppor-tunities for the guys are quite limited. Video-game rooms, pool halls, and these punching machines help to pass the time.

worked there for a month. I met a Puerto Rican there and lived with him for a year while I was going to the clubs.

Earlier, I had gotten an advance of 500,000 and sent it to my father for his medical costs because of the epilepsy. Then I met the Puerto Rican, Jerry. He helped me. Along with the money I earned from the other clients, I was able to pay it all back.

The Puerto Rican was a good man, very kind. He never hit me. He did what I asked him to. After hav-

ing been beaten and all, it was easy to fall for a guy like that. This guy told me first that he loved me. I told him, "You're a crazy guy." Every day he would tell me he loved me.

He was all right, but he would drink too much and pee in the bed. Every day I would wash the blanket. Every other day, he would wet the bed. He was always drinking. I thought: "Just don't mistreat me, and it's fine." I would clean up after him and take care of him. If I was out of his sight, he would be out looking for me.

Almost all the bars in the Dark Man's Zone (DMZ) are smaller and more run-down than those on the main strip less than one block away. At the same time, the atmosphere is friendlier.

How could he have run out on me like that? He must have been one or two years younger than I. I think maybe he left for his own good. I really wanted to live with him. I thought I was good for him. I thought about him. He was so good to me. I had really depended on him and believed in him. I didn't drink. I decided not to drink because it would only make things worse. If I drink, I go crazy. I became tough then. I became stronger inside.

Then I met up with the Puerto Rican again. I was worried. I had a lot of debts. We went and sat down. He said to drink up. He told me to eat. He said, "Let's not talk this time but meet again." I asked him why I should trust him. I said, "I don't believe in Americans any-

more." Then, two days later, he came back. I asked him if he had a wife. He said yes. She was Korean. He had a room in the Hyatt.

When he got paid, he would give me 100,000 won or 200,000 won, but he never slept with me. I continued to live by myself. He would come every day and help out. He would come during the evening and give me $20 or $50 and tell me to get something to eat. Since I wasn't wasting the money, the debt didn't increase.

Then Jerry said he wanted to spend the night with me. He wanted to go to an inn. After I finished work, I went there. He was good to me, but I didn't like it. People would tell me that I was crazy. "Do you think you're a high-class prostitute?"

The Silver Star Club is a country-western bar on the main strip. It has a great dance floor, and considerable quantities of beer are consumed each night.

In neighborhoods contiguous to the bar area, a U.S. serviceman may rent an apartment or room for his Korean woman for the duration of his tour of duty. This row of unfurnished two-room apartments is inside a walled compound, with the owner's modest house at the entrance. Each has a very small kitchen, with butane tanks for fuel and a small bath with a toilet and a shower head coming out of the wall. Rent is 200,000 won per month, or about $300. Electricity and butane are extra. There is no heat or hot water.

The Civilian Military Operations (CMO) mediates any confrontation between Koreans and U.S. service personnel. They use mobile phones, patrol regularly, and respond immediately and in force. A Korean-American serviceman is attached to each unit and serves as translator.

They told me to hold on to him. I said okay and lived with him for three or four months. He gave me money, so I was able to pay back the debt.

I lived with Jerry and commuted to work. Although he was good to me, I did not become close to him. What's the use of becoming attached to someone who left you because he didn't like you? I couldn't believe in him anymore because he had left me once. But Jerry helped me a lot. It was while I was living with him that Father passed away. My sister-in-law came and told me that Father was in critical condition. I went to see him.

My sister-in-law talked to my brother about what I was doing. My brother really beat me up. He said he was all finished with me. I told him that I was going to live all by myself, that I didn't have any brothers or sisters from then on. Since then, I've broken all rela-

tionships. When I came back, Jerry asked me, "What's wrong?" I couldn't answer him and just cried. He kept asking, so I answered that I had gotten a beating.

Since I came back, I've been living with Jerry without many problems. When I'd tell him not to get divorced, he'd say, "Are you saying that because you don't love me?" and would get on my case. So I say nothing about it. I couldn't tell him to do this or that now, could I? He helped me a lot. He helped pay for my teeth treatment. The hospital bill was 1,500,000 won.

Then the owner and an American got into a fight at the club. The American hit the owner because he didn't like a woman. He pushed away the people who were standing around, and the owner fell down the stairs and broke his head. He was taken to the hospital. They asked me to take care of the place. I was the only one they could trust. I asked

Papasans and security personnel
playing cards before work

Jerry to let me go and live there. He said he understood.

There are many incidents of fights when the GIs come. It starts because of a woman. The GIs have spent money on a woman but can't get satisfied and demand their money back. There are fights over that. It's a frequent thing.

When they fight among themselves, the women take sides and the fight gets bigger. In those situations, they're drunk and talk about their ranks. A man higher up in rank demands that a man lower than him in rank obey him. The lower-ranking man says, "You're the captain on

the base, but not here." These fights get rowdy.

I cleaned my room and gave everything away and went to the club with my small bag of clothing. I lived by myself again. The owner was rather tough and mean. I was kind to the men. I mean, everybody wants to have a good time—good food and all. So if they had no money, I would buy for them on credit. I told them they had to pay on a certain day if they had a conscience. I collected all the debts from the American GIs, and then I paid the women for all they had earned from the Americans.

The American GIs treat us better than Korean men. Of course, they also go crazy at times. But as for their treatment of women, I think they are better than Korean men. There are Korean men who treat us well, too. But I never came across a good Korean man—only the bad ones.

Through my club work, I got to know the Americans. Of course, there are the drunks who cause problems, as anywhere. But I could understand and accept that. There are Americans who live with you and in reality despise you, but in my experience, I haven't met too many

like that. There are many who just play with you. At the time, they want to use you. They tell you that they love you and all that stuff, but when they turn their backs on you, you're all alone.

In some American clubs, if you have no debt, they see to it that you incur some. If you had no debt, you would have the choice of going to another club, a better club. But if the woman has debts, she can't leave before she pays up. Escaping from a club isn't easy to do. The women with a conscience stay and work.

Many of the women in the clubs are two-faced. Some of the women

When not working, some of the women from the clubs have the freedom to hang out. Others may not be so privileged and are able to go outside of the club compound only when accompanied by security personnel from the club or with a *mamasan*. These women are trying to fix a broken pair of glasses.

stick by the owner. Others join together and stand up to the owner. There are tattletales who tell the owners everything. Then we have a big fight about who told what to whom. In the place where I work, none of the women squeal on one another to the owner. If we decide to do something, we do it.

Because I have gone through a lot, I would coach the new women. If we felt that a new women couldn't handle it, we would help her to escape. We would take her out. We'd tell her that this place wasn't for her. We'd help her go even if she had a lot of debt. We had many cases like that.

Not all the people in this business are bad. Just because people are in prostitution doesn't mean that they are bad people. They are here because of their family circumstances. I don't think it's evil. I don't think there are good and bad businesses. There's an old statement: Earn like a dog and spend it like the secretary of the treasury. I'm not ashamed of my work at all. I guess a person could be embarrassed by it, but I'm not like that.

It doesn't matter what others say, if our hearts are clean. Some people may disdain us and call us evil, but I think such people are the evil ones. They are spitting in their own faces.

New bicycle: two club women with the
child of one of them

Inside a bar on the strip

I think those who bad-mouth us are the bad people. That's my honest opinion.

I've been through so much suffering that if I were to think about a good future, I would think about what I've experienced and live accordingly. If I had money, I would help the poor and share it with them since I'm not going to carry it with me after death. I really don't dream of having a lot of money and living well. I just want to lead a normal life. What's the use of being greedy, anyway?

For me, it meant something to try to be a good daughter while my parents were alive—even in this kind of a place. Some children and parents fight over the family money. I think we should always live, trying to un-

derstand each other.

On the one hand, I dislike American GIs being in Korea, but they are human beings. They've also left their homeland and must be lonely. I hate the guys who are mean, but I feel sorry for those who are not. Sometimes the guys who tell you about their personal lives over drinks aren't bad. But then there are these nasty, mean guys who cause trouble when they drink. I don't like them. But they probably couldn't control what they were doing. They probably don't know what they are doing. After all, how uncomfortable are we within Korea when we leave our hometowns? I think there are good and bad people among the GIs.

For me, it would be okay if they

Mobile carts with rides will be moved from place to place and are quite popular with children. In this highly militarized part of the world, it seems natural to see a young boy in a helmet pointing his toy weapon at another. This is a neighborhood next to the bar area.

withdrew the troops. On the other hand, I think it's okay for them to stay, too. The women will not be able to stay in Korea if the Americans withdraw. I hear a lot about withdrawal, but I don't think it would be easy to do that.

I would like reunification, but the question is whether or not it would be a good one. If we are reunified and are able to live with a like mind and heart, then we could live happily. Nothing is greater than reunification if we can trust each other and depend on each other. If not, then it would be better to stay as today. If the result of reunification is not a better society, then it would be better not to have reunification.

---

1. Anyang is an industrial zone.
2. The 1989 exchange rate for the southern part of Korea was $1:660 won.
3. Lotte Department Store is one of the largest modern department stores in the center of Seoul. This is a major stop on the tourist circuit of Seoul.
4. One rice sack holds approximately 150 pounds of rice.
5. *Chusok* is a major traditional Korean holiday occurring in the fall.
6. Tong De Moon, which literally means "east of the gate," is a section in the center of Seoul. The city was formerly enclosed by a wall with four gates.
7. The cost of marriage is so high that it is common for working-class people not to get married. The Women's Legal Aid Center performs group marriages for poor people on Saturdays and provides counseling.
8. The women are required to provide their own room, often rented from the bar, for customers to come to and they must furnish the room with a bed, dresser, TV, and sound system in order properly to entertain the customers. This is one of the ways in which clubs get the women into debt.
9. Team Spirit is an annual military exercise conducted by the U.S. military forces with the forces of various other countries in the region.

MS. PAK

Uijongbu—Tong Du Chun area.

Age: 35

It is quite common to see tanks, ammunition trucks, huge gasoline tankers, and other U.S. military vehicles on the main civilian roads of Tong Du Chun.

At this stage, since we don't know what Kim Il Sung is thinking, I think it's okay for U.S. troops to be here.[1] But if our country could have lived depending on and trusting each other, it would have been great.

As far as I know, our country exists because the Americans helped us. However, if there were no U.S. or Soviet Union, or if Kim Il Sung had not gone to study in the Soviet Union, or if President Syngman Rhee had not studied in the U.S., our country wouldn't be divided along the Thirty-eighth Parallel.[2] And when we had the war, if Kim Il Sung had been stronger and there had been victory, we'd probably be a communist country, but we'd still be one. If President Syngman Rhee had been the stronger of the two and had provided real leadership, then it would have become the Republic of Korea—still one nation.

Isn't it true that the Americans and Russians are playing with us by placing us in the middle? So there is no need to say that you are helping us. You help us because you need something, too. I once had an argument with an American GI about these things. Then I read that the U.S. and Russia had made a deal. So there is no one who is right or wrong. You are in Korea to make money, not to help us. None of you who are in Korea are here to help us.

Since I've dealt with Americans, I've noticed that we Koreans are still poor and many go hungry. But Americans come here and they can eat whatever they want; they can do whatever they want to; they can buy whatever they want. Our country's people are still living three to four people in one room. Very few kids get to have their own rooms in their teens. Our country has developed a lot during the past eight to ten years, right? But even then, when Americans ask you to their houses and show you around, it's so different from our country's houses.

When you go to Itaewon, the commissioned officers have their own homes.[3] Poor people like us feel like we've walked into a castle. They have all kinds of liquor. When they come outside, the make fun of us with their $10 and $20. I can accept the fact that they have the ability to live like that. But in places like Itaewon, a single family uses the whole house. One man uses three rooms. Those with low ranks have a

Kid at play in the bar area

single room, but it still has a bath-tub and the facilities all work.

When you go to the U.S. Army base, everything is automatic. They can use as much electricity or water as they need. Meanwhile, the government tells us to save electricity and water. It's a world apart. Our men in the army have no hot running water in the showers. They don't have enough to eat; they sleep side by side with a light blanket. When I see the Americans living so well in such nice homes and comfort, I feel sorry for our soldiers. They have it so hard. If it weren't for Kim

Most factories will not hire married women and certainly will not keep in their employ a woman who is pregnant or has children. Thus, there is a large informal economy that underpins the larger economy, where women work at home and take care of their children.

Il Sung's viciousness, I think it would be a hundred times more profitable for our country if the Americans left.

The reason is that the Americans don't pay any taxes. They live comfortably because of us, too. They can rent a house [outside the base] cheaply. For most people [U.S. military personnel], the base pays for their rent. But the way they act with us shows that they despise our country. They think: "Koreans will lose their land if we aren't here. We are needed here because of Kim Il Sung. So we must be treated well. They can't live without us." I feel such thinking is really bad.

Many Korean women want to work with Americans in this line of work. I don't know about other countries, but our Korean men are a bit violent. I don't know how I should express this. For example, even a good person begins to show another part of himself when he starts drinking. Their true nature comes through. When they drink, they release the tension and stress from society. They act crazy and do as they wish. Americans aren't like that. Although they end up lying to you and deceiving you, Americans usually don't bother you and are friendly.

The women use contraceptives. The large majority are on the pill. There are some who use the loop, but it's not so effective. Americans have larger penises than Koreans.

Guys in a video-game room in the bar area

It's true that there are problems because their penises are larger. Things like the loop don't do the job. Something can go wrong inside. About 70 percent don't use condoms. Even those who use them stop using them once they start coming regularly since the women usually take the pill.

There are many women who can't take the pill. They throw up. So whenever they get pregnant, they have an abortion. Most people who have worked here for a long time have had ten or more abortions.

We heard that the first AIDS patient was a sailor.[4] There was one case of AIDS in Songsan this time.[5] The woman was young. She caught it from this life-style. Koreans don't have it. We got it from Americans. In all cases, it's related to Americans.[6]

While we're here, we don't receive Korean customers. So AIDS and syphilis and things like that come from Americans. In the old days, we didn't wash our underwear too often because there weren't such diseases among the Koreans. I have also lived with Koreans and had various relationships with them, but I haven't seen much disease.

Koreans don't know how to kiss and caress too well. If I were to compare their bed practices, Koreans usually go for the sex act, while Americans tend to kiss a lot and get messy. When I used to live with Korean men, they weren't that

The Social Hygiene Clinic is operated by the local Korean government. Women who work in bars that have U.S. servicemen as customers are required to have a weekly VD smear, a chest X-ray, and a blood test every six months, plus an AIDS blood test every three months. The women pay for the tests themselves.

For the checkups, you have to pay a membership fee every six months and now, for the first time, you have to have your picture taken. In the past, we paid W 500 or W 1000. Now we pay W 2,000. With the picture, it will cost W 3,500.

The [Korean] government provides the checkups. The U.S. government is not involved. What the Americans do is this: a GI goes out and sleeps with a woman. Any disease quickly appears on a man. At the hospital, they ask the man whom he slept with and from which club. After they find out the information, they go and find the woman and tell her to go to a clinic.

I think it's good that we get a weekly checkup of our bodies. It's just that we can't make money during that time we're in the clinic. If we have anything, we have to stay there for three days and receive treatment. On the fourth day, we get another examination. If we are okay, we can leave. If not, we stay another three days and get another examination. They let us out only after we're cured. They're strict about these things in every base area.

When we go to a hall, there is a debt system with the owner. You incur a debt by buying things. You also have to pay rent, food, and heat. Some owners settle the account once a month. Many places don't pay any salary. You have to sleep in order to make money. But it's the same yesterday or today. The smart person never gets tricked.

Every place I went, I never let them abuse me. When I listen to other women, I tell them, "Why did

messy. So I don't think the diseases started in Korea. In the Korean halls, they don't have to check for syphilis. But here, we have to have a checkup every week. It's very strict.

Gonorrhea occurs when you have stress or are tired after having sex. So if you don't have good feelings about having sex, you have to check it out and treat it. It goes away when the weather gets cold. But we don't have too many cases of syphilis or gonorrhea.

When I entered this work ten years ago, I had to get a weekly checkup. If we didn't and were caught by a worker from the Health Department, there was a penalty.

Studio 54, which gets going about 11:00 P.M., is a club where people go after most of the strip has closed down.

you let them do that to you. You should have done this and that." You can tell what people are like by looking at them. There are women who are into flashy things. They waste a lot of money. The owners usually take advantage of them. But if you look as if you have your wits about you, the owners won't try to trick you. You have to keep an account of your work, your debt, how much you've paid back, and how much you have coming to you the next month.

When I first entered this world, I thought that the Americans were well educated and great people. At first, I really treated them well. Even though they couldn't understand Korean, I called them "Mister" in Korean. I always used terms of respect when talking with them. Then I was tricked by them once or twice, and I saw many bad things happening—in fact, I saw people being killed.

Like once, an Amore cosmetics saleswoman was walking to her job one day. On the way, she saw an American GI burning trash; but it had a strange odor. She smelled hair burning, so she got suspicious. She called the police. They found him burning the body of a woman. He had killed her during a fight.

I try not to injure other people. No matter how bad men are to me, I give them three chances. If we try to understand and accept them, even those men won't mistreat us. The bad guys call us "bad bitches." They enter a hall and begin cussing out the people. I talk to them nicely: "You came her to drink OB [Korean beer]? You drink it when I give it to you." Then I tell them, "Don't talk bad to me. You're here in Korea to earn money. I'm here to earn money. So don't talk nasty to me." Then some kids say, "I'm sorry." But I think some Americans try to trick us and use us.

American GIs treat us this way because we're poor, uneducated, and have to make money through this

The P-Funk Club in the Dark Man's Zone (DMZ) is small, with just one woman working there. She works as a waitress, talks with the guys, may sell her sexual labor, and cleans up after each night's partying. A middle-aged Korean couple own the bar; the wife works as a bartender and her husband as the security person.

A bar owner

kind of life. They say they don't hit women while they're drinking in their own country, but they can do as they please since they are in Korea, a poor country. I think they overdo it at times. The American GIs make fun of us by saying, "Why are you so poor? Do you eat only *kimchi?*" and other things. Any human being, no matter if they live this kind of life or not, can be good and not be used by others. We may be poor, but we will live on our own power.

I have three brothers and one sister. I'm the oldest. My parents grew ginseng. All the people in the village lived off it. At that time, we were rich. Then our elder uncle went away and didn't come back for a week. He had gone to a gambling place and lost almost all the money. Because of my uncle, we went bankrupt. We sold our home and moved to Taejon City.

My mom worked so hard. My father had become discouraged by the farm failure and didn't work anymore. My mother worked as a bread

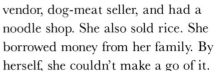

vendor, dog-meat seller, and had a noodle shop. She also sold rice. She borrowed money from her family. By herself, she couldn't make a go of it.

My father was a ladies' man. He was good-looking and had many affairs. When I was in the fifth grade, the villagers chased away the woman who was having an affair with my father. She worked in the local pub. Whenever my father came back from there, he would beat mother up. The villagers said that my mother was such a nice woman and chased the other woman away.

The woman came back to the village again. When I woke up after sleeping, mother was crying. Father wasn't there. He had gone to her again. I knew that much. I had heard she had come back. I went to my father's friend's house and said, "Please take me to where my father is." I meant to do something about it. I was thirteen.

We went to the inn. I began to shout, "You witch. My mother is working so hard to earn money. Why do you have to come back and make trouble for us." I shouted at her a little more and came home. Father came back the next day, but he continued to be a ladies' man, a butterfly.

During my second year in junior high, I dropped out of school. I had an uncle living in Seoul. I went to work at his dress shop. My brother kept writing me letters about things at home. Whenever I got a letter from him, I was so happy. I would burst into tears. I was so young then. The dress shop closed for the summer. I went home. I couldn't go

Four women are entertaining one guy, and the *mamasan* is nearby.

back to Seoul again. I didn't want to leave my brothers and my mother. I stayed home.

[When I was about sixteen], I had a friend who always bugged me to go to the movies with her. She liked a man who worked in the theater. One day, that man asked me out. He was very nice to me. We had fried wontons and Chinese cake. He picked up the food with the fork and gave it to me to eat. I was very embarrassed. I barely ate anything.

After that, he sent free movie tickets for us.

One Christmas Eve, there was a party in the village. We were having a good time. I had a glass of wine and fell asleep. It was a bit chilly, so I woke up. No one was there except that man. Suddenly, I was very frightened. I got up and ran out. He began running after me. Later he told me that if I had not run out, nothing would have happened. He said he didn't know why he had run

Rice paddies

Middle-aged women often work at construction sites. Their jobs may be physically demanding, their pay is about half that of a man doing the same work. Women employed in this way are almost always from rural areas, where a life of hard physical work is the norm.

Middle-aged women may also be employed hauling and delivering.

Older women in a village gathering at the end of the day to prepare vegetables for cooking and to chat.

This market near the bar area is quite large. One can buy fresh vegetables and fruit in season, peppers, spices, fish, meat, household and hardware items, and clothes. A number of the women from the clubs shop here, as do other women in the neighborhood.

after me. He didn't want to go all the way then. He had gone out with many girls and raped them. But my father was very strict with me, so he knew he'd better not touch me. He had just wanted to be good friends. He said that when he caught me, he decided to rape me.

I had on blue sneakers with white laces—I still haven't forgotten that—and red corduroy pants with a corduroy jacket and a hat. There was a zipper in the front. I had to pass by the dikes before I got home. There was a lot of snow. The dikes

went up, then came down to a ditch. We had gone down to the bottom. The water was frozen. I was caught. With ice as a bed, he went wild. He began right there. He was trying so hard to get my clothes off, and I tried my hardest to keep them on. I thought he was trying to kill me. I didn't know anything—I was so naive—I didn't know why. I fought with all my might. The zipper came apart and things tore. I got very tired and he was, too, so he didn't treat me badly.

It was past the curfew.[7] We went

This housing for agricultural workers is located in the valley outside of Tong Du Chun.

to an inn nearby. He asked the owner not to tell anyone that we were there. I was very embarrassed to be there. He raped me. I was beginning to have my period but the man kept coming. It hadn't been long since I had started having my period. It was a mess, because I continued to resist. It was horrible. Blood everywhere.

In the morning I went home. I had no strength left. I stayed home in bed for over a month. I thought I had a disease and was going to die soon. Mom thought I was sick and suggested we go to the hospital. I thought they would find out I had been with a man. What a horrible scene that would create. So I stayed home in bed. Mother was worried.

Soon after that, we moved. Mother and father had a new store in the market. They wanted to have a business. I thought we were moving because they knew about me.

The man followed us there. My father was angry. He beat me and gave the guy a few smacks, too. He said, "You're not my son, so I'm not going to beat you, but leave." My father kept beating me, saying "Why did you fall for a guy like that?" My father really loved me. I was young, so he was really angry and worried.

The guy came back. I met him while I was going to the bathroom [outside]. He dragged me away to an inn. We stayed for a few days. He wanted us to go to Chunjoo. He said, "We can make a go of things even if we have to work really hard. We can come back after we make some money." He was really making

Urban poor often build shanties on rooftops. This woman has just finished the day's laundry.

before, but in Chunjoo, he only had an occasional beer that I bought. When he got paid, he brought the money home. It was a good life. Then I got pregnant.

When I was almost ready to have the baby, I was homesick. I wanted to know what was happening, so I wrote to my aunt. My aunt and uncle visited me. They told me that my mother had passed away. I felt that my mother had died of heartache because of me. I didn't even know that she had died.

I couldn't visit home because I was about to give birth. I went to my in-laws' home and had the baby. My mother-in-law knew my mother from way back. She knew that my mother was a good woman, so she was very good to me.

When my baby had grown up a little, I told the man I'd like to visit my home. I said it would be good for him, too. When I said that, he began to drink heavily again, so we had a fight. My mother-in-law packed red beans, sesame oil, and many things. She sent a man to take me to the station. She told me to come back quickly.

When I got to Seoul, the kids were starving. After my mother died, my father had moved to Seoul. He took the children with him. He was really messed up. I cleaned the children up and took care of them. All of a sudden, one month had passed. I kept thinking I had to go back. But how could I leave them like that? I stayed one more month and another month. I couldn't leave. I just couldn't leave the kids.

My youngest brother was a couple

a case for himself. I didn't know what to do. I felt sorry for him then. It wasn't that I loved or liked him. I just felt sorry for him. He was talking about killing himself. Since I knew that I would get in trouble if I went home now, after several days, I agreed to go with him.

We went to Chunjoo. We had a very hard life. The man worked very hard in the cabbage fields. He drank of months older than my baby. When I was nursing my daughter, my brother would begin crying. What could I do? I had to nurse him too. My father was working in a real estate office in Hwagok-dong. I was working in my uncle's dress shop. It was hard to work even if I left the baby with others. It was far to the shop from where we lived.

A stepmother came to live with us to take care of my brothers. When she first came, she matched me up with another guy and we got married. I had a daughter [to this husband], who died soon after she was born. This daughter died, and my father sent my first daughter to the orphanage. I returned home one day and found that my baby was gone. She was two. I asked where she was. My father told me to forget about it. I said I couldn't live without her. He said he took her to an orphanage. I asked which one, but he wouldn't tell me. I nearly went crazy.

The man [husband] was suspicious of my fidelity. He wouldn't let me go to the market or the beauty shop to cut my long hair. He thought other men would take me away because I was so beautiful. At that time, to dry your hair, you had to brush it in the sunlight. We didn't have dryers. As I was brushing my hair, he would ask, "What are you doing brushing your hair outside? Whom is it for?" He thought I was trying to show off to another man. When he was in his right mind, he would say that I was beautiful when I was brushing my hair like that.

One day he said to bring a cup of water. He divided the water into two cups and began stirring it wildly. He said to drink this and die. He said if I didn't drink it, he would kill me with a bat. He said he would then drink and die. I was naive and stupid. I started to drink it.

Right after I took a sip, my mother-in-law knocked on the door. I guess she saved my life. I didn't have the courage to swallow it. I spit it out and opened the door. My mouth started to get swollen as I was going to the door. She asked what was wrong. She opened my mouth and shouted, "You've gone crazy again. If you want to die, kill yourself, but don't kill other people's children." She went out and washed some rice. She gave me the wash water and told me to gargle with it and spit it out. It neutralizes the poison. He was too much. I couldn't stand it. My mouth was really swollen. Mother-in-law had gone out to get some medicine. I was so afraid of living there, I left. I went to my uncle's house. [This husband] is dead now, so the marriage is over.

There was a *dabang*[8] that I had seen. It was called Doshin Dabang. I made a phone call. They hired me. I wasn't a hostess then with her fingernails painted and ordering people around. I was just a helper, so I didn't get good pay. I cleaned the place. I was still very young.

I saw that the hostesses did nothing in particular. They just had their hair up. My brain began ticking: we were out of rice—there was nothing to feed the kids—so I went to an employment agency in Young-deungpo and said I wanted to be a madam [hostess]. They told me to

One of the duties of women who work in the bars is cleaning up after a night's partying.

Men playing Go in a working-class
section of Seoul

go to Kimpo.[9] They said I would be
a madam and lady [waitress].

The place they sent me had been
a quiet *dabang* before. The business
wasn't very good there. But when I
got new customers, they never left.
The business boomed. I got to know
men only for money. When I had
a free day, guys would ask me out.
I promised to meet them one hour
apart.

I had moved the family to Shung-
pyung where the rent was cheap. We
didn't have a telephone. My father
stopped going to the office because I
sent money home. He was also sick.

Once, while I was working, everyone came—the whole family—like a
band of refugees. They had all kinds
of bags with books, kitchen utensils,

and clothes. I took them to a restaurant and fed them. I sat thinking
hard. It was a big problem. I had
already taken advances to send
home. My debt was high.

There was a Mr. Park, who had a
fish farm on his land. At that time,
people were into raising eels. He had
a small cottage on the fish farm. I
asked him to let my family live there
until I earned some money or at
least until the next month. He agreed.
I took them there right away.
I took eggs, rice, and other things
to them.

Then, a man loaned me the
money to get my own place. I would
pay him back with interest. It was a
tavern, tearoom, *dabang* and ginseng
teahouse all rolled into one. There

were only four tables. We had to bring the water from a mountain well. I got up at 4:00 A.M. to carry water down with my stepmother. The business started out well. I must have paid the loan back within a month.

I realized that while the customers were drinking, they would ask for girls. Then they would go to a brothel. I didn't like losing customers. I hired a woman. The woman I hired couldn't have been better. It was such a good business, we decided to move to a larger place. We leased a house, and I hired two women. They were good, too. We made a lot of money. I moved to a house with ten rooms and hired ten more women.

I was twenty-one or twenty-two, but I had brains. If I saw one thing, I knew ten things. I must have been meant to be something. I was good with the customers. I had a cook, but I got rid of him and cooked my-

self. I was doing a great business. We were in competition with the larger brothels. The name of our place was Oknyu Place [House of Jade Women]. The women kept the money [they earned from men] for themselves. If they didn't want to go out, they didn't have to. I paid them a good salary since I have been through it.

My father was ashamed of us, so he didn't come. My stepmother came and helped out. Then she said she wanted me to get her a roadside tent-bar.[10] She said she would like to support herself. I agreed to buy her one.

Then Father said he wanted to spend 200,000 won for *Chusok*. If someone spent 100,000 won for a party, people thought they were filthy rich. It would be as if we were showing off our wealth. At that time, I was short of money. I was skimping on my meals in order to save money. How could a parent ask such

Women work in their houses as part of the informal economy. This wool has been dyed. After it has dried, someone will pick it up and take it to another woman's place, where the next step in the process of making a garment for sale will take place.

a thing? Did he know how I had earned it? That's what made me hate him. I was really sad and angry. I left home. I took only a small bag with some clothing.

Wherever I went, I left word with my eldest brother. I was gone for a few days when he came looking for me with the news that Father was in the hospital unconscious. I had left home because he had asked for some money, and now this had happened.

I didn't think he would die, I thought he was just sick. Since we didn't have any medical insurance, we just gave the hospital the money it demanded. I wanted him to recover, so I spent the money. I thought the money would heal him. But he just didn't get better.

After fifteen or twenty days, the chief doctor asked for a guardian. The immediate guardian was my stepmother. She went in to see him. She came out sobbing and kept saying, "It's all over." She said that we didn't have enough money to keep him in the hospital. He couldn't live long and would die quickly. So for everybody's sake, they told the family to take him home. That's what I heard later.

If they had told me that then, I might have tried other ways to cure him. I'm angry about that even today. Since he wasn't her first husband and since life was so difficult and he couldn't work because of his illness, she just let him die. That's the only way I can explain her action. She remarried soon afterwards. She wanted him to die so she could get on with her life.

Strangely, everyone came the day

he passed away. I thought it was okay and took a nap. They woke me up. Father was beginning to move around. He had gotten a little better. He began to ask for things, like fruit. They say that when people ask for something, it's like their preparation for the afterlife. He was struggling. He kept saying he wanted to go the bathroom. He had tubes running out of his body. How could he move? How could he go to the bathroom? He raised hell for about an hour.

My aunt and uncle told me to bring the doctor. The doctor kept looking at him and pinching him here and there. Mother cried and cried. I asked the doctor, "What's happening? How is he?" He said my father was dead and told me to start mourning. I couldn't talk then. It was as if the sky had fallen and the earth had quaked. I must have aged ten years. I felt that it was my fault that my mother had passed away, and I had tried to be a good daughter to my father. I really couldn't believe he had died. I kept touching his face and his arms and legs. They were cold.

I was really sad. I went crazy. I had no desire to live. Our neighbor encouraged me. If he hadn't helped me, I don't know what I would have done. My sister wasn't with me then. She hadn't even come home. She had fought with stepmother and left. I was exhausted for a month or two. We had lost all the money. I had lost my father. But what is there left to do but live, since we are human beings?

After father died, I had a dream.

A man relaxing in a working-class area of Seoul

In the dream, father kept saying that he would take mother and the baby with him. I would shout "no" and begin crying. Then I would wake up. Some people say that means the family will break up. I asked stepmother about it. She said we should have GUT.[11] I told her to have one, but I really didn't like it.

The spirits exist. I personally experienced it. In the GUT, there is a part when the spirit wants to have a "lion dance." The family would be seated and the "lion" would enter the room. The spirit would descend on the shaman. Unless the spirit was punished and became afraid, it would not leave the place. The shaman was tied together with a rope and we were trying to untie her, but it wouldn't loosen. No matter how hard the strong men pulled the rope, it wouldn't come untied for about thirty minutes. When they finally got the rope undone, the man living across from our house began to foam at the mouth. He was old and weak. Usually spirits attack weak people.

We made preparations for the hundredth-day memorial service. Stepmother took care of the housework and cooking. Our neighbor had a big mill. He brought a sack of rice for us. All the rice was gone in less than a month. I remarked that it was strange: even though we didn't eat too much rice, almost all of it disappeared before the month was out.

At the hundredth-day memorial service, all the relatives, including uncle and aunt, gathered. In front of them I told my stepmother: "I have tried to accept and treat you as my parent, but nothing is as important to me as my brothers and sister. You are selling the rice these kids need. I can no longer consider you my parent." Since she had lived with our father and we had lived together, I gave my stepmother the house we had leased.

We left with only our clothing and nothing else. We went toward Kimpo airport. We rented a room. I had to get a job in order to live. I went to a *dabang*. I kept Myung

Midnight on the main strip of the bar area. People are going to Studio 54, a large late-night bar and dance club. *Mamasans*, left and right, who procure for women working out of hotel rooms or brothels, are looking for customers with whom they will negotiate a price. They then take the man to the woman's room.

Sook at home so she could cook for us. She was young but good. I worked, but we couldn't survive on the *dabang* wages. I brought knitting work at night. I'd finish and take it in early in the morning on the way to work.

When my father passed away, the youngest was five. He wrote in his diary: "On the way from school, I had this strange thought. Why don't I have a mother? Other kids all have their mothers. My friends go to school holding hands with their mothers. I wish I had a mother. Where did my mother go?"

I didn't ask him about it, but I always talked about the fact that we had to make a greater effort because we didn't have a mother and a father. "Mother and father are up in heaven and living well there. They are looking down on us. If we are bad and hang out with the wrong crowd, mother and father would be

very sad. We should always live the right way. It may be wrong for me to say it, but our father was not a father like other fathers. When you grow up and become mothers and fathers yourselves, you should try to become the best mother and father."

"Our mother was a really good woman. She couldn't pass by a poor person without helping. I'm sure she is in heaven. But father lived on what mother earned when she was alive. He was an intelligent man. He was discharged after the war as a sergeant. Many people called him a great guy. So he became very proud and expected everything to be given to him. He didn't do anything."

"Don't live like him. It doesn't matter how smart you are if you don't try. In any good work, to make it good, you have to give your best effort." I always told them that they shouldn't become objects of other people's scorn or do bad things.

They're all healthy and good kids.

When I came home, the kids would all be asleep in a row. When I saw them like that, I felt tired but also responsible. My eyes would droop but I tried my best to finish more knitting. We barely got by with the food and school tuition. I was always getting two months' advance pay and in deeper debt.

Our situation was very difficult. At the *dabang*, I earned the highest wage. I worked conscientiously. The owners liked me. But *dabang* income wasn't enough. There wasn't one day when I didn't worry about money. Honestly, you have to get around with men and do things if you want to earn money. I was very careful to do it without the kids knowing. As they got older, I didn't want them to know how their sister had lived.

In *dabangs*, a lot of men try to pick you up. I had two days off every month. One day, I was in a bad financial crunch, so I made an appointment with I don't know how many guys—one per hour at this and that hotel. As I talked, they would give me money to eat and so on. I couldn't count the money while I was with them. I just put it into a bag. It was W 600,000—a lot of money. But I don't know who gave how much. I was so busy that day. On the next rest day, I would do the same thing. I had a lot of fun—the money—my body. So the money situation improved a little. After father passed away, I was a loser. I didn't care about my body anymore.

Because my father had been such a butterfly, I've never wanted to

The bar area is full of specialty tailor shops. Patches, such as those shown here, are especially popular with the guys.

have an affair with a married man. I still don't. I think about what pains it can bring. I had no male friends. I just made money. But there was this man. He was married. He kept telling me to eat good food and take Korean medicine. He seduced me. He must have been fifty. It was a long relationship.

I always went home every night for the kids' sake. Although Myung

One large disco in the DMZ is rather posh. Couples dress to the nines. The couple on the left is headed that way.

Sook could cook, she didn't know how to make the side dishes. So I cooked at night. I had to do the wash and iron their uniforms. I don't know if they'll realize it when they grow up, but with all my strength, I tried my best to raise them.

Once, a person I'd known from an agency[12] called and said I should try something different. They said it paid well. We'd make up the women and put beautiful Korean dresses on them and have them sit inside the windows. If they sat there, the customers would come in. I'd match them with a woman and send them to a room. If there were many people, I'd let them know when twenty minutes had passed. Then they would have to go into another room and have sex again. It went on for

twenty-four hours with no time to rest. The women would grab a nap here and there.

I thought I should know what the women were doing. I did it myself for two days. If there were ten guys, I'd have to take in ten. If a hundred men, then a hundred times. In general, you can do about twenty men. I'd take a drinking table and drink with them. Then we'd go into another room and make love. After we finished, we'd leave quickly so another couple could go in. Then I'd come out and try to direct the traffic.

They also had a show. As they went up to the table, there would be cucumbers, eggs, paintbrushes and so on. The women would do a show and then make love right after that.

The owners wanted me to hurry the women along—make up their faces again to sit down in the window and receive the next customers. If they didn't sit in the window, the customers wouldn't come in. But so many customers—it just isn't something human beings should do. It was like they were just lying there with their legs apart. The women were getting tired. So I'd tell them to rest a little. It was driving me crazy. Some of the customers would mistreat the women.

What surprised me was the fact that these women had to endure this for money. I felt as though I hadn't suffered anything in comparison to them. Yet they stayed because the money was good. I guess there are worse places.

One day, I just gave up. Only a few people with the stomach for it could work there. I couldn't stand it any longer. These were my sisters living like this! I'm willing to work hard, but I just couldn't bring myself to force these women who were so tired to receive another customer. I slept in bed all day.

The owner came and asked me, "You really can't do it?" I said, "I can't. These women aren't animals. They're human beings." He said he would bring me the money I'd earned. They didn't want me to let the secret out. I said thanks and left. I couldn't believe there were places like that. No matter how good the money is, I felt I couldn't work like that.

Then someone from an agency in Seoul told me about the Commissioned Officers' Club. That grabbed

me. After all, I'd given up on my body. I've given up on marriage. I was twenty-six, so I still looked young. If I wanted a job, I usually got it. I called and went in.

I'd heard that Americans have large penises. I didn't think about doing it with them. I thought I would work as a waitress and earn a lot of money. But those people were honest—they told me everything. They said I would earn a lot. I thought about it: "*Dabang* isn't enough. If I work here with the Americans, people would look down on me. If I lived away from my kids

Guys have lots of stories about accidents in training, and others where someone "bought a piece of the farm." The serviceman on the left was taking part in war games with his unit. Another unit mistakenly fired mortars into their area. Everyone dove for cover, and this fellow's ankle got tangled up in a tree trunk. He was lucky, he said—only broken.

Almost to a man, the guys will say they hate the military—the way it treats them and makes them work. At the same time, almost to a man, each is extremely proud to be an American and to be part of, as they say, the greatest fighting force in the world.

and sent them money, it would be okay." I thought I would work for a few years until the children finished school.

They said I would be going to Tong Du Chun.[13] The man, a woman, and I went together. It looked like a nasty neighborhood. The surrounding rooms were small, and they only had a bed in them. But the owner's room was well furnished. The place they called a hall was like a shack with a few tables. I'd been to many *dabangs* but this was the worst. I mean, you know when you've crossed the line.

I told them I didn't want to work in such an inferior place. If the place was low-class, it would draw that kind of client. I said this was going too far. They said we should go to another place. They realized I was twenty-six with a lot of experience.

They brought me to Osan. It was a small place, but it had a dance floor. There were a lot of American GIs. I'd never seen an American. Some were huge. They were dancing up a frenzy. At that time, I thought that Americans were number-one citizens—that they had a big country and were better educated. They probably spend a lot of money. So I thought I would earn money there. I was also afraid.

As they danced, the lights flashed and they took their clothes off. It was the first time I'd seen a nude dancing place. They said I should go to work tomorrow. I asked for a W 600,000 in advance. The interest rate was 10 percent. They said the room rent was W 30,000. And [I had to buy] a lot of other things, including the heating coal. With the remainder of the W 600,000 advance, I paid for the kids' living expenses and took care of some loans.

I began working. I was like a spectator. I just sat around. I didn't even smoke. Blacks would approach me and say things. Whites, too. Then the owners came and said they'd been wrong about me. I wasn't the right material. They said, "That guy has the hots for you. Do something about it." I saw that it was a black man. He was a bit old, too. Whew. I asked what I should do. The owner said I should drink with him. He gave me juice in a large OB beer mug. Then the man said he would like to sleep with me.

If there was man who liked you, you just had to drink juice out of that huge beer mug. Your money went up the more you drank. After sleeping with a man, we would write it down and leave the money at the

This couple live together in a neighborhood next to the bar area.

club. The money from sleeping was to your credit, but they could subtract it from your debt.

The owner said I would be lucky if I slept with a black man the first time. I told him I couldn't do it. He said I had to do it. I told him I would think more about it. I finished work for the day and returned home. I lay there all by myself quietly and thought. There was no salary.

I thought: "If I do this with Korean men, someday it might get in the way of my brothers' advancement. What if my brothers get married and somehow a member of the bride's family, an uncle or cousin, recognizes me from this kind of work? It's a small world. I don't want to mess up my brother's lives that way. If I'm going to earn money

by having sex with men, I might as well do it with Americans."

I realized I had to use my body to make money. I accepted the black man, and we went home. I didn't know his first name or last name. I was shaking. He came in and sat down. We could do it in bed or in the living room. He kept calling me to come. I said I had to go to the bathroom. I thought about it in the bathroom. "If I do it with him, will my skin turn black?" All kinds of things. I wondered how big his thing was. I'd seen other people doing it with them, and they looked dark, too. But I had already been paid. I resigned myself to doing it.

I came in. He was on the bed naked. The light in the room had a red bulb. Because of the red light, his

Three *mamasans* returning to their bars
after an early dinner

black skin shone, and his large eyes
flashed in the light. I just couldn't
go in. I sat by the door and began
crying. It was too cold outside. He
still told me to come. I shook my
head and cried. But he was very
nice. He told me to come and just
sleep. I said no. I couldn't go. I just
sat there. Then he put on his clothes
and left. I gestured to him, "Where
are you going?" He said he was leaving and wanted me to sleep, to get
on the bed. I was so thankful. I followed him out and said good-bye.

I thought about it: "That man
was really nice. A Korean man
would have said that because he had
paid, he wanted something out of
it. He would have been angry." I

thought a white man would be okay.
I went to work again. The man
was there. I told the owner that I
couldn't do it with him if it killed me.

Then a large white man came and
began talking to me. He had huge
shoulders. He asked my name, and
the girls around me told him. I
didn't know anything in English. In
junior high they never taught you
anything. They taught you the al-
phabet, but I couldn't carry on a
conversation.

He gave the owner some money
and told me to do it with him. The
owner warned that I had to do it.
When we went home, the Americans
always took their clothes off. We got
ready to sleep. He was gentle. I wor-

ried about how I could handle his body, but he helped me. He was good. I was good.

He continued to come. He was good to me. He bought me things when the merchants dropped by. Whenever he came [to the club], he'd come home and sleep with me. He gave me money. He taught me English in a fun way. He was really nice. He was good to the other women. He had six stripes. He was the golf and volleyball coach. He was around twenty-six, like me. One month passed and another, but the owners didn't like my getting a regular customer. They were afraid I would start a family. Whenever he came, they shut the door in his face. They made him angry.

I was taking the pill during those two months. He told me not to take it. He threw it in the garbage. But I took it secretly. I bought a new pill almost every day. I couldn't talk [in English]. I couldn't fight with him. He told women who spoke good English to tell me to stop taking the pill. Then he bought two word picture books, one in Korean and the other in English. Through the books he told me not to take the pill. He wanted to have a baby. Since I was getting on in years, he thought I should have a baby, too. But at that time, I had no thoughts of getting married. I only wanted money. I was always thinking that I had to earn so much to send it home. I always counted my money. I always knew how much I had coming to me. Twice a month, I paid the interest and brought money home.

Then one day, he couldn't make love so I fell asleep. After a while I awoke to find him still sitting around. I put on a dress and went outside to change the coal. When I came back in, he wouldn't help me undress. So I told him that he couldn't even make love. I slept in my clothes. I may have been a little cruel. He woke me up, saying that he was leaving. Usually, he left without telling me. I said fine.

He had two uniforms in the closet. He took those, boots, and four hundred dollars he had left there in an envelope. I thought nothing of it. We Koreans don't end rela-

Shooting pool and marking time

tionships that quickly even if we are angry—especially since we had been together for several months. He didn't come back that evening. He didn't come to the hall. I thought maybe he was busy at work or something had come up.

I waited a week. He still didn't show up. I decided I couldn't wait any longer. I told the husbands of the other women living in the house to look for him. They said they couldn't find him. I went to where he worked. They didn't know, either. I went to the gate of the base and waited for him. I'd go there at the time work started and when work ended. It was cold standing there in the early morning. I did that for many days. He still didn't come. He was my only customer then. I cried.

His name was Douglas. He was my first love. No one had been kinder than he, particularly after you've known Korean men. He had treated me well, like a baby. I depended on him a lot. He used to come and give me $20 every day. He bought me clothes and other things I needed. He even bought me things for my brothers and sisters. I was deeply in love with him. I cried every night—going from this room to that room. I wrote a letter. I said I wanted to see him. There were men who went from *dabang* to *dabang* and sold jewelry, necklaces, and other accessories. They knew Douglas well. They'd always seen us together. I gave the letters to those vendors, asking them to give the letters to him if they saw him.

One day the owners talked to me, saying that Americans were liars. I shouldn't trust them because they'd say they love you and the next thing you know they're saying the same thing to another person. They were saying I should meet another guy. But I kept waiting for Douglas for over a month. I cried every day. I'd go to the hall, but I would stand outside looking for him. I didn't feel like working there anymore, and I couldn't go on like that. I had been late in sending the last living expenses home. I decided to make money.

I decided I wanted to change halls. But the owners said I couldn't leave. They said I had to pay back the agency fee of W 300,000. I had a W 600,000 debt remaining. They were demanding that I pay W 900,000. I argued with them. I said, "I'm not a three-year-old baby. In Korean law, there is no agency fee of W 300,000." Agency fees are around W 50,000. I said W 300,000 was out of the question.

I said I can go anywhere I want to. I moved to a new place with a woman I knew. When I changed halls, I found out that the rent had been too high and that other places paid a salary. I told the other women, "Never pay for agency fees." I told them to come to me if anyone demanded agency fees. I'd fight for them. Several women came.

Other people would say that they'd seen Douglas. I thought maybe I'd see him, too, and went out once in a while. Once, I was coming back from somewhere and wondered why I couldn't see him

Late at night a guy negotiates with two *mamasan* procurers about the price of a woman

when others could. In the hall, there is a picture of a woman on a motorcycle. A guy is chasing after her. I told the woman with me, "Wouldn't it be great if I were like the woman on the motorcycle and men were chasing after me?" Then the women said, "Hey look, there's Douglas." I told her, "You're crazy. You're trying to make fun of me."

But it was true. There he was with

Inside a bar on the strip

his big shoulders. There were three women with him. He kept looking at me and talking with them. I couldn't hear anything because of the music. He came to our table nonchalantly. He asked what I wanted to drink. I said I'd like a juice. My friend and I drank the juice while he drank liquor.

My heart was beating wildly. I didn't know the language. I couldn't say anything. He asked how I'd been. I said okay but my eyes began to get bleary with tears. He was acting normal. He patted my back and

said, "Let's go home." I thought I would go home and talk with him with the picture book. We came home. So, with the dictionary I asked him, "Why are you angry? Why didn't you come?" He said, "Don't say anything." We slept. In the morning he said he was going. I asked him if he would return. He said, "I don't know." He left.

I kept waiting for him. My debts piled up. Then, I decided again that it wasn't going to work. I calmed down. I had to earn money. I knew not all Americans were like that. I slept with them. Since our club closed early, we went to other clubs with GIs. Then someone said, "Hey, Douglas is in the bathroom dead drunk." I was there dancing. I went and shook him to wake him up. I think he must have been on some kind of drugs. He was smashed. He seemed glad to see me. I told him to sit down at the table because I wanted to talk with him.

I asked him why he had taken my heart but never returned. I said he was a liar. I had barely learned how to speak like that. He said he loved me, but he wanted to have a baby and marry me. He said that I didn't like to have sex with him because he was so big. For him that was the most important thing. But he said he didn't dislike me. At that time, I didn't know anything about sex—I just did it for the money. He said I didn't love him. I said I had to earn money. He said we two couldn't make it together. He said, "Let's remain friends." He wouldn't come back after that. I lost a lot because of him. All Americans are like that. They are.

I got another friend. He had come from Japan for a three-month vacation. When I meet men, I meet great men. He was very kind. He bought me things to eat and gave me money. We had a great time. He really made me believe in him. I was still very naive, so I really believed people. He was over thirty years old. He said he had to go but would be back the next year. After he left, he didn't write.

I accepted reality. I've met many Americans in this business. All of

Women and others working in the bar area shop at a large market nearby. There are also trucks and cars that go through the bar area, each with one or two items for sale: fish, eggs, fresh corn, peaches, seaweed, watermelons.

them are good liars. At the time, if we make them feel good, they'll say anything. They're paying money to sleep around, so they'll tell lies to feel good. In reality, we're the fools. But why do they have to tell lies like that and fool people? It's because we have these lowly jobs. That's the only reason.

I was good to these Americans. I cooked for them. One man said that he was divorced and had a child. He told me that I would make a great mother to the baby. But he never brought any money. I told him that I couldn't go on like this. I told him that he had to pay me for the time we'd spent together until now. But on the day he said he would bring the money, he had another excuse.

I told a sister who spoke good English to talk to him. I told her the story. The sister talked to him. She told him to take his wallet out. There was money in there. "So, you were trying to get a free ride?" I said. "There's nothing free here. You have to pay for living expenses."

Boys coming home from school

He said I was so good to him, he thought he could get by on nothing. If I did so much, he should have paid up. He had played around with me.

Because I was far from them, the kids were in bad shape. Sangjin was in junior high. The youngest was in elementary school. I visited them once. The walls had become black. I asked why. A matchbox had caught on fire, and the fire spread. They were in a basement then. Everything burned up. That's when I decided I couldn't leave them alone. Anything could happen. So I moved them close to me. Since I could see them every day, I gave them good food. I always gave them something, even if it was candy.

Then I sent all of them back up to Seoul and transferred them to another school. I moved to Kunsan with the woman I had worked with at the first hall. It got better after that, little by little. The kids would come to get money, or at times I would go up with the money. But the trip from Kunsan to Seoul was tiring.

I always tried to send some money. I worked all night. I earned pretty good money, but growing kids eat so much. I had fed them so well from early childhood that they ate a lot. Their mouths had become high-class, so it took a lot of money. They had to have meat at every meal. They didn't eat leftovers. I just wanted them to be healthy, normal, and happy.

When I visited again, it was a mess. I found that my oldest brother was wasting the money. He was renting another room for himself and his girlfriend. He didn't have a good job. He just couldn't hold down a job. He was young and had no experience. He wanted W 300,000 to start a business. I had given him the money, but he spent it all on other things. He asked for W 500,000 again. I told him to go to college, but he said that would be too much of a burden for me. He wanted to make money. I got an advance and gave him some money. But now, he's all messed up. Like father, like son? That's the only reason I can think of.

I didn't think about meeting a good person to marry. I didn't want to get married anyway. But there was a really good man. Because he was so good, I thought about marrying him. He was divorced. He had one kid. He said that his mother was president of a large company. Her income was high, and he was the only child.

He wrote to me. He came back after a year, but I couldn't marry him. There was no one around to take care of the kids. I could have gone to the U.S. and sent money, but the kids couldn't live by themselves. I couldn't face the fact that something might happen if I wasn't around. I told myself that I would get married after Sangjin finished school. I'd educate them more before I went. I thought: "I have entered this kind of work. My brothers don't have any responsibilities so they can get married easily. I'll take care of them until then."

1. Kim Il Sung has been president of North Korea since it was founded in 1945.
2. Syngman Rhee was the president of South Korea for the early part of the U.S. occupation until his overthrow by the student-labor movement in 1961.
3. Itaewon is a section of Seoul that is known to most foreigners as a shopping area.
4. According to Yu Bok Nim from My Sister's Place, the first AIDS case was an American lecturer at a university.
5. Another bar area outside a small U.S. base.
6. According to Yu Bok Nim, 50 percent of all AIDS patients in the southern part of Korea are women who sold their sexual labor to American GIs.
7. At that time in Korea, everyone had to be off the streets beginning at 12:00 midnight. Anyone caught on the streets would be arrested.
8. A *dabang* may be a tearoom and/or a drinking place from which women may sell their sexual labor.
9. Kimpo is an area outside of Seoul where a major American Air Force Base was located during the Korea War and afterward. It is now Seoul's international airport.
10. A tent-bar is a roadside eating place.
11. GUT is a shamanistic ritual to drive out evil spirits.
12. A job-placement agency, as mentioned earlier in the story.
13. A small city with a large bar area immediately outside U.S. Camp Casey.

Okinawan farmers spreading out recently harvested bundles of rice on metal road barriers. The bar area is about six blocks away.

Okinawa

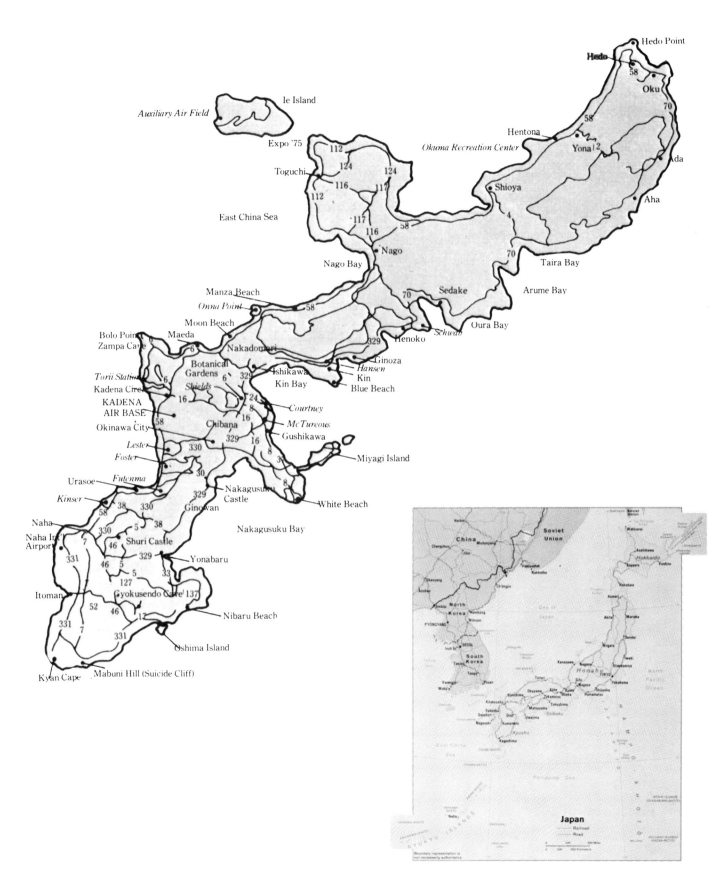

The 1989 exchange rate in Okinawa was $1 = 140 yen.

OKINAWA THEN AND NOW

Saundra Sturdevant

Arriving in Okinawa in June 1988 to do the work on this project was a relief. In the Philippines, the low-intensity warfare of the Aquino government permeates every-day existence. In the case of the urban population, there is the threat of potential violence and coups. In the countryside, it is real violence that has generated approximately one million internal refugees during the Aquino years.

Being in Okinawa again was also a great pleasure. Volcanic in origin, Okinawa looks amazingly like 1950s Hawaii before development began. There is the great beauty of high cumulus clouds over the Pacific, clear blue water, sandy beaches, palm trees, blazing sun, and the liquid sunshine of the rain and the flowers: white ginger, bougainvillea, blue morning glories, salmon-colored hibiscus. And there is the gentleness and kindness of the people.

Okinawa entered the consciousness of most Americans at the time of the Battle of Okinawa: a three-month campaign that ended on 23 June 1945. The photos of W. Eugene Smith in which he sought to show the agony and suffering of U.S. Marines as they fought from cave to cave, using satchel charges and flamethrowers to rout re-sisting Japanese soldiers from their hideouts, are the touchstone. If Smith had not been wounded twice and immediately evacuated, he might also have captured on film some of the devastation that the war wreaked upon the peoples of this country.

Approximately one-fourth of the entire Okinawan population was killed during the Battle of Okinawa. One of the themes that runs through contemporary Okinawan assessment of the period is that Japan used Okinawa, sacrificed Okinawa and Okinawans, for the defense of mainland Japan. The military orders from the mainland to Japanese commanders on Okinawa bear out that judgment: the battle was to be drawn out as long as possible, thus giving Japan more time to prepare for the U.S. invasion of the mainland.

One of the horrific aspects of this holding action was the intense Japanese indoc-trination of the Okinawans regarding the savage behavior that they could expect from U.S. occupying troops.[1] The Japanese offered an alternative solution to capture: the murder of one's family and suicide. How many of the approximately 150,000 Okinawan deaths were a result of believing this propaganda is not clear. Okinawans have just recently begun to talk about this period in their history—about the deaths, about being survivors.

An Okinawan woman cleaning up an area by a sea retaining wall. She's listening to a local radio station that plays Okinawan music and gives news and information in the Okinawan language.

At the end of the day, older Okinawan women may play croquet. Here, a group of women players wait their turn.

June 23, 1945, marks the end of the Battle of Okinawa, where approximately 150,000 Okinawans, one-fourth of the country's population, were killed as the U.S. and Japanese military fought for control of Okinawa. People of all ages observe this anniversary of the war's end with antiwar demonstrations as well as gatherings with family and friends, where offerings of food, drink, and prayer are made to those who died.

Large demonstration turning the corner in downtown Naha, the provincial capital. Demonstrators are protesting the announced visit to Okinawa of the Japanese Crown Prince, Akihito. Anti-Japanese feeling stems from hardships endured during the colonial period, the deaths during the Battle of Okinawa in 1945, and increasing Japanese economic and cultural domination at the present time.

This bitter residue is one of the main pillars of Okinawan distrust of their Japanese rulers and is strongly manifested in anti-emperor and anti-war sentiments. The other is the brutal colonial period itself that began in the late nineteenth century and ended with U.S. military occupation after the Battle of Okinawa. During the colonial period, the Japanese did their best to stamp out the distinctive Okinawan culture, history, and language. As was the case with Korean opposition to Japanese colonial rule, the resistance of the Okinawans was continuous and manifested in a number of ways. And, as in Korea, Japanese suppression was always immediate and thorough.

Antiwar sentiment is pervasive and has recently found political expression in the election of a new governor, Masahide Ota, who ran on a platform that included the withdrawal of U.S. troops from the island. Ota has since found American officials unreceptive to his proposals for a reasonable timetable for this withdrawal—a stance that reflects, as the Persian Gulf War demonstrated, the great need as perceived by the American military for bases in Okinawa.

The U.S. military occupation lasted until 1972, when the U.S. returned Okinawa to Japanese authority. This period lasted twenty years longer than the seven years of U.S. occupation of mainland Japan. Reversion came as a result of intense antiwar pressure occasioned by the Vietnam War: antiwar groups, labor unions, political parties, and antibase groups formed a powerful coalition to remove U.S. bases from Okinawa. As it turned out, a tactical compromise was made: reversion to Japanese control. Once that was accomplished, so the argument went, it would be easier to pressure the Japanese authorities to remove the bases. That was not the result.

There continues to be a considerable U.S. military presence in Okinawa. Although the 145 bases constructed by the Americans during the occupation had dwindled to 46 by the mid-1980s, these account for 75 percent of the total number of U.S. bases in the whole of Japan. And more than half of the 60,000 U.S. troops stationed in Japan are actually stationed on Okinawa.

Thus, Okinawa—not mainland Japan—continues to be the forward-most commandpost of U.S. military might. The primary mission of the U.S. Air Force and the Marines on Okinawa is to respond immediately in defense of the U.S. presence in Japan, the southern part of Korea, and the Philippines. Rapid Deployment Forces train constantly and are ready to be shipped immediately to the Middle East or to Korea, if needed. Of the approximately 20,000 Marines stationed on Okinawa, 10,000 were sent to Saudi Arabia during the Persian Gulf War.

Kadena Air Force Base is extensive and compares in terms of size to Clark in the Philippines. And now that the U.S. has given up Clark, it may be that Kadena will bear more of the overall defense load. Headquarters of the 313th Air Division, the forward command for the Western Pacific, is at Kadena, as are strategic-reconnaissance aircraft, nuclear-capable aircraft, and tactical fighter wings and squadrons.

Frequent antiwar demonstrations take place on Okinawa, and Kadena is one of their targets. In 1986, a well-planned demonstration of more than 20,000 Okinawans joined hands, making a ring around the Kadena base. That day the driving rain was so fierce that it was hard to see the next person in the chain. To make sure that the ring was complete, the demonstrators twice stretched out their bodies, reaching to join hands to complete the ring.

Okinawan antiwar fervor, as demonstrated in the drive to remove Kadena, is reflective both of the harsher aspects of the history of the two peoples since 1945 and of the role that Kadena plays in the global strategy of the United States. The issue of nuclear weapons is central: the U.S. has acknowledged that prior to reversion of Okinawa to Japan in 1972, nuclear weapons had been stored on Okinawa.[2]

Since reversion and the U.S.-Japanese agreement stipulating that the U.S. must request permission before bringing nuclear devices into Japan, the two governments have refused to comment on the nuclear issue. It wasn't until May 1981 that Edwin O. Reischauer, the American Ambassador to Japan during the Kennedy administration, publicly affirmed that Navy aircraft carriers with nuclear weapons aboard regularly docked at Japanese (and Okinawan) ports.[3]

The threat of nuclear annihilation is a part of contemporary Okinawan consciousness. Okinawa is termed the "Nuclear Bull's-eye." The fear is that again Okinawa will be the battleground for someone else's war. Many on Okinawa argue that this again is a situation in which Japan would be sacrificing Okinawa for the sake of the defense of Japan, for in a nuclear war Okinawa would not be just a battleground—it would be destroyed.

This reasoning follows from the fact that it is Japan that made the treaty with the U.S. in which the greatest number of U.S. bases and personnel are not on mainland Japan but on Okinawa. And it is Japan that looks the other way at the continued—and assumed increased and updated—presence of nuclear devices on Okinawa. Finally, it is Japanese Self-Defense Forces who train and plan with the U.S. forces on Okinawan soil.

Many Okinawans find this history, together with the impressive Japanese economic growth and increased military spending, cause for concern. Apprehension has heightened since the early 1980s as increased joint U.S.-Japanese military operations have taken place, ranging from Japanese naval and air force participation in RIM-PAC (rim of the Pacific) exercises in 1980 to full-sized joint maneuvers integrating the U.S. and Japanese navies in the late 1980s. There is an unease with these developments and with the extensive contacts between the defense and economic establishments of both countries.

The everyday presence of the Americans is pervasive. On the highways and central streets, U.S. military personnel wearing combat fatigues move in military vehicles from one camp to another or to maneuvers somewhere in the islands. U.S. Marines practice amphibious landings in Fukuchi Reservoir, a principal source of fresh drinking water. And the sound of aircraft is constant, be it the *plop-plop-plop* of helicopter blades, the high-pitched whine of jet fighters, or the deeper roar of

Kadena Air Force Base is one of the largest in the Pacific. Before the construction of Kadena, this area was prize agricultural land. Okinawans have sent delegations, petitioned, and voted numerous times trying to get the U.S. military to leave the islands. They also demonstrate: in 1986 more than 20,000 joined hands to form a ring around Kadena.

These huge U.S. military communications structures are called "Elephant Cages" by Okinawans. Being a volcanic land, Okinawa has little flat land suitable for cultivation.

View of Yomitan, where U.S. forces landed in 1945, from atop Okinawan clan tombs

During the U.S. Occupation period and into the Vietnam War, signs like this notified U.S. personnel that the sanitary conditions in the establishment were first class. U.S. personnel were allowed to enter, drink, and purchase sexual labor from the women working inside. Establishments without this sign were off-limits. Military Police patrolled and enforced this distinction.

bombers. Apartments housing U.S. personnel have huge U.S. flags painted across their tops. Statues of Uncle Sam and the Statue of Liberty, advertisements for the American Bakery, discos, pizza parlors, used-car lots, and stores selling surplus military equipment abound. In many ways, it is a case not of the U.S. having a military presence on Okinawa, but of Okinawans living within a U.S. military preserve.

There is no denying that the historical, geopolitical, and economic considerations inherent in the U.S. military presence are extensive. At the same time, it is clear that a military presence has a life of its own that has an impact in many ways upon women. Many of the ports and bases that once belonged to the Japanese Imperial Navy, for example, are now the preserve of the U.S. Navy. And the areas around these ports and bases, where women previously provided sexual labor for the Japanese military, have subsequently provided similar labor for American military personnel. The treatment of Korean women in Okinawa graphically exemplifies this commodification of women's sexual labor.

When U.S. forces occupied Okinawa, the Japanese military offered them Korean women, many of whom they had kidnapped and dragooned from their fields and homes to serve as *Chong Shindae* (Women's Volunteer Corps) for Japanese troops. The Japanese military policy was to acknowledge, provide for, and control the sexual expression of its troops. Between 1937 and 1944, some 200,000 Korean women were taken to provide sexual labor for Japanese soldiers in China, Southeast Asia, and the Pacific islands.[4] It is not clear how many Korean women were used in Okinawa, but during the Battle of Okinawa approximately 10,000 of them were killed. Those that remained were the ones whom the Japanese offered to the Americans.[5]

During the American occupation, Okinawan women provided sexual labor for U.S. military personnel. With more than 150,000 people having been killed during the Battle of Okinawa, the number of families not intact, with family providers dead and injured, was enormous. And this toll does not speak to the psychological traumas that incapacitated many of the survivors who had witnessed the months of intense slaughter.

The task of providing shelter, food, and medical care in an economy controlled by the U.S. military and where the U.S. dollar was the medium of exchange was exceedingly difficult. Women who sold their sexual labor during this period were mainly widows and daughters of families left with few resources to make their way in an agriculture- and fishing-based economy. This work continued during the Korean and Vietnam Wars, when it is estimated that between one in thirty to one in forty Okinawan women sold their sexual labor.

The labor of these women directly or indirectly was a primary source of income that fueled much renewed economic activity. In the early 1970s, the total amount generated by sexual labor was the largest of any industry in Okinawa. According to the Legal Affairs Bureau of the Government of the Ryukyus, the number of full-time prostituted women in 1969 was 7,362.[6] Although the number was actually much higher, Shimabukuro Hiroshi, an Okinawan writer, takes the figure of 7,000 women

Okinawan woman returning home after work mopping and cleaning a restaurant in the Kin bar area

and calculates that if each earned an average of $20 per night, the annual income from this labor would be about $50,400,000. The income from sugar-cane production, the largest industry in Okinawa in 1970, was $43,500,000.[7]

With reversion to Japan came implementation of Japanese laws and a bureaucracy to administer these laws. Legislation had declared sexual labor illegal in Japan in 1956, and, with reversion, this prohibition was extended to Okinawa. As in Japan, implementation was a considerable problem. By the mid-1980s, it was Filipinas who provided entertainment and sexual labor for the U.S. military. The bar areas where they worked were outside each military base and separate from the area where Okinawan women sold their sexual labor to Okinawan and Japanese men. Despite the location, the *yakuza* or those in alliance with the *yakuza*, were in control.

Due to the nature of the work, it is difficult to determine precisely when Filipinas began to be imported for this labor. It is clear, however, that the process began in the mid-1970s, after reversion, and had to do with the U.S. dollar–yen exchange rate: commodities in Japan became too expensive for the salaries of U.S. service personnel. On the Philippine side, the Marcos years saw the export of labor become a viable means of earning foreign exchange. Filipinas could be found working as domestics and child-care providers in Hong Kong, Taiwan, Singapore, Kuwait, and Saudi Arabia. Men from industrialized countries were purchasing Filipinas as mail-order brides. And by the mid-1980s, some 100,000 Filipinas worked on the Japanese mainland as entertainers and providers of sexual labor. Another 4,000 worked in the bar area outside around U.S. military bases in Okinawa.

1. With respect to combatants and noncombatants alike, the Pacific war was a total war in ways that the war in Europe was not. See John Dower, *War without Mercy* (New York: Pantheon, 1987).

2. Declassified materials show that nuclear weapons were stored on Okinawa, Guam, and Iwo Jima beginning in the mid-1950s. *The Nation*, 13 August 1985.

3. *New York Times*, 11 August 1985.

4. Originally, the Japanese military estimated that each woman would take in twenty-nine soldiers daily. But like a number of other miscalculations, the reality was that women often had to take in seventy to ninety. This situation became clearer in early 1992 when Yoshiaki Yoshimi, a history professor in Japan, established the fact that beginning in the mid-1930s, upwards of 200,000 women were lured or dragged to Japanese battlefronts across Asia. They were mostly children and teenagers from Korea. Others came from China and a few from Japan. Yoshiaki Yoshimi's research establishes the fact that the Japanese military was in control of this process and that it was official policy. It was not the work of entrepreneurs, as had been previously asserted. During Prime Minister Kiichi Miyazawa's subsequent trip to Seoul, he was forced to apologize for Japan's role in these events. That is not sufficient. Korean women and their allies have formed an organization, The Korea Council for the Women Drafted for Military Sexual Service by Japan. They demand that the Japanese government reveal the truth of the situation, give a real apology, and provide reparations. The Japanese government conceded the first of these in July 1992.

5. William T. Randall, *Okinawa's Tragedy: Sketches from the Last Battle of WWII*, (Ginowan, Okinawa: Oma Books, 1986).

6. Takazato Suzuyo, "Women in Relation to the Base Situation in Okinawa," unpublished manuscript presented at the International Abolitionist Federation, 2nd International Congress, Vienna, Austria, 3–6 September 1984. Takazato Suzuyo has worked and written on the situation of Okinawan women selling their sexual labor. This manuscript, which she gave to the authors, provides the source for much of the historical information on the topic. Takazato Suzuyo worked for a number of years as Municipal Councilor in Naha, Okinawa. One of her main responsibilities was counseling women who had sold their sexual labor when Okinawa was under the control of the U.S. military, prior to May 1972. In 1989, she was elected to the Naha City Council.

7. Ibid. Takazato Suzuyo cites Shimabukruro Hiroshi, "The Actual Situation of 'Sex Industry,' Okinawa's Biggest Industry," as the source for this data.

KIN: THE BAR SYSTEM

Saundra Sturdevant and Brenda Stoltzfus

Kin is the bar area outside U.S. Marine base Camp Hansen. Filipina women work in the bars as six-month contract workers. On the edges of the bar area are rundown hotels where a few older Okinawan women sell their sexual labor. The bar system described here applies only to the bars with Filipina women in them. The information comes primarily from conversations with these women.

Promotion agencies recruit women from the Philippines to work in the bars. The promotion agencies are Japanese and/or Okinawan owned, generally by *yakuza*, with offices in Manila. Filipinos work as recruiters. The bar owner pays the promotion agency to do the recruiting, then the promotion agency pays the woman's salary. The Filipino recruiters receive a commission of $100 per month from the salary of each woman whom they recruit. The woman's salary before this commission has been deducted is $350 or $400 per month. Travel expenses to and from Okinawa are also subtracted from her earnings.

The Filipinas working in Okinawa are legal contract workers. When a woman is recruited in the Philippines, she must learn to dance with a group of women. She attends dance classes and then auditions in front of judges. If she passes, she gets a blue card with a number. When her number comes up, she is given a visa and brought to Okinawa. In contrast to this system, in mainland Japan, many of the approximately 100,000 Filipinas are working in the country illegally on tourist visas.

The Filipinas in Okinawa are hired to be cultural dancers; before they go to Okinawa, the women believe that cultural dancing is what their work will be. When they arrive, they are placed in bars by the promotion agency. They have no choice with regard to which bar they will work in. Usually on the first night, they are required to dance nude or partially nude, and alone. The majority of the clubs employ only two or three women, although a few have up to eight or ten. In the past, the women always danced nude. But with pressure from women's groups in the Philippines, Japan, Okinawa, and the women themselves working in Okinawa, nude dancing is now illegal. They do continue to dance topless in the majority of the clubs, however, and completely nude in a few of them. Those clubs with totally nude dancing always attract more customers. Okinawan immigration does checks approximately every month to see if there is nude dancing, but the bars are forewarned of the visit and either comply or close down for that evening.

In the club, the woman has a quota of 400 drinks that she must sell to American customers per month. The drinks cost the customer $10, and the woman receives a commission of $1 per drink if she meets her quota. If she does not make her quota, she receives .50 per drink. The bar owners give the women two days off each month and either provide food or money for food.

The women are not forced to go on bar fines but are free to do so if they choose. Bar fines range in price, usually from $100 to $150, and are less common than other ways of selling sexual labor. In some bars, there is a "dark room" or dark corner where the customer may purchase whatever form of sexual labor he desires, thus eliminating the need to pay bar fines and take the woman out.

Housing is either above, behind, or near the bar. In the small bars, the owner either sleeps on the premises in order to watch over the women or, at the end of the work night, locks the women in their room. The rooms have bars on the windows. If the housing is farther away, the women are escorted to and from the clubs in a vehicle and are guarded.

In November 1983, two Filipinas were killed when the Upper Lima Club caught on fire and they were not able to get out of their room because the windows were barred and the doors locked. Because the owner was insured, he was able to take the money and modernize the bar. The families of the women received nothing.

Depending on how controlled they are by the club in which they work, some Filipinas may also go on dates with Americans during the day. Arrangements are made with the customer in the club for a meeting place. In some cases, the women are not allowed out of the club even during the day when the club is closed; in others, they are free during the day as long as they sleep each night in their room.

Because, legally, the promotion agencies bring the women to Okinawa as cultural dancers, they provide neither contraceptives nor education about them. If a woman becomes pregnant, however, the promotion agency will make the connections for her to obtain an abortion and will then deduct the cost of the operation (about $385) from her salary. If a woman gets pregnant and does not choose to have an abortion, her contract will be considered broken at the point when she is no longer able to work. She will, of course, have to pay for her return trip to the Philippines.

The Philippine consulate holds periodic meetings with the women to see if there are any complaints or problems. Theoretically, if there is a complaint, someone at the consulate will talk to a representative of the promotion agency; then the promotion agency will talk to the bar owner. However, if a woman reports, for example, that she has been made to dance nude, she is bound to be harassed by the promotion agency and may not be allowed to return for a second contract.

Even though conditions are very difficult for the women, they do usually want to return for a second contract because the money is better than what they can make in the Philippines. A Filipina can earn much more in Okinawa than she could as a clerk in a department store or even as a teacher in the Philippines. Besides, as a result of working in Okinawa, she is automatically stigmatized.

The Kin bar area is not racially segregated to the extent that bar areas in the Philippines and Korea are. However, there are some clubs that are predominantly Euro-American, which usually play hard-rock music; clubs favored by African-Americans play more rap and may have a dance floor.

The areas where Okinawan women sell their sexual labor are separate from those where Filipinas work. U.S. service personnel are prevented from entering these areas and purchasing the sexual labor of Okinawan women. The *yakuza* patrol the streets and enforce this separation. Recently, however, there have been some Okinawan and Japanese customers in the clubs servicing U.S. military personnel.

ROWENA

Age: 30

I was born in Pampanga, but we often moved back and forth between the province and Manila.[1] My father is a jeepney driver. We used to have a jeepney, but it was sold because we had no money. My mother went around selling different things [as a street vendor].

My mother and father were always fighting because my father didn't want my mother to work. My mother was selling *halo-halo*. She would buy cooking bananas in the market and sell them along with *halo-halo* at a table. My father didn't want her to work. My mother wanted to work. She said, "How will we survive if I don't work. You're lazy."

My father didn't want to have a boss; he wanted to be the boss. Every time the drivers went to work, the owner had them sweep out the jeepneys. He didn't want to do that.

Pool is a favorite activity for young males. Most neighborhoods and barrios have a pool hall or tables set up on the street.

Women and children in the barrio

with us in Pampanga very long. They went to live with my grandmother on my father's side in Manila. We girls stayed with my mother's mother.

Sometimes my mother would go to Manila. She left us in the province. We were still small. We cried and cried. My grandmother took care of us. When my mother arrived, we were very happy. It was as if we hadn't seen her for a year. Sometimes she would go to visit my father's siblings in Angeles. They were rich.

My mother was pregnant when they separated and we moved back to the province. She gave birth in the hospital. I was studying in grade five. I was in school in Manila, but when they fought and we moved to Pampanga, my studies got messed up. My father heard the news and came to the school. He said, "Go to your mother." I told my teacher that I had to take care of my mother, who was giving birth. I was eleven then.

My father returned to Manila because he had work there. My mother returned home to my grandmother. She had just given birth and was already washing clothes.[2] There were a lot of clothes because there were so many children. I was the one who operated the pump. I was still small. I wasn't able to wash that many clothes yet. Then she started bleeding. There was a lot of blood.

When my mother gave birth to Heidi, they put some gauze inside her and didn't take it out. Her body developed an infection from the gauze. She got sick with a fever. Her

He asked why he should sweep; his work was to drive. My father also liked betting and playing billiards.

Once, they fought very seriously. My mother took all of us children and went home to Pampanga. My father ignored us because of his pride. My two brothers, the youngest and the eldest, didn't stay

fever was very high until she was no
longer able to move her body. We
took her to the hospital for a checkup. We borrowed some money. When
we left to go home, the doctor gave
her some medicine. She couldn't
move any part of her body anymore.
She was crying, "It hurts, it hurts."
If you touched her hand even lightly,
she would cry.

I was the one who took care of my
mother and smallest sister. I would
get up and give my mother her medicine at about 1:00 or 2:00 A.M. I
had to hold her head up. My mother
was a large woman and very heavy.
My sister would also be hungry. I
fixed her milk. I had a difficult time
then. I was also studying. Sometimes I didn't go to school because
my mother was sick. How could I go
to school? I took care of my sisters
because I'm the oldest girl. The

oldest in the family is a boy. I'm
the second.

We were to be pitied because
sometimes we had no money. My
mother had no money because my
father was in Manila driving
jeepneys. My grandmother also
didn't have any work. My grand-
father was too old. My grandmother
depended on her sister, who sold
food. She gave us side dishes to go
with the rice.

One day, my grandmother's sister
came to the house and gave us some
bangus [a type of fish]. She loved us.
She said, "How is Puring?"

"She's sick, ma'm."

"Why didn't you tell me? Your
mother might die, and you haven't
told me yet. Go rent a jeepney."

We rented a jeepney and took my
mother to a hospital. I didn't go
along because I was taking care of

my youngest sister, Heidi. My next-oldest sister wanted me to take care of my mother at the hospital. I said, "I can't take care of Mother in the hospital. I have to stay with Heidi. You be the one to look after Mother."

We sent my father a telegram that our mother was in the hospital. About three days later he arrived. He went straight to the hospital. Our youngest brother, Aling, was with him but he was still small and had to wait outside.

My father went up. My mother said, "Where is Aling?"

"Downstairs. The doctor wouldn't let him come up. I'll take him to *Ate* Lolong in Angeles."

"Okay, and then you come back here."

My father said, "How do you feel?"

"Look, I can move now. You know, we must pray because I'm getting well."

"Okay, you get well. I'll take Aling to Angeles first."

"Okay, and then come back. I'll be leaving."

"You keep saying you are well. You are not completely well yet."

"Look, I can move now." My mother laughed.

When they arrived in Angeles, my younger brother went to my cousin's room. They were playing. My father was talking with his sister. Then my cousin ran out and said to my father, "We saw Aunt Puring. We saw Aunt Puring." My father had a premonition. He went to the hospital.

When he arrived there, my mother wasn't in her bed. He said, "Where's the patient who was here?"

The other patients said, "When you left, sir, she died. She's downstairs." My father cried. He went downstairs immediately. They had put her in the morgue.

I was taking care of the youngest. My other sisters were playing. We heard my grandfather crying while he was still far away. He said, "Oh Puring, Puring, Puring."

My grandmother embraced us immediately and said, "Oh, my grandchildren, you poor things. Your mother died so early." We all cried.

My mother's body was embalmed inside our house. We cried and cried, especially me. During the vigil, a lot of people were sleeping there. But I couldn't sleep. I watched over her body. They say it is bad if everyone is sleeping and no one is watching the dead. I really watched over her, but I was also afraid. Sometimes I would get in bed between my sisters.

[At the burial] I said, "Ma, I'll go with you." I tried hard. Two of my aunts held me. My mother appeared to me after the burial. It's true that on the third evening, the dead person will appear. We were all sleeping on one bed. My sister and cousins were beside me. I was in the middle. I couldn't sleep. My body was very hot. The wind was strong. I covered my head, but something took off the cover. I saw that my mother was floating in the air, a spirit.

My mother also appeared to her sister and to Heidi. My father agreed to let her be adopted by our aunt since she had no children. I

A barkada

couldn't care for her because I was studying. My mother would play with Heidi. Heidi said, "Mama, Mama." We cried when she was like that. We dressed her in red because my mother might take her since she was still small. Then, my aunt talked to my mother. She said, "Puring, don't take your child. We won't abandon her." My mother no longer appeared.

My father took us to Manila, to my grandmother [his mother]. The one who loved us was my grandmother on my mother's side. My grandmother on my father's side did not love us. She was terribly strict. We were studying. I'd get home at 6:00 in the evening, and there would be all these questions. "Why are you just getting here now? Maybe you were out with the boys." She would hit me if I wore shorts.

I did everything . . . the ironing . . . the cooking . . . washing all their clothes. I washed countless clothes. I also went to school. I couldn't go out and play on the street. We had a hard time there. When my grandmother was in the hospital, I was the one who took care of her. I was still studying. I got thin.

She got to be too much. I couldn't take her strictness any longer. I ran away. I stayed with a classmate. This classmate had a brother who wanted to get to know me. I married this brother. I was fifteen then— fourteen going on fifteen. I was very young. Before, whenever someone was courting me, my father always said, "Don't talk to him." He was very strict. When you are restricted, you rebel even more.

My father sent my uncle who was a colonel at Camp Aguinaldo.[3] He came in a car with his secretary. They had guns. My father didn't talk to me because we were angry with each other. He stayed inside the vehicle. It was my uncle and his secretary who came into the house with guns. They said they were going to take me with them. I really didn't want to go with them. They left.

I got pregnant. My stomach grew larger. I was nauseated. Being nauseated is difficult. I couldn't get up. I was always throwing up. My stomach grew larger. I gave birth on August 14, 1980. My child was very fat. A boy.

My grandmother died and was lying in state. My child was only three months old. He was very fat. My father and I had not talked; but when he saw his grandchild, my child, at the wake, he made up with me. We hadn't been speaking and then all of a sudden, he picked up my child. He really liked carrying him around. He said he was happy with his first grandchild. But my father still didn't like my husband. We lived together but we weren't married. It's good that my father didn't agree to the marriage because if I had married that guy, I wouldn't have been able to leave him.

My husband was also a jeepney driver. Every time he went out to drive the jeep, he would ask me for money. We had nothing in the house

then. We were still new together. My mother-in-law had given us a small room. I bought a fan and casette and blankets on installment. I paid that debt before I gave birth. Then, when I gave birth, he pawned them. He started smoking marijuana and drinking cough syrup. I had a very difficult time then.

When he went out to drive the jeepney, you could expect, in the evening before he came home, he would go out with his *barkada*. They would smoke marijuana. They were already high when they were driving. I would wake up about 1:00 or 2:00 in the morning and look for him. I would wait until all the jeepneys were in the garage. I didn't eat. I would always wait for him to eat. I was very thin. I was very angry. I swore. I said. "This motherfucking man—I'm going to leave him." I would look for him. My feet, I don't know how, took me to wherever he was. I walked. I didn't know where he was, but I would go straight there. He would be in a restaurant. I would swear at him, "You motherfucker. I'm hungry."

Just after I got out of the hospital, after giving birth, it was my birthday. I was beside the window. Our house was upstairs near the street. I saw my husband. He was walking on the street. Someone talked to him about taking some people to Makati.[4] He said, "Okay, I'll do it. Get in." All of them were children.

I called out to him, "Don't you drive! They're all children. Look at yourself. You can't even walk, and you want to drive? You might have an accident with your passengers."

He got angry. He took his *chinelas* . . . they're very thick . . . and hit me very hard on the head. I called my mother-in-law. She said, "You motherfucker. Your wife just gave birth. Get out of here. You are a fool." It was good that he left.

Later, he went to the gas station and bought a container of gasoline. He spread the gasoline all around the house. Many people live there. The first place he lit was our kitchen. It burst into flames. I was sleeping. It was good that my mother-in-law was there. She said, "Fire! Fire! Hurry!" She got a large blanket, immersed it in water, and put it on the wall.

He hid. Our *baranguay captain* was looking for him. They called the police. He said, "Totoy, come out now. You're surrounded." Reporters were there taking pictures. I was in the paper. I have a towel wrapped around my head because I had just given birth and might get damp with dew. That's bad. His mother talked to the *baranguay captain* and asked him not to arrest my husband. The *baranguay captain* showed compassion and agreed.

My mother-in-law said to him, "Get out of here. Go to your aunt in Munoz."[5] We looked for a house in Bagong Barrio.[6] The place where we lived was good, but I had a hard time because we weren't with my mother-in-law. It was just the two of us and my child. We had nothing to eat. He was still taking drugs all the time. I was sick of him. My mother-in-law left us alone. She said it was so that he would learn.

When I got some money, I

A family in Tondo, an urban poor section of Manila

cooked. I would hide the *ulam*. I taught my child, "When your father arrives, tell him you are hungry and haven't eaten."

The child was big already. He was smart. He said, "Papa, I'm hungry. Mama and I haven't eaten yet."

Neighborhood men getting loaded together on the street

He got angry and said, "Mother-fucker—why? Where is the money?"

I said, "You haven't given me any money."

I really felt sorry for my child. Sometimes our *ulam* was only *titse-ron*.⁷ I said, "My child, we have no money. We only have *titseron* for our *ulam*."

He would say, "Yes Mama. I like that."

But we did have rice. We had plenty of rice. It was only *ulam* that we didn't have. We would dip the *titseron* in vinegar sauce and let that drip on the rice. We had a portion of rice from my mother-in-law. Every Wednesday and Sunday, I would go to my mother-in-law. She would buy us rice and some *ulam*. My mother-in-law was kind. She bought us clothes for Christmas.

My mother-in-law sold clothes in Baclaran⁸ with another woman, Baby.⁹ Baby said, "It's up to you if you want to go to Japan. You are still young. Your beauty is being wasted if you stay with Totoy. You'll only get beat up and go hungry."

I thought about that. I said, "*Ate* Baby, put in an application for me."

"Talk to your mother first. Maybe she won't agree."

I talked to my mother, "Mother, I want to go to Japan."

She said, "Okay."

I talked to Totoy. He did not agree: "Japan, Japan. You can't leave."

I said, "Mother agreed. I'm going to Japan. You can do whatever you want with your life. I'm going to Japan."

[While I prepared to go to Japan], I would get up in the morning, cook, clean the house, and give the child a bath. Afterward, we would eat and I would put the child to sleep. My husband had nothing to do. He didn't have any work. All he had to do was watch the child. I was the one who did everything. At 1:00, I went to the promotion agency. I left the child. I said, "You take care of the child. He's sleeping now."

I was at the promotion agency from 1:00 to 5:00. When I got back to the house, I was tired. Everything was scattered around. It's because he's a man. He doesn't take care of things. I had to clean again. My husband had been in the vacant lot drinking. He had nothing to do. My child had played inside the house all alone. He was only two years old, still small. He might have fallen. I cleaned him up. He was very dirty.

I still had to cook. I would feed the child and put him to sleep. Sometimes he didn't want to sleep. Before he went to sleep, he wanted me to lie down next to him. I would massage his back so he would be able to sleep. Then, I would wash a full container of clothes. My husband would just get drunk.

I finished working at about midnight, but I still had to carry water. You have to walk down a small alley before you come to our house. You walk by other houses. I always wore shorts then. I was very thin. My body was beautiful. Someone there liked me. His name was June. I didn't know he liked me. I had a friend, Mira. He said, "Mira, introduce me to Rowena."

[One day] Mira came to our house. She said, "Rowena, someone wants to meet you."

I said, "Who?"

"June."

"Who's June? I don't know him. I don't want to. I have a husband."

"I'm just talking about meeting him."

Sometimes Totoy didn't come home. He washed jeepneys at the Shell station. One evening, I was introduced to June. He said, "Let's go eat at the Burger Machine. Come on."

It was good that Totoy's brother was staying with us. I put the child to sleep and said to my brother-in-law, "Ray, please watch the child. My friend is calling me to go out."

We went to the Burger Machine and then to Shakeys. We drank until dawn. It was the first time I'd had alcohol to drink. I got drunk. My brother-in-law was still awake. He was waiting for me.

I said, "Ray, is Totoy there?"

"No, he didn't come home."

"Thank goodness. If he had, he would get angry with me." I had brought Ray some fried chicken.

"Where's that from?"

"Mira took me there. We ate and drank. It's good Totoy didn't come home." My brother-in-law was nice to me because I was the one who washed his clothes.

When Totoy came home the next day, he had some money.

I said, "You have money? Why? Did you wash a lot of jeepneys?"

"No, I pinched this." While he was washing a jeepney, a taxi pulled up. He watched the taxi driver filling his tank. He saw the man get out his wallet, and it had a lot of money in it. He grabbed the wallet and ran. He had done everything by then—drugs, and now stealing. He was very thin, and his eyes were sunken from taking drugs.

One evening, Totoy's drinking companions told him, "*Pare*, you'd better watch your wife. Keep your eye on her, because she's being chased by the men around here. You don't know it, but Mira is her pimp." He got drunk that evening.

I was carrying a container of water. Totoy came out and said, "Motherfucker, come here."

I said, "Why? I'm tired. I haven't finished carrying water yet."

He hit me. He was really hitting me. It's a good thing my child didn't wake up. I forced myself not to cry. I had a pain in my stomach from his hitting me there. He was hitting my face. I put my hands over my face. He forced my hands away. He hit me in the eyes. I got black eyes. My brother-in-law didn't interfere because then they might fight. It was a fight between us.

I was in bad shape. I prayed, "Please wake me up early so I can run away." The next morning, I got a paper bag and put all my clothes inside. I asked my brother-in-law to look after the child. He had seen everything.

I ran away. I called my mother-in-law. I said, "Mother, I'm not going home. Totoy beat me."

She said, "Go home. If he beats you again, leave and don't return."

I went back. He beat me again. I left and did not go back. I lived with Baby in Kalookan.[10]

He looked for me. I heard someone calling, "Rowena, Rowena." I looked out through a hole [in the wall of the house] and I saw Totoy. I called Baby's mother. I crawled under the bed with the new puppies. The dog had just given birth. It's good I didn't get bitten.

He said, "Where's Rowena?" I want to talk to her.

"She's not here. We pity your wife—we saw her black eyes. You don't care about her. Rowena will not go back to you. You have no shame."

I worked at a club in Kalookan called the Pink Panther. I was a receptionist. Baby was still my manager then [for Japan]. I would give her money for food because I was staying there. Sometimes I gave money to my child. I would go to my mother-in-law's house if Totoy wasn't there.

At the Pink Panther, there were two managers. One of them liked me. Before they let a woman entertain customers at the tables, they want to have sex with her.[11] I went to a different club.

After I was there a few days, the manager from the Pink Panther came. I left there and moved to the Las Vegas club.

The club was large. The managers there know people who work in Kalookan City Hall. I had only come to work once when one of them said to me, "Don't leave. I have something for you." A little later, he asked me to sit down with some people from City Hall. I got to know Danny and Boyet. No other women were at the table yet. Danny gave me his phone number. He was kind. I always called Danny. He liked me. He was older. I don't have young boyfriends, always older ones.

I was still practicing [dancing] to go to Japan. Someone arranged for me to go as a tourist, TNT[12] to Osaka. Danny and I were very sweet at the airport. I cried. My clothes were very beautiful, all white so that I looked like a tourist. We pretended we were only sightseeing there, but we were really going to work. I didn't know that the work was selling sex.

I wasn't able to actually get there. I cried and cried when I left. That's bad. If you cry and cry, you won't be able to get where you're going. When we arrived at the airport in Osaka, we were deported. When they looked at the passport, they said, "Who is your sponsor?" I told them the name of the Japanese man. He was frightened and nervous. He went ahead of us. We were being held at the airport. They paged the Japanese man. They asked us, "What kind of work do you have here?"

"None. We're only tourists. We're just going to look around." We had "show money," $1,000.

"Do you have any money?"

"Yes, here—$1,000." It really was $1,000. It was a thick wad.

They still wouldn't believe us, so they sent us back to the Philippines. I didn't know if I should laugh or cry. My friend said, "Motherfucker, we were there in Japan and now we're going home. It's as if we were just out for a stroll." When we arrived home, our manager was angry with us.

I called Danny. He came for me. I had nowhere else to go because I couldn't return to Baby's house. The people there knew I had left. It would have been embarrassing. And, Baby and I had argued because I had applied with a different promotion agency and gone to Japan.

We rented a room in a house. The rent was P 450. But Danny didn't sleep at our house because—this I didn't know before—he was married. He would come when he left work at 5:00 in the evening and go home at 10:00 in the evening. I slept there alone. We had nothing, not even a fan, because we were living together for the first time. Danny was kind. From the time I first got to know him, he was kind.

The other manager said, "Come with me tomorrow. I'll let you audition." I was accepted and danced for them. I was able to come here on July 7, 1988. I wasn't here long, though—only three and a half months when they sent me home because I was too fat. But now I'm fat again, and they haven't sent me home. I'm even fatter now. I should only be here for six months, but I'll be here for eight months.

Danny thought I wouldn't come back. He cried. We moved to a house in Kalookan and stayed together. His wife found out about us, so we broke up and I went to Japan again.[13] I didn't have much money. I

Many clubs attempt to control completely the women's movements. Here, a van is bringing the women to work at the Club Hawaii. Late at night, or at dawn, the van will return and take them back to their rooms.

do [cultural] shows. When I arrived, I was shocked. There were only two women, and the club was dead. The clubs in the Philippines are better than here.

On my first night, they made me dance alone. I thought we would dance in groups. I cried on the stage. There were a lot of people. Our *papasan* said, "Take off your bra. Take off your bra." I cried. I didn't want to take it off. The *papasan* said it was better without panties . . . you would be number one.

I said, "Motherfucker. Number one is without panties. That's your problem."

He always told us, "The women at the Champion,[15] they have a lot of money because they are smart. You, you don't like money." The women at the Champion have sex inside the club. That club has a dark room.

A dark room is a dark place in the club. It's not a room—it's just very dark. There are some chairs and a curtain. You can't be seen there. If a man wants to pay for a woman, you go to the dark room. That is the woman's work. If she wants to make a lot of money, that's up to the woman. If you go the dark room, you are paid $20 or $30 worth of drinks. It's only for a short time. When it's done, you come out.

In other clubs, the owners force the women. There is one club where that is really the work of the women. Everyone knows the club. The women don't know it will be like that [before they come]. The *mamasan* forces them. The women get mad. They don't want to do it. They cry.

pushed to go back in order to make some money. I really wanted to return. It was good that the two old ones [bar owners] requested me.[14]

I didn't know what the work here would be [the first time]. We were taught to be cultural dancers. There were many of us practicing and auditioning for dancing. When we auditioned, it was in groups. What we knew was that our work here would also be in groups. I expected the clubs to be large and that we would

But you do it, or you'll be sent home. One woman was kept prisoner inside that club. Sometimes she wasn't fed for three days because she didn't want to do it. She said that wasn't her job. The promotion agency is the one who places the women in the clubs. You can't move if that's where you're put.

When *papasan* is drunk, he gives us a hard time. We tremble when he's drunk. He has no shame. Once, he hit me on the leg—hard. I yelled, "Ouch! Ouch! Ouch!" I ran to the bathroom and locked the door. He pounded on the door and tried to make me come out. I didn't open it. I said, "I'm shitting." He sat on a chair and lay in wait for me. I came out very slowly and carefully. He chased me and slapped me. He really wanted to hurt me.

My American husband came to get me.[16] I slept at his place. He was very angry. He said, "Fuck *papasan*. Motherfucker." The next day, my husband went to the club. He said, "Come here, *papasan*. I want to talk to you. You're full of shit. You're chicken shit. Come here." *Papasan* didn't want to go outside. "Don't hurt Rowena again. Motherfucker. I'm the one you'll have to fight. The women work for you, and on top of that you hit them." He was really angry.

The other day *papasan* was putting my husband down. "That guy," he said, "don't talk to that guy. He has a wife in the States and a kid." He's divorced. His wife is asking when he's going to send the papers to the lawyer. I was in his room when his child called long distance. *Papasan*

Dating

said, "That guy is always in the clubs. He's a butterfly. Life in the Philippines is better. While you're here, you'll earn lots of money. When you go home to the Philippines, you'll be happy. If you marry him, you'll be miserable."

My salary is $400 a month, but I only receive $290 because $10 is deducted for insurance and $100 for the manager in the Philippines, at the promotion agency. The promotion agency pays our salary.

In order to meet the monthly quota for drinks, women spend a good number of their nonwork hours contacting servicemen on the base to get them to come to the club to drink and chat. Quotas range from 400 to 500 drinks per month.

We have a quota of 400 drinks per month. One drink is one ticket. If you sell 400 drinks, you get $400. The price of the drink is $10. We only receive a commission of $1. If you don't make quota, you only get half your commission. For example, if you sell 300 drinks, you get $150. I only made quota a few times.

At our club, there is no bar fine; but if we want to [go with an American], it's possible. We're the ones who decide. If we don't want to, we are not forced by the *papasan*. They pay the owners. For example, the customer pays $100 or $200. If it is $100, we get ten tickets for drinks. The owner decides how much it costs.[17] My husband paid for me

once when there was a party. We left the club at 6:00 in the evening. My husband paid $50 so that I could leave the club. It was $50 because in one day, we have a quota of ten drinks.

We really can't leave the room.[18] We have to be there. If we leave in the evening, we get fined $100. One time we were caught. I have a Filipino friend who was stationed at Schwab.[19] He was going home. He said, "Let's go out for a little while and get something to drink because we're going home soon." We went out and had a drink at midnight. It was myself and my companion from that club.

A room above the club. A number of clubs house the women above the club in which they work. Windows and doors are barred, and a woman's coming and going is controlled by the club owners.

We got home at 1:00 A.M. When we went upstairs, we opened the door very carefully. We had to try not to make any noise. The door made a loud sound. It's noisy in the evening. During the day, it's not noisy. We went up the stairs very slowly and carefully. I carried my shoes so that the heels wouldn't be heard. The stairway is cement. When I turned on the light—I was still holding my shoes—there was *papasan* at the door.

He said, "You, you are number 100. You are not number 10, you are number 100 now." Before, you were good, but now you have no shame. We didn't say anything. He said to my companion, "You, you're teach-ing Rowena. Before, she wasn't like that. She was number one. Now, you're the same." He was really an-gry. We were very frightened. He said, "Tomorrow, you will have a fine of $50. Both of you." He was drunk. He didn't know what he was saying. The next morning, he didn't know what he had done, but we didn't talk to him. Before, we were not strong, but when I got to know my husband—no more. It was as if I became stronger inside because of him.

The Philippine consulate had a meeting with us last year to see if we had any complaints about our work. They would talk to the owners [about our complaints]. They asked

Rowena's *papasan*

Sometimes, you can save a lot of money. It's up to the woman. If the woman wants to earn money—wants to do it with a man as often as every day—when she goes home to the Philippines, she will have a lot of money. There is a woman who works in one club, everyone knows her, who is an eleven-timer. *Papasan* is always comparing us with this other woman. He says, "There are women in that club who make a lot of money. One has four children. She is old, thirty-eight already, but she looks young."

I said, "She does blow jobs. We're still afraid of that."

In some clubs, there are blow jobs for $30 or $25. If there is a man who is getting horny, he says to a woman, "Okay, I'll pay you $50—you do everything." He'll give it to the *mamasan*. The women at that club are very popular.

I have a lot of complaints about the club. One evening last month, the owner was drinking. He started drinking about 10:00 in the evening. By 1:00, then 2:00 A.M. he wasn't home yet. At 3:00 he still wasn't there. We couldn't sleep because we knew he would give us trouble. We covered our faces to pretend we were sleeping, but our eyes were twitching.

A little later, he said, "Rowena, come here."

I said [in English], "People are sleeping. You sleep now."

He said, "You don't like money. You no smart."

"I like money. Me, I like money. I've had a lot of drinks. I've already made quota."

if we have enough help, if our bathroom is clean, if we have a day off, and if there is a dark room. They also asked if our club has a bar fine. They asked each club, one at a time. The women were shy. They didn't want to speak. They didn't say anything.

Maybe the women were afraid to tell the Philippine consulate because they don't do anything. They are also afraid Filipinas will lose the work in Japan. In the Philippines, if you work [in a club], you might earn P 200 in one evening. We're paid in dollars here. When you go home, you have thousands.

"Bullshit. Tomorrow, after tomorrow, you're going home." He was always saying that. He thought he could scare us.

"Yes, go ahead and send me home." I answered back because we were sleepy. "Go to sleep now. People are tired."

"What? Tired? How did you get tired?" He was trying to insult me. I was grinding my teeth in anger. "How many drinks did you have?"

"Twenty-four."

"You, you are bold now. You only had twenty-four drinks."

This motherfucker. He still wasn't happy. I had already had twenty-four drinks. It was way past the quota. He was a demon. I was grinding my teeth. He pounded on the bed. I ignored him. I thought: "Motherfucker, starting tomorrow I won't talk to him." Maybe he thought I was sleeping but I wasn't. I didn't talk to him. He pushed me over to one side. I was facing him. I didn't speak. Maybe he got tired. He left and went to sleep.

The next morning, we didn't speak to him. He knew what he had done. Sometimes he doesn't know what he is doing. Sometimes he knows. I frowned at him. So far, we haven't spoken to him. If he speaks to me, I frown at him. He's always telling my companion, Sally, "Don't listen to anything Rowena tells you. If you do what she says, you'll get pregnant. You won't have any money. You'll go home and have an abortion."

There are women who are afraid of what their parents will do if they go home pregnant, so they have an

Dating

abortion. It's possible here. They are sent home if they're pregnant. They have to pay. That's why the women don't tell the promotion agency if they're pregnant. But some women want to continue the pregnancy.

The owners don't know that I'm always with my husband during the day. It's possible to go on dates, but we are always told at meetings [of the promotion agency] not to go inside the base. They say it is so the women will not get pregnant. The Filipinas here like to go inside the base. It's okay with the Americans.

I got to know my husband here at the club. My companion introduced

Dating

with him. He was very kind. He was only a dog with his people [subordinates]. You have to be strict in your work. From the time I got to know him, I didn't go out with anybody else—only him. If you go out with other guys when you have a boyfriend, the boyfriend will find out and won't be serious with you. He will also bullshit you if you bullshit him. The two of you will be bullshitting each other.

I should already have gone home last June 10. We decided that my husband would go to the Philippines this July to get my papers [for marriage] taken care of. He needs to be there to make it fast. But I couldn't go home. They extended me. There are only two of us in the club, and there is no replacement for me. Our manager pressured me. I didn't want to agree. I said, "*Kuya*, I can't have an extension. I want to go home. I don't like it here because of the way our *papasan* behaves. We make our quota, we should be fed well. We used to have two days off, now we only have one [per month]. Our *papasan* treats us as if we were stupid."

Our manager said, "Try to get along with your *mamasan*. Come to the promotion agency [if there is a problem]." Our promotion agency is kind. "Come on. There are no women."

My husband said, "Rowena, you have to decide if you want an extension. Look at how the *papasan* behaves." I also wanted to go home because we had plans to get married.

I went back and forth. I went to

us. She went and talked with him. It was cold. It was December. I was shaking. He bought both of us drinks. He asked me to sit at the table with him. He kept looking at me. We talked. He asked what kind of cigarettes we smoke and bought us some. He bought us roses and lots of drinks.

If I had a customer when he came to the club, he would get jealous and angry. After I was finished, I sat my husband and then to the manager at the promotion agency . . . to my husband . . . to the manager. My manager was really pressuring me. I said to my manager, "*Kuya*, you talk to my husband because we are going to get married. I'm having trouble."

They talked. The manager said, "We want to extend Rowena. Please go along with it." My husband said, "You know why I don't want Rowena to extend, because their *papasan* beats them. How many times has he hit Rowena? How many times have I lost my head in that club. The old man never changes. But I shouldn't be the one to decide. She should made the decision. I'll stand by her, but it's up to her to decide."

My manager said, "You'll only be delayed going home by four weeks."

I said, "Okay, I'd might as well earn as much as I can."

My manager gave me the phone number of the Philippine consulate so that If I have complaints, my husband or I could call there.

They say the Filipinas won't be able to come back to Okinawa because the Americans look down on them since their work is to have sex with different people. Even the President of the Philippines says the Americans look down on the Filipinas, because the work of the Filipinas is only like that [selling their sexual labor]. In the Philippines, if people from the province find out you have been in Japan, they say, "Oh, you have sex with people."

The Filipinas say, "Why should we listen to you? We won't be swallowed up by what you say." Some of the Filipinas work here because they want to help their families. They feel sorry for their families.

Maybe they should continue it because if the Filipinas can't come back [to Okinawa], they will be in bad shape. They won't have any work. The only work would be in the clubs in the Philippines, but you don't earn much there. You wouldn't be able to support your family. Here, you earn a lot in six months. If you work twice [two six-month stints], you'll be able to build a house.

I came here because I had no money. I was forced to work in a club because I didn't know of any other work. I worked in a garment factory before, making clothes. My salary was 50 centavos for each piece. I would be paid every week. Sometimes I earned P 150, sometimes P 300 per week, if I turned out a lot of pieces. I got serious about coming to Japan because of the money. Here, you earn dollars. Think about it, only one click and you earn $300.

The club owners here will also lose business if there aren't any women. The Americans will only spend their money on their own drinks, about $3. If a woman makes quota, how much goes to the club? Thousands. In one month, 400 drinks—I think that is already a thousand.

My Filipino husband wants to come back to me now because I have money. He wrote and said, "Forgive me for what I did to you. I blame myself. We love you." He is trying to make me care about him again. He thinks he can change my feelings. I won't go back to him be-

Service personnel getting loaded and getting into the music at the Rock America Club

cause I have had so many bad experiences with him.

If he saw me, he'd be shocked. When we separated, my face was gaunt. I was very thin. My eyes were sunken. He wouldn't know me. When I was a young woman, I was beautiful. I'm not bragging. He got me then. My body was beautiful. My legs were beautiful. He ruined that. He's the one who ruined my body. My neighbors would say to me, "How could you like him? You're beautiful. He must have given you a love potion."

I said, "I don't know." But, I didn't really like him. I had run away from home. I stayed with him because I had no place to go and

was confused about my family. My father and I didn't understand each other. I was only fourteen then.

The American customers I talk to say they want Filipinas because Filipinas take care of them. Some of them are divorced. Filipinas really do take care of them—not like American women who, even if they are married, go their own way. They also say Filipinas are affectionate.

I met one American in the club. He was new. He introduced himself and asked if I wanted a drink.

I said, "Why not?"

He said, "Will you talk to me if I buy you a drink?"

"Yeah, I'll talk to you. Okay, buy me a drink."

One tactic the women use to try to make their monthly quota is to hang out in front of the clubs to get the servicemen to come inside and buy drinks.

He said, "I wanna marry you." I had just met him. "I wanna marry you. I'm divorced. My ex-wife, she bullshits me."

He said he saw his wife in bed with another man in their own house. He almost killed her, but he sent her away and now he needs another woman to marry. He said he wants a Filipina. It was like he was playing. He said, "I love you."

I said, "Why do you say you love me? You just met me this evening. You don't know me yet."

He said, "Yeah, the first time I saw you I loved you."

I thought: "This American is bullshitting. He is really a bullshitter." They are bullshitters. The Filipinas are also bullshitters.

He invited me on a date right away. He said, "May I invite you somewhere tomorrow?" Afterward, he'll say the same thing to another woman. He'll go to another club and invite another woman . . . another date.

Some of the Americans, if they really like a woman and ask her on a date, they'll only eat in a restaurant. They'll take her to a store and say "If there is something you want, tell me." Some of the Americans are kind. I know if a man is kind. I watch him first and listen to what he says. If he is not stupid, I know right away. If I see he's stupid, I don't go near him. If I know he

During the afternoon, before going to work in the bar, some women are allowed by the bar owner to have freedom of movement. The women, like the guys, do not speak Japanese, can't use public transportation, and, thus, stay in the bar area. This is a time when it may be possible to play, to have fun together.

is kind, I approach him and talk to him.

Sometimes, I teach Sally. When she first arrived in the club, she had a customer. He bought her a lot of drinks. The next day he came back. He didn't come inside. She said to her present customer, "Excuse me, I have to talk to my customer. I'll come back." She went to him at the door: "How are you?" She kissed him. She talked to him for about ten or fifteen minutes. Every day she did that. In the end, he didn't come

back. He didn't drink. He didn't buy her drinks because she went to him at the door.

I told her, "When your customer comes, don't approach him. Don't run to him. They will think you really like them. They won't come back and won't buy drinks because you already talked to them. Don't talk to them. Let them come in. Just sit there and say, 'Come and have a drink.' They'll come in if they really like you." She lost her customers at first but when I taught her what to do, she started to make quota.

She's afraid of our *papasan*. He got angry when she didn't sell enough drinks. Before, when I had twenty drinks and she only had seven, he said to her, "You, you're going home now. You don't have any brains." He always got angry with her. She was new. She would sit there looking forlorn and crying. I felt sorry for her and showed her the ropes.

I'm always teaching Sally. I'm always building up her inner strength. I tell her, "Don't be afraid of *papasan*. He can be frightened. Fight him. Watch what I do." I answer back to our *papasan*. I fight. I said, "You fight, too. If you're afraid, he'll frighten you even more. He knows you're afraid." Now she fights back.

It's good that she has a companion like me. Some of the other women don't bother to teach you. When I was a first-timer, my companion didn't teach me anything. I learned myself. I was afraid. I said to her, "Christy, teach me. What should I do? How does it work?"

"You just talk to the Americans." That's all she taught.

Every morning she would leave at 10:00. There were only two of us at the club. She left me alone in the room. I cried. For two weeks I cried and cried. She would arrive when we opened the club. She had already taken a bath.

Her customers would arrive. I didn't have any customers. Once, *mamasan* said to her customer, "Sit down here. You buy her a drink." He bought me a drink. I didn't say anything. She had a customer already. She would look at me nastily. When her boyfriend arrived, she said, "Look at Rowena. She stole my customer. He bought her a drink." It wasn't my fault. If he hadn't wanted to buy me a drink, he wouldn't have. She wanted her customers to be only hers even if I didn't have any. She always wanted to be the highest earner, to sell the most drinks.

When Sally was new, I said to the customers, "Buy her drinks. She's new." I was always helping her. If I had a customer and she didn't have any drinks yet, I said to my customer, "Buy her a drink. She hasn't had any drinks yet." If I had a customer, he was also her customer. If she had a customer, he was also my customer. We gave to each other.

She's lucky. When she had just arrived here, I took her along when I went out with my husband. We'd go to Kosa and walk around.[20] She'd be on one side of my husband and I'd be on the other. We'd all hold hands.

I'm close to Sally. She's like my sister.

The bars here are different from the bars in the Philippines. Where I worked in Manila, there were a lot of

women. They would sit at a table in the corner and wait. There were maybe six floor managers. There were Filipino customers and sometimes foreigners. Sometimes the customers were military and police.

There were Filipinas dancing nude in groups. It was all the way. They were called models. Here it's only half nude. There were customers who were looking for someone to sit at their table. The floor manager would go to the back and look for someone beautiful or intel-

The women's need for friendship and support is heightened by their being in a foreign country. Sometimes working in the same bar will result in bonding; at other times, there is competition.

Returning to the Philippines. Six months is the usual contract period for work in Okinawa. This van is loaded with a woman's purchases for herself and her family. One package is addressed to Tondo, an urban poor area of Manila.

ligent. They had a flashlight. They would flash the light on a woman's face and say, "Come here." The woman would sit at the table. If the customer liked her, she would stay. If not, she'd go back and they would look for another one.

There was also a stage. If there was a fast dance, the women would dance. Even women and women would dance. The customers would watch and if they liked a woman, they would tell the manager, who would shine the flashlight on them, "You, come here." I was a receptionist, but I didn't stay long. I worked there for about three months.

Here there are only a few women in the clubs. Some have twelve, some eight, some four, some two, and some only one. There is no floor manager, only the club owners. The owners also tend the bar. When a

customer comes in, the women entertain him. If he wants to buy a drink, the woman sits down. I choose. I don't like the stupid ones. We're the ones who approach them—not like in the Philippines, where the floor manager is the one to approach them.

In the Philippines, if you don't want to go to work, or are sick, you can be absent but you won't earn anything. You can't be absent continuously. If you're absent today, you must work tomorrow or you'll get a warning. If you don't work for three days or a week, you'll lose your job. Here, if you don't go to work, you are fired.

But, you earn less in the Philippines. Here you earn dollars. In one month, you can earn a thousand. You get paid by the month. Even if there are no customers and you don't sell any drinks, you still have your full salary.

In the Philippines there is no salary—only commission from the drinks.[21] For example, if the drink costs P 45, you keep half. You have tickets for the drinks. At closing time, you count your tickets. They give you the money every evening, so you have money the next day. Here, you get paid by the month and the food is free. The situation of the women is more controlled here, but you earn more.

1. Pampanga is the province just north of Manila; travel between the two is easy.

2. Almost all clothes washing in the Philippines is done by hand; only the wealthy and foreigners have washing machines.

3. Camp Aguinaldo is one of the large military camps in Manila.

4. It is common for people to rent a jeepney for special excursions, especially for groups. Makati is the large business district of Manila.

5. Munoz is an area of Manila.

6. A poor urban area of Manila.

7. Fried pork skins usually eaten as a snack.

8. Baclaran is an area of Manila where people go to buy clothes cheaply. They are sold in the street in open-market style.

9. It appears that Baby is a recruiter for Japan.

10. An area of Manila.

11. In some clubs, the managers have sex with the women before they entertain customers.

12. TNT is an acronym for *Tago ng Tago*, which literally means hide and hide. It is a euphemism for being an illegal worker or immigrant in another country.

13. The women from the Philippines do not distinguish between Okinawa and Japan. When referring to going to work in either place, they say Japan.

14. Bar owners may request of the promotion agency that a woman return to work for them. If she agrees, she is automatically accepted again.

15. Another club in the same area. (See also Janet's story, p. 282.)

16. The women will sometimes refer to Americans as their husband, or more literally, their spouse, if the relationship is relatively long term.

17. The procedure for bar fines differs among bars. (See also Janet's story, p. 282.)

18. The rooms are often at the back of or above the club. In this case, the room is upstairs in a building across the street; the bar owners also stay there.

19. Schwab is a small Marine base about thirty minutes from Camp Hansen. The Filipino is a Filipino in the U.S. Military. He speaks Tagalog and lives in the Philippines, which would indicate that he was recruited from the Philippines. Such recruitment is one route for Filipinos to obtain U.S. citizenship. There are an allotted number of Filipinos recruited each year.

20. Kosa is the bar area outside Kadena Air Force Base.

21. Rowena is describing her experience in clubs in Manila, which is not necessarily true of all clubs in Manila or elsewhere in the country. Conditions vary widely.

JANET

Age: 21

I was born in San Fernando, Albay. There were seven of us: six girls and one boy. I'm the second eldest. But because my eldest sibling is married and has a child, I'm the one acting as the oldest. My mother is a house-keeper. My father is a farmer. We have land that belongs to my grand-father, my father's father. It is only a small plot. There are twelve siblings in my father's generation. The land was divided up, but some of them live far away and are married. The ones who live far away have other ways of earning a living, like a store or a jeepney or a tricycle. My father is the only one who has become a farmer. He's the one who uses the land, but it isn't in his name.

We plant vegetables and rice. Because we were poor, the children needed to help. When I was old enough—in elementary school—I sold vegetables. Sometimes I sold them in the market, sometimes I walked around selling. I also helped

Fourth of July at Kin, Okinawa. Camp Hansen Marine Base Open House

plant corn, root crops, rice, and vegetables. On Saturday and Sunday, when we didn't have school, we helped. The girls, too. Sometimes in the province, we don't use a stove. We use wood to cook with. Sometimes we have to carry water. Those are the things we did when we weren't in school.

During my first year of high school, I studied at night and worked during the day as a waitress in a restaurant. When I arrived at school, I was tired. Sometimes, even if I knew the answer, I didn't answer because of fatigue. I just sat and listened to the discussion. During the second year of high school, I worked making handicrafts during the day. At night, I went to school. After school, about 9:00 or 10:00 in the evening, I would sell cigarettes, peanuts, and soft drinks at the fiestas, dances, and school programs.

When I was older, I quit school. I kept working in order to help my parents a little bit. I worked as a saleslady in a department store in Legaspi, where I stayed at a boardinghouse. I think I was there for more than two years. Our salary was P 32 per day. Every payday, I gave money to my mother. My younger brothers and sisters were still in school. We had root crops and corn [to eat], but the money was not enough [for school expenses].

In 1987, there was a bad typhoon in our province. Our house was destroyed. My sister came to see me. She asked to borrow some clothes because all their clothes were wet. I was the only one who could help them. Nothing had happened at the

Pounding rice to remove the husk

boardinghouse. It was a large building, so the typhoon didn't damage it. I had hidden P 50. I gave it to her because I felt sorry for them.

Another saleslady had been saying before, "Let's go to Japan."[1] Her family was also poor, and she needed money. After the typhoon, I changed my mind and thought seriously about it. She convinced me. I made

Entrance to the bar area seen from
Camp Hansen

myself strong inside. We went away
to Manila. My friend knew whom
to approach in Manila. We practiced [dancing] and applied to go
to Japan.

Before I came here [to Okinawa],
I thought it was bad. People say
that the women who work in clubs,
especially in Japan, are very bad. I
had not yet been to Japan, so I was
afraid. What would it be like? And
I heard that Japan was not good
for Filipinos because of the war.
My parents experienced the war, so
they have bad feelings toward
the Japanese.[2]

I thought maybe I wouldn't be
able to do it, but I needed the
money. I thought: "Many Filipinas
go there, and they are able to come
home doing well. They come back
the same as the left, so what they do

there must be okay." The stories I
heard were about group dancing.
They didn't tell us everything. Even
though I felt some apprehension, I
was mature in my thinking and
knew that what I did there would be
up to me. So I made myself strong.

My parents didn't know I was
going to Japan. I lied to them because I knew they didn't approve of
that kind of work. I wrote to my
mother: I said that I worked in a
store, but I was practicing dancing.
Before, when I was working, I sent
money. I borrowed P 50 a day from
the manager in order to continue
sending money home until we left,
and for cash. We stayed with our
manager as tenants. Daily lists were
kept of our debts. We will pay them
when we go home.

A *bakla* at the promotion agency,

Bakla toasts Marilyn Monroe

Ten Story, is the one who taught us how to dance. After practicing dancing, we had an audition at the promotion agency in front of the Japanese. We had to dance and show our personality. The owner of the promotion agency is Japanese, but there are Filipinos who work there. There are some half Filipino and half Japanese. We practiced for a month and a half and then passed. Soon it was time to leave.

When I was about to leave, I went home to Bicol. I couldn't endure going to a faraway place with my parents not knowing. We talked. I convinced them that it depended on the person—what she would do in Japan. To this day, my mother thinks I work in a large restaurant that has shows. I said, "We dance and sometimes the band requests certain songs. We also sing." They still don't know that I'm working in a club. They really wouldn't like that. Maybe if I don't come back to Japan, I'll tell them the truth.

When I first arrived in Okinawa, all I saw was mountains. I thought it was supposed to be beautiful in Japan. But it is like my home province—it is lonely.[3] The scenery here is almost the same as in the Philippines.[4]

November 1988 was the first time I came here. This is my second time.

Kin Beach is about a thirty-minute walk from the bar area. Servicemen come here alone or on dates. Marines practice maneuvers in the dense vegetation in the distance.

When I was a first-timer, I hadn't done this work yet. I was nervous. There were a lot of people. My companions pushed me onto the stage. There were four women then. I was the fourth. They said, "You're next."

I said, "How do I dance?" Even though I had practiced before coming, we had practiced in groups.

Here it was solo. They pushed me: "Your turn."

"I don't know how. How?"

I danced. I didn't do what the *mamasan* wanted. She was angry. They stopped the music. I was shamed on the stage. There were a lot of customers. I really cried. I thought: "This is what it's like to work in a club. I didn't know." I thought about my mother. I didn't want to cry because I saw the customers. It was obvious to them that

I was new, a first-timer. Even in the Philippines, I hadn't been inside a club before.

When I first came, we had to be nude all the way [while dancing]. Now it is banned to go all the way. It's only topless. They banned it because the Philippine consulate said Filipinas were being treated like pigs here by the Americans. There are customers who really look down on the women. Sometimes there are customers who are crude toward us. We fought to have it be only topless in order to reduce the crude treatment.

The majority of the women want to dance only topless. But some of the others say they were used to going all the way nude, and you earn more if you go all the way— more customers will come to your club. It is slower now, maybe because the women aren't going all the way. Maybe the customers like all the way. For us, it is only on the stage and to the waist.[5] Maybe only those who like you will have the patience to come and buy you drinks. I think it's better to go only halfway so that even if it's said that we are working in a club, at least we are trying to preserve morality.

When I returned to the Philippines for the first time, I was only there a short time—only three weeks. I had already signed the papers for my second contract. I had my period but it only lasted one day. I thought: "Why only one day?" My American boyfriend also came to the Philippines. We met in Olongapo for two evenings and a day. He had two weeks' duty there just at the time I was also going home. We stayed in a hotel, and I was nauseated and dizzy: I was already pregnant.

I went home to Bicol for only four days. I told them the same thing—that I was working in a restaurant. We didn't have very much time to talk. There were a lot of people around because we baptized my niece, the first one.[6] We were busy. We didn't talk seriously. We didn't have time to talk just as a family. So, what they know is what I told them before. It hasn't changed.

I didn't feel like coming back here again because the earnings are less now; and if the earnings are low, the time is wasted. I don't know, maybe if I had enough money, I would study again. I would go back to school or start a small business. That's my dream. When I was still in school, my dream was to be a

Posters like this depreciating the women, the culture, and the country where U.S. service personnel are stationed are ubiquitous in each of the bar areas. Hats, shirts, and banners carry similar, but more concise, messages.

nurse. I wanted to help children. But, it's no longer possible.

I didn't tell my boyfriend that I was pregnant in Olongapo; I told him here. He works at Tori Station.[7] He told me he would help me. He said he would marry me. He made promises like that. After two weeks,

Okinawan clan graves and Tori Station communications tower

he didn't come anymore. I called his office. They said he was in the States.

I was angry. Of course, I was depending on him. It was as if my hope had suddenly been cut off. I went to his house. The truth was that he had not gone back to the States. He was still there. The man lied to me. He was only hiding from me. What he did to me was painful.

I said, "Why don't you want to take responsibility for what happened, and you know you are the one who got me pregnant?" He was divorced and had one child. He said he wasn't ready to have another family yet. I said, "Why didn't you tell me. You made promises that you would help me. You know my situation. You know I need money. I came here to work, not for that [sex]. You didn't say, 'I will give you $100 or $300 so that you can go home.' I called the office and they said you were in the States. But you had

not gone home to the States, you were hiding."

He came back and said he was sorry. He says he will return to the Philippines in order to marry me. I don't know. I lost some of my love for him, and I don't want it to happen again. What if I got pregnant again and he hid again? It really hurt. Why didn't he tell the truth. I said, "Once is enough, twice is too much."

In May, I thought I needed to go home because my stomach would be getting large. I would have to break my contract with the promotion agency. If I didn't finish my contract, I would have to pay the promotion agency. That was my problem—where would I get the money for a plane ticket. It was good that I had a miscarriage on May 7. I didn't abort, it just miscarried. Maybe it wasn't the right time.

Maybe the Lord intentionally let me get pregnant so that when the man was playing with me, I got to know the person he really was. If I hadn't gotten pregnant, maybe the relationship would have gone on until now. I wouldn't have known that he was just playing with me.

If I had wanted to have an abortion here, that would have been possible. I would tell the promotion agency. They have a doctor. But I was afraid. If I hadn't miscarried, I would have continued the pregnancy. That would have been difficult, too, because I'm helping my parents and siblings. We're still poor. We don't have enough to live on. Of course, I would tell my parents that I was pregnant. Maybe they would have been able to accept it. After all, the baby was already there.

Before that there was a Mexican—a Marine. He was my second boyfriend. He's in the States. He wrote. He doesn't know my background, because it's still painful. I still can't get rid of that pain. It's as if I sometimes lose my trust in the Americans, because I might fall in love again and trust again, and the man might leave me again. After one time of love the men change their minds.[8] It's not like at home where we think that if you spend time with a person, if you love a man, you want only him. With them, we don't know how their minds work. Nothing happens. Then, you get pregnant and are left. It's difficult.

Never mind getting pregnant as long as you don't get AIDS, because if you happen to get AIDS, they say you are luckier if you just die. I haven't heard of anyone here with

AIDS. I don't know, maybe there is VD, but it's easy to recover from that. There is medicine. If you have symptoms now and go to the doctor right away for treatment, you can be well in twenty-four hours. You just go to the promotion agency. There is money deducted from our salary for insurance. If you get sick and go to the doctor, it's free from the insurance deduction. But if the cost is too high, you'll probably have to pay.

Some say that AIDS is an illness of bad people, and if you are a good person, you won't get it. In my opinion, even if you are a good person,

The guys are young, most between the ages of seventeen and twenty-four. On Okinawa, bikes are an additional, and welcome, form of recreation.

Because so many bars are successful in fully restricting the movements of the women, communication is exceedingly difficult. Here a serviceman talks with a woman through bars.

They say it's not but it is. It's possible to go on bar fines. It depends on you. If you want to go, you can go. If you don't want to, that's up to you. There are hotels, but with my boyfriend, we would go to a house. I have also had Japanese customers. Last December, when they had vacation, the Japanese men came here.

The bar fine is paid to the *mamasan*. My boyfriend paid $200. If he pays $100, the woman gets credit for twenty drinks. I'm the one who raised the price. *Naku*, you do that and then you only make a little bit. If he pays $200, the woman gets forty tickets. If it's only a small amount, I don't go. You're the one to set the price because the *mamasan* agrees to small amounts and large amounts. When it comes to me, I really raise the price. Sometimes, I have them pay the bar $50 and give me $150.

We have a quota of 500 drinks each month in our club. When I was a first-timer, I could make quota but not now. No matter what I do, I can't make quota. It's very difficult to get drinks. You have to play games. "Buy me a drink . . ." They hold on to you. They kiss you. If not, you won't earn. If you don't kiss a customer, he won't like you and won't buy you drinks. He won't come back. Sometimes, even that isn't enough. They want to take you out and use your body. Even just talking—if you don't talk to him because you are tired of talking, he won't come back to you and buy you drinks.

Before, our commission per drink was 50 cents. We're the ones who end

you only have to have sex one time and you might get AIDS.

I don't use birth control. I know about it, but here in Japan I don't know where to buy the pill or condoms. The promotion doesn't help because it is supposed to be forbidden to go on bar fines. But you fall in love sometimes. Something happens. Some Americans don't like to use a condom. Our *mamasan* gave me some condoms.

The promotion agency says that going out with Americans is not part of our work, but it really is.

Bikers

up poor . . . we're the ones they make money from—and then they don't pay. We fought to make it a dollar. That's what we fought for at the Philippine consulate. It was approved that the bar owners should raise the commission because the work Filipinas do here is so difficult.

The Philippine consulate visits the Filipinas to see what their situation is like here. We formed a group, and all the women who work in the clubs brought forward what our problems are. We said the commission should be raised, even just a little. It should be made a dollar. The women said, "It's true that we are used, so our commission should be raised." We also fought for a night off from work, or if we work on our night off, our tickets should be doubled. That wasn't approved. But some of the bars in other areas are doing that. Also, in Kosa they still strip all the way.[9] They go all the way at the Champion, too.

The Philippine consulate lets us know when they're coming to find out what our problems are. They are like our guards here. The consulate talked to the promotion agencies, and they talked to the bar owners. They had a meeting and told the owners we were not to dance nude all the way. I think they frightened the club owners because they said there would be visits by immigration. The women come through immigration as group dancers or models, not to dance nude.

Beauty shop in the bar area

Just the other day, someone came from immigration. Our bar closed because there are supposed to be three women here, but there are only two of us, and we are supposed to dance in a group. Other clubs had the women dancing in groups the evening immigration came. The owners knew the immigration people were coming because the promotion agencies told them so that they would be prepared. Sometimes, an owner is caught. Sometimes immigration people come in civilian clothes so they won't be noticed. They see what the situation really is and know that the club owners are lying.

We don't choose what bar we will work in. The promotion agency tells you where you will work. It all depends on luck. I have some friends at [club] Washington. We learned that there are dark corners. They can do anything with the customer there—things to get the customers to keep coming back. In our club, it's too light. There are no places to

hide or dark corners or dark rooms. One customer said to us that it was better this way so that we wouldn't be abused. We're ashamed to do those things. The women at other clubs aren't ashamed because the *mamasan* is the one who gets them to do it. I think their quota is also very high. I think if they don't make quota, they are sent home or given a penalty.

At least, our situation in this club is a little better than in other clubs. Our *mamasan* is kind. Anytime we want to go out, we can tell her and go out. If you are hungry and want to go buy some food, she'll let you go. There are other clubs where the women can't leave. The others say we are lucky. At least, people don't look down on us that badly.

I don't know if there will be replacements when we leave, but I've heard that there won't be any more. About a year ago, our manager was fighting to keep the women coming to Japan. They were fighting Cory [Aquino] because Cory said Fili-

MPs, the guys, and Okinawan Provincial Police at night in the bar area

pinas in Japan are being treated like pigs. Maybe Cory doesn't like the women coming to Japan. Our manager said she should give the women jobs, then, because of the [economic] situation of Filipinas. How will these women who have worked here earn a living? Will Cory give them work? The news I heard was that women from Korea would replace them.

I think the women should be able to continue to come. For us, this has been a big help. I think it should continue so more would be helped. And, it's up to the woman whether or not she allows herself to be abused or exploited. You have to make yourself respectable so that you won't be abused. If it's stopped,

we should be given work. We would change. We wouldn't work in a club anymore if we were given work that's adequate. I would like to study so that I could get a better job even though I used to work in a club.

I've been able to go to Olongapo because I met my boyfriend there. We walked around. I had come from being in the bars here in Okinawa. The clubs in Olongapo are much better: bigger, more people, more women, more beautiful, different colors, many people walking on the streets. There are always people in Olongapo. Here, there are only a few. They also said that when there is a ship, business is good. But they say that the work in Olongapo is worse than here. My friend who

The Champion Cabaret, *right*, is run by an Okinawan woman who worked in the bars during the Korean and Vietnam Wars. The Filipinas who are assigned to work at the Champion are forced to dance nude and sell their sexual labor inside the club in corners darkened for that purpose.

The bathroom at the Champion has multiple uses. A small room on the other side of the door may be the dark room. The sign reads: "Attention—After 2:00 no one may stay in the kitchen or go out. Ask permission first before peeing or shitting. Make-up time starts at 3:30, thirty minutes for two people."

used to work in Olongapo said, "There is no comparison between the work in Olongapo and here." Here, she has only experienced half of what she experienced in Olongapo.[10] She is married now and lives here.

I want to get married because I think that is part of my life. Of course, I want to have children when the time is right for me. But if it will only cause problems and headaches, better not to. It would be okay if my husband were a Filipino, but I don't want to be in the same situation as my family when we were very poor but just kept having more children. You get even poorer. Most Filipinos have children and more children. Like my family:

there are many brothers and sisters, but my father only earns a small amount of money. We didn't have enough. From the time we were small, we've always been poor.

What I experienced, I don't want to continue to experience. I want my life to be better. I want to be able to take a rest once in a while in my life. I want to be able to help my family, not abandon them. Maybe with Americans, there are also some like that [poor], but you have to look for one who will be able to help you and will understand.

Another thing is that if you marry a Filipino, they don't like it if the woman already has [sexual] experience. They'll have a lot to say about her—gossip. That's why it's proba-

Guys and women hanging out in front of Andy's before work in the afternoon. Andy's is a clothing store run by a Pakistani.

bly better to marry an American. Whatever your experience, it's okay with them. They don't mind what you've been through as long as you are honest with them. I have a difficult time trusting Americans, but I guess you have to try to see if he loves you.

This present boyfriend of mine left last May. I have to understand him. He said I was okay. He trusted me. At least, I wasn't like the other women he couldn't trust. He said he would marry me. He still writes me. Maybe it will continue. If he is honest with me and doesn't bullshit me, maybe he will be the one. But I don't know. It's difficult to trust anyone because I was hurt once.

I know Americans really like to have a good time. If they aren't having a good time, it's like their life seems boring to them. They are fond of barhopping. But some are okay. There are some Americans who help the women, who understand your situation. They know how to empathize with you without only being interested in your body. They are also interested in what's inside you. There are some Americans who are crude, who just bullshit. They only want your body. They are blunt. They say, "Is it possible to use that? [the woman's body]." I don't agree. Would I just waste my body? I think about myself. I try first to see if he loves me, if he's able to help me.

Before, when I hadn't worked in a club yet, I thought that the women

Men on the street bar-hopping

who do were bad—dirty. I was disgusted by them. When I was small, if a man had sex with a woman and they weren't married, I thought that was bad. In the province, if a man has sex with a woman, they have to get married.[11] If you have sex outside of marriage, it's as if you're a bad woman who has ruined her life. You're repulsive to look at.

I think I'm still conservative in my thinking. I still feel the same toward the women who work in the clubs. But because my mind has been broadened, I doubt what people say. It might just be gossip. I think it depends on the woman and the reasons. She might not have done that because she wants to. The

women come here to work, to earn money, not to play around. Even me—I came here because I need the money.

I would like to go home, but it isn't possible yet. I have to finish my contract. We come in a group. When you are a first-timer, you're taken care of. You'll be escorted to the airport. After you're on the airplane, it's up to you to get off at the other end. You'll be picked up at the airport and escorted here to the clubs—to wherever you'll be working.

If you're beaten up or something by the owners, you can go to the promotion agency or the Philippine consulate. We aren't supposed to be beaten or hurt by the Japanese be-

Filipina returning home, being taunted by two guys. The packages lined up belong to a number of Filipinas also returning home.

cause we are contract workers here in Japan. I haven't heard of anyone being beaten by Americans, or anyone killed. If they were caught doing that, they would be in big trouble and sent home.

I take care of myself even if there is trouble at the club because of that. I don't want to allow myself to be abused or exploited by another person and lose my self-respect. I show others that no matter what, they must respect me. I haven't changed my opinion of myself. I want to continue to respect myself so that others will respect me whether they are Americans or anyone else. Even if they have an education and I work in a club, I will not

be abused or seen as small or as a pig. I don't treat myself like a pig so that I will not change my opinion of myself. I take care of myself even if they say I am only a hostess. Some say, "She is a hostess, she works in a club, but she is beautiful inside. She looks respectable."

It's because I don't have sex like some of the other women who are wild. It's as if they see themselves differently. But if you are simple and respect yourself even in your movements and words—if you are careful in your movements and speech—even if you are a hostess and work in a club, you will be respected.

If I'm abused, I get angry. I swear. I show them that they can't

Hats and shirts displaying these messages are ubiquitous in each of the bar areas.

The great mobility of U.S. forces allows servicemen the opportunity to party in a number of playgrounds. The Armed Forces radio station in each country continually broadcasts information about flights to various R&R spots in Asia. After being stationed in-country for about six months, a serviceman can fly on military aircraft. Ten dollars gets you from the Philippines to Pattya, Thailand.

push me around. Whatever they say to hurt me, I say something to them that's even more painful. They think I won't fight back. If you are abused and you just laugh, they get used to it—especially those who are bull-shitters. That's why, if they say something that is painful to my ear, I swear at them. I show them they can't treat me like that. They will say, "Ah, this one is different." You have to frighten them. It's because some of them are crazy. There are some who are crazy no matter what you say—they keep on talking bad. I don't talk to them again because sometimes I can't control my anger.

This is because of my family, my mother and father. Isn't it true that married couples fight? But we grew up without hearing any fights. Maybe they did fight, but they didn't let us hear it. Another thing: I grew up for almost twenty years living with them and didn't hear my parents swear or say bad words. Our family was very quiet and peaceful. We were brought up that way. I only learned swearing from other people, especially when I came here. Sometimes I use words when I need to, to people whom you should swear at. But otherwise, I don't use those words.

Our life [in the province] was beautiful and happy. The only thing was that we didn't have enough money. If we had not been short of money, I wouldn't have come here to Japan. I wouldn't have made myself strong inside to come here if we had had enough to live on, but we really didn't.

1. The Filipinas working in Okinawa refer to Okinawa as Japan. They do not make a distinction. At this point, before they leave, they may not yet have known if they were going to Japan or Okinawa.

2. In 1941 and 1942, Japan took control of the Philippines. During that time, the Japanese military subjected Filipinos to horrendous abuses. Many Filipinos who carry memories of the war still dislike the Japanese. (See also Manang's story, p. 98.)

3. The term used here, *malungkot*, can mean the contrast of the quiet province with the hustle and bustle of the city; or it can mean lonely and sad. It can, but does not necessarily, mean both.

4. Okinawa and the Philippines are both Pacific islands. They are not very far from each other, about a two-hour direct flight by commercial airlines.

5. In some clubs, the women dance nude on stage and when their turn is finished, they are required to walk nude around the club while the Americans are free to feel them or do other things.

6. Only some Tagalog words distinguish gender; no pronouns do. In this case, the gender of the child being baptized is not clear.

7. Tori Station is a communications base on Okinawa.

8. The meaning here is ambiguous, although she seems to mean sexual intercourse.

9. Kosa is a street outside Kadena Air Force Base. It is a bar area.

10. The implication here seems to be that the women in Olongapo experience more abuse of various kinds than do the women working in Okinawa.

11. In the provinces or in traditional culture, a man may rape a woman in order to marry her. Once raped, she must marry him whether or not she wants to. (See also Linda's story, p. 137.)

DISPARATE THREADS OF THE WHOLE:
AN INTERPRETIVE ESSAY

Saundra Sturdevant and Brenda Stoltzfus

Sexual Labor and Global Feminist Sisterhood

At an international solidarity conference in the Philippines, one woman called a meeting, posing the question: Is sisterhood global? The group was made up of women from industrialized and Third World countries. After about twenty minutes, the woman stopped the discussion and pointed out that during those first twenty minutes no woman from a Third World country had yet spoken. All the women who had spoken were from industrialized countries.

When Adul de Leon, a national leader of Gabriela, returned to the Philippines after attending another conference in the U.S., she said, "Brenda, when you return to the States, you will have a hard time with the women's movement there.[1] They spend all their time arguing about whether or not prostitution can be a free choice. We women from Third World countries got really bored with their fighting. Our issues around prostitution are different."

Adul's comment raises the persistent issue of dominance and power. Who sets the agenda? Who defines the issues and questions? Who speaks? Who benefits? To have a voice in decision making, theorizing, planning, and discussions is to have power or the possibility of power. Adul identified one manifestation of this issue. Gender relations, some feminists argue, is the classic and most profound arena in which dominance and power are apparent. Race, class, and sexual orientation within the women's movement in the United States are others. Yet another may be found at the heart of the very arguments that Adul was so bored with—the issue of free choice.

The 1980s and '90s have seen rapid growth around the world of organizing by prostitutes, with prostitutes, and about prostitution by feminists and activists. The rise of prostitute groups has challenged various feminist analyses of prostitution. Until prostituted women began organizing, their voices were not heard by feminists. A quote from the Second World Whore's Congress clearly expresses the ambivalence that prostitutes from industrialized countries feel toward feminists:

The International Committee for Prostitutes' Rights (ICPR) realizes that up until now the women's movement in most countries has not, or has only marginally, included prostitutes as spokeswomen and theorists. Historically, women's movements (like socialist and communist movements) have opposed the institution of prostitution while claiming to support prostitute women. However, prostitutes reject support that requires them to leave prostitution; they object to being treated as symbols of oppression and demand recognition as workers. Due to feminist hesitation or refusal to accept prostitution as legitimate work and to accept prostitutes as working women, the majority of prostitutes have not identified as feminists; nonetheless, many prostitutes identify with feminist values such as independence, financial autonomy, sexual self-determination, personal strength, and female bonding.[2]

Prostitute groups and prostitutes from industrialized countries are demanding their own voice, and therefore the power to define their own issues. Prostitution, they argue, is work that can be freely chosen. Variations range from claiming that "whores are the most emancipated women, the only women who have the right to fuck as many men as men fuck women," to prostitution as one choice among many difficult choices under the obvious conditions of discrimination and oppression of women.[3] Prostitution and marriage are both economic choices; both provide sexual services to men, and the possibility of violence against women is inherent in both.

The other viewpoint in the fight described by Adul holds that to accept prostitution as a form of woman's work is to accept the notion of women's bodies as commodities, an idea at the core of male dominance and violence against women. Furthermore, as long as there is prostitution, there will be rape; anything that can be bought can also be stolen.[4] Prostitution and marriage are again compared, both being the primary institutions through which women experience oppression or where female sexual slavery is practiced.[5] A woman who is forced into some form of prostitution and/or cannot get out is a victim, subject to sexual violence and exploitation.[6] Because prostitution perpetuates the view of women's bodies as commodities, women who choose prostitution freely are not acting in a socially responsible way.[7]

This severe judgment of prostituted women as not acting in a socially responsible way increases the polarization between "good" and "bad" women and further stigmatizes women who sell their sexual labor. Even though prostitution and marriage are compared, the judgment appears to come down severely only on prostituted women, not on married women. In this view, the only way for a prostituted woman to be legitimate is to take on the victim identity and image. And the victim identity presumes the desire to leave prostitution.[8]

The desire or demand that the woman leave prostitution is understandable in that it often arises from anger at the limited options open to women, and at the dehumanizing aspects of their work. At the same time, this desire or demand reflects a distancing of the woman selling her sexual labor. So-called rehabilitation is often spoken of as simply a matter of providing alternative jobs. It's far from being that simple.

We really know very little about the physical and spiritual wounds that result from the isolation, the grief, the denial of human rights, and the breakdown of family and other human relationships that come in varying degrees from the selling of sexual labor. From her work counseling Okinawan women who provided sexual labor for U.S. military men over an extended period of time during the Vietnam War era, Takazato Suzuyo writes about the woman who has ongoing delusions of sexual persecution and becomes greatly agitated and unusually nervous twice a month, on the fifteenth and thirtieth—paydays for U.S. troops. Or the woman who has yet to find a drug that will allow her mind to rest at night and not be filled with images of being raped by gangs of U.S. soldiers, which is what providing sexual labor to twenty to thirty men per night amounts to. These may or may not be extreme situations, but they are not unusual.[9]

As Adul points out, discussing the sale of sexual labor within the parameters of free choice is oversimplified; it does not address the social context within which the women act. The voices of prostituted women from Third World countries may not echo the voices of prostitutes from industrialized countries. Their voices and agendas may be very different.

Perhaps the greatest failure of both arguments is the tendency toward generalization. Kathleen Barry, for example, has done tremendous work in documenting situations of female sexual slavery; but she tries to extend an analysis based on her work to all forms of sexual labor, without including the voices and issues of prostitute groups. And prostitution groups organized in industrialized countries, though they have made great strides in challenging laws and the stigmatization of prostitutes and prostitution, have wrongly generalized their experience to all prostituted women, without taking up the issues of prostituted women working in Third World countries or as migrant women in industrialized countries. Amid the discussion on choice at the Second World Whore's Congress, one voice, a migrant Filipina, spoke about the right to choose not to be a prostitute.[10] Thanh-Dam Truong succinctly articulates, "The broader environment in which prostitution takes place is not uniform. It is necessary to avoid the reduction of prostitution to any single manifestation."[11]

Compare two situations of sexual labor: the courtesans of Lucknow, India, and a Filipina in a *casa* in Manila. The Filipina, whom we shall call Liwayway, was tricked into going to Manila from her province with the promise of good work as a maid. She was placed in a *casa* in Manila, where she was literally kept prisoner and forced to sell her sexual labor to foreign men who came to the Philippines as tourists. She eventually escaped through the help of a customer and began working in a club in Olongapo, also selling her sexual labor.

According to research done by Veena Talwar Olenburg, the courtesans of Lucknow were women who had left their "respectable" world due to various hardships.[12] Their goal was autonomy and financial independence from men. These women, as perceived by Olenburg, were able to create a counterculture and community. The sale of entertainment and sexual labor to men functioned only as the financial base for their community, which was the center of their lives. Their closest emotional ties were among themselves. Some admitted to being lesbian and others chose not to discuss details of their private lives. In summation Olenburg writes:

> That sexuality competes with economics for priority in the struggle against gender inequality is not surprising. That male sexual control and aggression is neutralized in a setting where the heterosexual sex act is mere routine, and passion and pleasure are simulated or distanced, is perhaps, an essential mechanism that women, both wives and prostitutes, have universally used to preserve their emotional integrity and dignity.[13]

Feminists from industrialized countries have often stressed the harmful aspects of separating one's sexuality from one's body. Kathleen Barry comments, "Where there is any attempt to separate the sexual experience from the total person, that first act of objectification is perversion."[14] Taking a very different view, Adul once recounted the political detention, torture, and rape of a woman under the Marcos regime. As a survival technique, the woman learned to distance herself from her body during the repeated rape sessions. Adul commented that this ability to distance oneself was something that perhaps should be taught to women in the Philippines who might be political detainees in the future. And it might also be useful to women selling their sexual labor.

An analytical framework for the sale of sexual labor cannot be developed in a vacuum. The context in which it takes place is of critical importance for how analysis is done. And voices of the women selling their sexual labor must become part of the analyzing. This essay describes the sale of sexual labor in the context of colonial empire expansion and U.S. military, political, and economic presence in the three countries. Although it is based on the women's stories and, hence, their voices, they are not yet participants as theorists and, therefore, the analysis is incomplete. But, given the prevailing silence about women selling their sexual labor outside U.S. bases in Asia, it is a beginning that points, one hopes, in the direction of empowerment.

VD and the U.S. Military

As early as 1902, toward the end of the three-year war between the Philippine Independence Movement and the United States, Governor-General William Howard reported that every military post in the Philippines had "houses of prostitution."[15] At that time, the U.S. military sanctioned and facilitated the existence of brothels, due to the "physical necessities" of the troops, and required weekly VD examinations by American physicians and surgeons of women working in houses of prostitution.[16] This procedure did not result in lowering the disease rate; by 1917 the military reported that 17 out of every 100 soldiers in the Philippines had venereal disease.

Within the United States, a similar procedure was followed. Among U.S. troops involved in the border war of 1916 with Mexico, about 30 percent or 288 out of 1,000 troops were infected. Again, it was military medical officers who inspected brothel women every two weeks and issued each a certificate validating the lack of disease.[17] With World War I and the need for combat-ready troops, physicians within the military found that their primary focus was not treating the injured but keeping men fit for action through control of venereal disease. A number of military officers attempted to aid in this effort by sponsoring houses of prostitution for their men.[18]

The situation was deemed critical, and policing of women selling their sexual labor was extended to the civilian sector. By March 1918, thirty-two states had passed laws requiring compulsory examinations of all women employed in this labor market. In practice, authorities sought to detain each infected woman until she tested negative. Legislation was also passed to place young women and girls convicted of prostitution in detention centers.[19]

A notable antifemale rhetoric accompanied these official military and civilian efforts. It was the woman selling her sexual labor who was accused of "draining the virility" of the men. In an age when Darwinism ran high, the women were not infrequently portrayed as being genetically feebleminded or tainted in some way. Although the women selling their sexual labor near military installations in the United States were often ill-educated migrants from rural areas, the guys were clearly the ones who had to be protected, the ones to benefit from "draining the red-light district as one would drain a swamp." Definitely there were "good girls" and there were "bad girls." "Bad and diseased women can do more harm than any German fleet of airplanes" was a popular slogan.[20]

"Draining the swamps" would continue to be a tactic up through the end of World War II. Speaking before the House Committee on Military Affairs in March 1941, Chaplain William R. Arnold, chief of chaplains, United States Army, intoned:

"The uninstructed, the weak, and the struggling should be protected from the propinquity of alluring temptation. The vicious should be restrained and disciplined. The chaplains of the Army pray and labor to develop spiritual stamina in their men, and they ask you to club the snouts of the ravening wolves at the gates of our camps and posts."[21]

These images may appear extreme, but they reflect the growing antifemale hysteria focused on prostituted women. These were extended to include "victory girls," "good-time Charlottes," and the "girl next door" during World War II. These non-prostituted women were increasingly pictured as seducers and spreaders of disease. No guy was safe from them—until the development of penicillin in 1943, that is.

The military began widely using penicillin in 1944. If the guys could not "say no," then they were instructed to take a prophylactic. Pro-kit stations were virtually everywhere, and condoms were distributed en masse; approximately fifty million condoms were sold or distributed free during each month of the war.[22] One military study reports that during the course of the war, some 80 percent of unmarried and about 50 percent of the married men engaged in sexual intercourse.

The U.S. Military in Asia: Post World War II

Since the end of World War II, the U.S. military has been involved in two large-scale wars in Asia. The need for "rest-and-recreation" (R&R) facilities has been and continues to be a major component of civilian and military policy formulated to ensure that support systems are in place for U.S. military personnel on duty outside the United States. Access to indigenous women's bodies has been recognized as a necessity. No longer is there disagreement between, on the one hand, those in the military and their civilian supporters who advocated and put into place R&R facilities and, on the other hand, those who cautioned against such practices or advised that they be located a reasonable distance from military bases.

It is important to note the paucity of information on the topic of the sale of women's sexual labor for either the Korean or Vietnam War periods. One looks in vain for a monograph or even a chapter in a book, scholarly or journalistic.[23] This is true for sources in English, Vietnamese, and Korean. Those interested in this topic have begun to search out literature that may contain situations in which a woman is selling her sexual labor. Comprehensive oral histories have not been collected; and the photographic record is no more helpful. Virtually identical photographs of women, on the streets or in the clubs wearing bikinis, have been taken again and again during the course of some forty years; and we know no more than we did after viewing the first such photo.[24]

There are hundreds of works focusing on the devastating course of these wars and their impact on the lands, the peoples, and the fabric of society of those involved. But it is amazing that so little is known about the lives of the millions of prostituted women in these two countries. Nor is there any study of the nearby countries of the Philippines, Thailand, Taiwan, and Okinawa and Japan, which experienced a tremendous growth in the sale of women's sexual labor during these years.

We can ferret out some details and recall others from memory in order to describe some aspects of the nature of this work during that time. As we have stated, by 1944, the U.S. military no longer considered syphilis and gonorrhea deadly diseases. They did continue the policy of providing pro-kits, condoms, and educational warnings against the prostituted women that would necessitate the use of these items. This policy continues into the present. So, too, does the policy of U.S. military direction in policing, examining, treating, and certifying the women providing sexual labor to U.S. troops.

In both the southern part of Korea and the southern part of Vietnam, there were great numbers of women selling their sexual labor. U.S. bombing left nothing over one story standing in the northern part of Korea, and the ground war itself produced great numbers of dead and a massive dislocation of population and refugees. A similar situation existed in Vietnam. There, coupled with the ground war, the U.S. bombing policy was designed to create instant urbanization, and thereby control. It did work on the level of urbanization: village people fled the air-borne reign of death, and the population of the cities swelled.[25] Ten million people out of a total of eighteen million became refugees during the years 1965 through 1973.[26]

During the wars, both Korea and Vietnam became highly militarized societies. The vast majority of indigenous men were fighting or actively supporting those fighting, the economies were geared to war, and a large presence of American troops was constant. Refugee women seeking to provide for younger siblings, dependent children, older relatives, and themselves took what work they could. In 1975, when the U.S. military left Vietnam, there were an estimated 500,000 women selling their sexual labor in the southern part of the country.[27] We do not have comparable figures at armistice in 1953 for the southern part of Korea.

The manner in which sexual labor was sold varied. At one end of the continuum, there was the woman who worked as the "wife" of a guy while he was in town or in country; she was called a "key woman," because the guy had a key to her place. The time span for this arrangement could vary from a week to a year, the latter being the period of a tour of duty. This situation had advantages for both the woman and the man, but it was unstable. Problems were those of consistent payment of rent and other monies to maintain the woman, violence, abuse, alcohol and other drug use, needs of the woman's family, questions of pregnancy and abortion, the man's being a "butterfly."[28] For the woman, being a "key woman" was better than working in the bars or a brothel; but her position was so precarious that a rupture in the arrangement meant that she would be back on the street or in the bars. This kind of arrangement, with its attendant difficulties, continues today in Tong Du Chun and in Olongapo.

These "key women" were few in number compared to those who worked in the approved/legal bars and brothels. A greater number worked on the streets and in off-limits areas. In order for a bar or brothel to be approved and licensed to provide entertainment and sex for U.S. military personnel, the women working there had to undergo periodic medical exams for VD, and, if found positive, undergo treatment. Bars and brothels not approved and licensed, or those with too many women testing positive, were off-limits. In Vietnam, there was a sign inside many of the bars saying that women who wore a certain badge were "clean" and thus could be purchased for their sexual labor.[29]

Vietnam also had "recreational areas." At Lai Khe, there was a one-acre compound surrounded by barbed wire with American MPs on guard at the gate. For security reasons, it was open only during daylight hours. There were two barracks inside. Each had two bars, a bandstand, and sixty curtained cubicles in which Vietnamese women lived and worked. Many of these women were refugees; others had previously worked in Saigon. They were recruited by the province chief who took a payoff and channeled them into town where the mayor of Lai Khe also got a cut. The Americans "kept their hands clean" by leaving the procurement and price arrangement to Vietnamese. The Americans, however, regulated the health and security aspects. Army medics checked the women once a week for VD.[30]

In areas not necessitating such control, both in Korea and Vietnam, signs outside authorized bars and brothels indicated which were approved. U.S. Military Police patrolled the areas, tried to keep the peace in the approved facilities, and checked to see that no personnel were using the labor of women in bars that were off-limits.

A similar system existed in Okinawa from the beginning of the U.S. military occupation through the period of the Vietnam War. Although during the Korean War the U.S. Air Force based squadrons on Okinawa that flew bombing missions over the territory of the northern part of Korea, it was during the Vietnam War that the Okinawan R&R industry experienced its greatest growth. B-52 squadrons, based at Kadena Air Base, bombed the northern part of Vietnam; and Army and Marines from Vietnam took R&R on Okinawa. The U.S. military used the "A" sign for "approved" to indicate which bars and brothels were legal. More than 1,200 carried this "A," and the Legal Affairs Bureau of the Government of the Ryukyus reported in 1969 that there were 7,362 full-time registered prostitutes working. Actually, the total number of women selling their sexual labor was about twice that.[31]

Yakuza, or gangs related to *yakuza*, controlled the sale of Okinawan women's sexual labor during this period. Control was exercised primarily through physical and psychological terror and intimidation. Once the women had been placed in a brothel, the brothel owner exercised another form of direct control over them through the "advance loan system." Under this system, the owner paid the gangs a certain amount of money for the woman. This purchase amount became the woman's debt, to be worked off through sale of her sexual labor. One women who worked in Kin, the base area of our study, describes her situation during the Vietnam period:

"Most customers are soldiers from the base. Within a year I became quite ill [perhaps a case of VD] and had to stay in bed for a whole month. As my advance loan grew, and as I was afraid of taking soldiers who had returned from Vietnam, I moved from one place to another. Finally I arrived at this place, Kin, seven years ago. I don't know how it worked, but my advance loan never diminished, even though I had twenty to thirty customers a night. Instead, the sum increased, because an additional $5 or $10 was added as a fine whenever I had my period or was pregnant and couldn't take any customers . . ."[32]

Although it is clearly U.S. policy to have women's bodies free of disease and available for men in the military, it is the economic, political, and social realities of the host country that determine how access to women's sexual labor is to be accomplished. If the host country is sufficiently disrupted by war and/or economically impoverished, there are women who will become prostituted. We have seen how this was the situation in Korea, Vietnam, and Okinawa during specific time periods. If local women are not available, or not available in sufficient numbers, or if the country is economically powerful and the women therefore too expensive, the occupying military must provide its own women. The French military in Vietnam had mobile brothel units of Algerian women. By the time the Americans replaced the French, the country was disrupted by war to the extent that sufficient numbers of Vietnamese women were available.[33] In present-day Okinawa, Okinawan women are too expensive. Thus, women from the Philippines are brought to Okinawa to provide sexual labor for U.S. troops. Okinawan male leadership defends this commodity importation on the political and moral grounds that the U.S. military demands women for sexual labor. If Filipinas did not provide it, the military guys would use and threaten "respectable" women of Okinawa. The Filipinas provide a barrier that ensures the safety and well-being of Okinawan society.[34]

The U.S. Military in Asia Today

Today, in both Korea and the Philippines, the Social Hygiene Clinic (SHC) system is used to try to ensure "clean" women for U.S. servicemen.[35] All bar areas outside a U.S. base have a SHC. All women selling their sexual labor in those areas must be part of the SHC system, with identification to prove their legitimacy and therefore "cleanliness." Women who do not have such an ID are subject to arrest. Bars, brothels, and massage parlors that do not require their women to have these IDs are declared off-limits by the U.S. military and consequently will have no business. The SHC is the avenue for doing business.

In both countries, the woman is given a medical check-up before receiving her ID passbook. Afterward, she is tested—once a week in Korea and every other week in the Philippines—for VD, gonorrhea, and syphilis. In Korea, if she tests positive, she is quarantined in the hospital until she is "clean." In the Philippines, she is given medicine and prohibited from going on bar fines until she is "clean." In addition, the women are required to have a chest X-ray and blood test every six months and an AIDS blood test every three months in Korea and every six months in the Philippines. If a women tests HIV positive in the Philippines, she is given virtually no information about what that may mean.[36] According to the SHC, she is prohibited from going on bar fines. However, the economics of the woman's situation dictate that she does continue to go on bar fines.[37] In Korea, at this point, there is no information available on what happens to the women.

The U.S. "keeps its hands clean" to a greater or lesser extent in both countries. In Korea, the SHC receives no funding or assistance from the U.S., but the U.S. military does participate in spot checks of women's VD identification cards and conducts sanitary inspections of the bars.[38] In the Philippines, the SHC is a joint project of the U.S. Navy and the Olongapo City government. In both countries, local women who are with American military men may be stopped on the street and asked to show an identification passbook and/or a night-off pass.[39] Failure to show these forms of identification may mean time in prison for the woman.

This system of control is made possible only through a cooperative working relationship between the U.S. military and the local government and bar owners, who are members of an almost exclusively local male elite.[40] It is they who benefit—

financially and politically—from the control and regulation of the prostitution industry. Through regulation of disease, local authorities are also able to ensure that the women will have a difficult time operating independently of the bar or brothel system. Within bar and brothel systems, the owners earn more money from the sale of the women's sexual labor than do the women themselves.

In contemporary Okinawa, as in Japan, the *yakuza* continue to control the bar system, with the cooperation of Okinawan bar owners and Philippine immigration officials. The promotion agencies are the "legal" means through which recruitment, training, and employment of women is carried out. The U.S. military appears to have less involvement with the bar system here. Because the women are working outside of their own country, they are completely dependent on the promotion agency. They do not know the language and do not know their way around outside of the immediate bar area. They either live above or behind the club, often locked in their rooms at night, or they are ferried to and from their rooms in vans operated by the bar owners.[41]

Because the women are in Okinawa as legal contract workers, a veneer of legitimacy must be maintained by the bar owners and promotion agencies, although everyone knows what the reality is. As Janet says in her story, "The promotion agency says that going out with Americans is not part of our work, but it really is." The most popular clubs are the ones where women dance completely nude, as opposed to topless, and where virtually any form of sexual labor can be purchased right inside the club. Women who happen to be assigned to these clubs by their promotion agency may rarely leave the club. All clubs receive warnings prior to "surprise" visits by immigration officials to ensure the bars are conforming to regulations. On those nights bars either conform or close down.

Prostitution around U.S. military installations in Asia has been effectively legalized regardless of the laws within each country. Like legalization elsewhere, it has enabled a high degree of regulation and control of the sale of women's sexual labor and of control over the distribution of profits from that sale.[42] For a woman to be legal, she must be licensed and therefore part of the system and subject to its stipulations about where and how she works and who benefits from her work. Women who are not licensed are illegal and therefore at risk. A women who is not licensed may be put in prison or forced to pay fines, bribes, or to provide sexual labor to local policemen.

Such extensive control of prostituted women has clear political benefits. Manipulation of this large percentage of the population becomes relatively easy. During the elections of 1986 in the Philippines, women employed in the clubs of Olongapo were required to report to work on election day and were kept at work until they voted. Trucks ferried the women from the bars to the voting place and back again. They were informed that retention of their jobs depended upon voting for Marcos. Prior to the elections, pro-Marcos and pro-Aquino parades periodically drove through the bar area. One woman lost her job for showing the pro-Aquino hand sign to a parade as it went by.

This high level of control also perpetuates the isolation of prostituted women from the rest of society. It depends on and maintains the polarization of women and the silence with respect to the sale of sexual labor outside U.S. military bases. Women in Okinawa are told not to talk to journalists or anyone of that type.[43] Although threats of violence are not specifically articulated, it is clear that the women are frightened. Women in the Philippines could lose their jobs for any indication of rebellion or refusal to comply with bar regulations. They might also lose their jobs for participating in any event that appears to be even remotely antibases, or for associating with someone known to be antibases or feminist.[44]

AIDS and the U.S. Military

Nowhere is the isolation, polarization, and silence more clearly seen than on the issue of AIDS. The assumption of the U.S. authorities and the guys is that women selling their sexual labor around U.S. military bases are the source of the disease, that they are the ones who are spreading it. Aboard ship in the briefing that the guys get before liberty, they are warned by their officers: "There's AIDS out there. If you're going to dip your wick, take precautions."

AIDS is indeed out there. But the women are not the source of the disease. They didn't have AIDS before. Who brought AIDS to them? Who are the carriers?

In Korea, the number of known cases of HIV and/or AIDS is reportedly under twenty, about half of which are among women who sell their sexual labor to U.S. military personnel. In Okinawa, there are no known cases of HIV or AIDS among the Filipinas; but there is no testing of the Filipinas before they go to Okinawa, while they are there, or on their return to the Philippines. Ostensibly their work in Okinawa is not the selling of sexual labor, so there is no monitoring.[45]

In the Philippines the U.S. Naval Medical Research Unit Two and the Philippine Ministry of Health began testing registered women in late 1985 and early 1986. In the tourist areas of Manila, Baguio, Davao, Cebu City, Iloilo, Bacolod, and Zamboanga, these tests failed to show any HIV positive cases.[46]

A number of women selling their sexual labor in the bar areas of Olongapo and Angeles City, the town outside Clark Air Force Base, tested positive for HIV. In Olongapo there were six. The SHC performs blood tests on the registered women every six months. The woman pays for the test herself. By late 1988, some fifty women had tested positive.[47]

This is certainly a conservative figure. Due to multiple exposures, lack of medical care, and general socioeconomic deprivation, the problem of measuring the spread of the disease is considerable. A number of bars also contract with moonlighting Navy medical personnel to provide in-housing testing. And there are perhaps as many unregistered women working on the streets as registered women working in the bars.

It would appear from the Philippine experience in the Olongapo-Angeles strip that the military men were the source of the HIV found among the women. Many

Filipinos argue that the fact that the U.S. Navy sponsored this study, the first of its kind in Southeast Asia, was tacit admission of the Navy's guilt.[48] In late 1986, responding to pressure from the women's movement and health organizations, the Philippine Ministry of Health asked General Fidel Ramos, a friend to and beneficiary of the presence of the U.S. military, to obtain a guarantee that all U.S. service personnel coming into the Philippines be tested for HIV.[49]

The military's policy, put in place late in the Reagan administration and perhaps partially in response to the efforts of General Ramos and others in Asia, is to test everyone posted to duty outside the U.S. Those already abroad when this policy began were also to be tested. If anyone tests HIV positive while on duty outside the U.S., he is to be evacuated immediately to the U.S.

Military personnel report that this policy is in place. The guys report that testing is done after each liberty, and that those who test HIV positive have indeed been evacuated.[50] However, the question arises—given HIV's latency period of several months to several years—how effective could any testing procedure now in place be? An average of ten U.S. Navy ships a month dock at Subic, home port of the Seventh Fleet. One typical porting pattern is to put in at Subic on the way to or from East Africa to Honolulu, San Francisco, or San Diego. The guys routinely get liberty at Mombasa, a port serving both the British and American navies. Some 40 percent of the women selling their sexual labor in Mombasa are reportedly HIV positive. After liberty at Mombasa, the guys return to their ship and are tested for HIV.[51]

Among the guys, the level of denial is high. There is the commonly seen poster: "ATTENTION: Due To A Recent Epidemic [of] AIDS Ass Kissing Is Temporarily Prohibited." On a more personal level, guys will liken AIDS to ". . . some disease . . . come out of the air conditioner . . . or something . . . it's here, then it's gone . . . AIDS is like that . . ."[52] Others will say that it's an old disease; it's just that they've given it a new name.

Lack of reliable information accompanies this high level of denial. The fact is that the military is not doing a good job of educating its troops to the reality of contracting HIV and developing AIDS. Basically, the guys are told to use condoms, and that's it. But there's great resistance to using condoms. On the strip, a guy will take them, blow them up, and wiggle them on either side of his head and say he is a rabbit. This type of behavior may begin to change as the reality of AIDS becomes clear.

AIDS testing by the U.S. military in the Philippines has followed the pattern of disease control in attempting to protect U.S. personnel, but it has also attracted local attention.[53] In Olongapo ten women working in clubs gathered together and drafted an AIDS petition demanding that, because AIDS was clearly brought to the Philippines by U.S. military personnel, the men also be required to carry ID passbooks showing that they are free of the disease, and that the U.S. take financial responsibility for the health care of women who test HIV positive and their children.[54] These women gathered 600 signatures of their coworkers in the clubs. Women's groups, health groups, and church groups in Olongapo, Manila, and Angeles circulated petitions that expressed support for their petition.[55]

In Olongapo, AIDS testing began in January 1986. In February 1986, Ferdinand Marcos was taken out of the country by U.S. aircraft and Corazon Aquino became president. One of the first actions taken by Ms. Aquino was to replace Marcos supporters in local government offices with her own supporters until local elections could be held. President Aquino replaced the Olongapo mayor, Richard Gordon, a staunch Marcos loyalist at the time, with a strong Aquino supporter, Mr. Macapagal. Mayor Macapagal quickly began AIDS education programs, and large signs went up all over Olongapo about AIDS. AIDS was also very much in the national press, often with allegations that the U.S. military was bringing AIDS to the Philippines. This focus on AIDS was partly a result of Gabriela efforts to bring the issue into public awareness. But it was bad press for the U.S. bases, and the base negotiations were not too far away. Everything changed with local elections the following year. Gordon won the elections, although there were allegations of massive cheating on both sides. Within months of Gordon's administration's returning to power, the AIDS signs disappeared and little was heard about education. Silence was again installed in Olongapo.

That silence may be increasingly deadly, especially when one recalls the recent history of venereal diseases. We have already briefly discussed the increase in the incidence among U.S. military men of VD, which accompanied acquisition of territory and colonies—an increase that reflected the difficulty of maintaining forces on foreign soil as well as better diagnostics.[56] In this respect, the U.S. experience mirrored that of the Europeans, for whom the spread of venereal diseases was a direct result of marshaling of great armies to secure formal and informal acquisition and control of markets and colonies. Fueled by capitalist industrialization, the British, French and Germans succeeded during the nineteenth century in establishing varying degrees of control over much of Asia, Africa, and the Americas. Among troops stationed abroad, the venereal disease rate mushroomed.

It was reported to have been on the rise among British troops since at least 1823.[57] During the Crimean War (1854–56) the British Army suffered more casualties to venereal disease than they did on the battlefield.[58] In India the military moved to control prostitution in the colony's 110 military areas. The focus was on the presumed source of the problem: indigenous women selling their sexual labor to the troops. The women were to be regulated and controlled through a system of inspection.

Although these actions were justified due to the strategic needs of the British Empire, the measures did little to alleviate the problem within the ranks in India or elsewhere.[59] By 1864, one out of every three illnesses in the British Army were venereal in origin, and admissions to hospitals for gonorrhea and syphilis reached 290.7 per 1,000 of total troop strength.[60]

As British troops came home, the incidence of venereal disease rose among the women selling their sexual labor around domestic military posts and naval dock-yards. And it would spread to women not in this labor market. So pervasive were gonorrhea and syphilis during the nineteenth century that the International Medical Congress meeting in Paris in 1867 had declared venereal diseases the "new cholera" of the century.[61] This cholera image was apt, especially given the prognosis of syphilis, for it's ravages upon the human body are not dissimilar to those of today's AIDS.

Regulations enacted at home were similar to those implemented by the military abroad, as political leaders, such as Lord Acton, and influential medical sources, such as the *Lancet*, agitated for regulatory legislation. The Contagious Disease Acts of 1864, 1866, and 1874 followed.[62] At first these acts were seen as exceptional legislation to control the spread of venereal disease among enlisted men and targeted specific military areas in England and Ireland. The War Office and the Admiralty administered the acts, with army and navy surgeons performing the examinations of the women identified as diseased prostitutes. If a woman was found to have a venereal disease, she could be detained in the local general hospital for up to three months.[63] Increasingly, the state used the acts to police the working-class areas where the women lived and worked, areas where labor organizing was on the rise.

If VD was the cholera of the nineteenth century, AIDS may be the cholera of the twentieth century. In the contemporary era of AIDS, mobility of the U.S. military is far greater than that of previous armies. When we see the demands made upon the U.S. military today to guarantee the functioning of a global capitalist economy, it is clearly a situation that elicits grave concern. As things now stand, AIDS will continue to spread among indigenous women selling their sexual labor to U.S. military personnel; and, increasingly, the impact will also be visited upon women in the U.S. and elsewhere, both in and out of this labor market.[64]

The Women and the Economy of the Bar Areas

The sale of women's sexual labor is at the base of the complex economy surrounding the bar areas around the bases. The bar and brothel owners gain financially from the sale of liquor and food and, of course, from the women's sexual labor. The grocery, liquor, and Mom-and-Pop stores in the area are also dependent on the bar traffic. Restaurants, short-order takeout places, ice-cream parlors, T-shirt and hat shops, and pool halls also abound. Clothing stores and shoe stores that cater to the women, who must dress up for work to attract the guys, are plentiful. So, too, are tailor shops where the guys can get beautiful silk, leather, or polyester clothes designed and sewn expertly for extremely reasonable rates. There are always a number of music shops with the latest tapes and low prices on Japanese and Korean stereo components, photo shops with good deals on cameras and lenses, and shops selling designer sunglasses and prescription lenses. And there are the ubiquitous vending machines, video parlors, drugstores, and venereal-disease counseling businesses.

The sale of women's sexual labor also supports the local economy through rent to landlords; wages to women laundering clothes and sheets and washing and ironing the GIs' uniforms, undergarments, and socks; and income to local men who provide security in the hotels and clubs or work as waiters in restaurants. Local men also shine and repair shoes, watches, cameras, umbrellas, and handbags. There are the barber shops, usually old-fashioned-looking, where a shave and a back and neck massage are cheap. And in Olongapo there are the ever-present street vendors— older women, older men, Aetas, and children—selling single sticks of chewing gum or one cigarette; English-language newspapers; fried peanuts, bananas, and peas.[65]

In short, the whole economy is based upon the sale of women's sexual labor. Business establishments in the bar areas cater to the needs of the women selling their sexual labor and to the guys purchasing the same. The goal is to make the guys feel comfortable, to get them to consume. On weekends, or when a unit returns from two to four weeks of field training, or when Team Spirit forces are in country, or when a carrier is in port, the atmosphere is one of a street carnival. The photos of Mardi Gras show the extent to which this can go (see p. 54).

Owners of various establishments stand to make a considerable amount of money. Local and national governments gain through taxes applied to liquor sales, hotels, and various consumables. A number of foreign corporations, especially American, gain directly through sale of their products or through franchises: Wendy's, Straw Hat Pizza, Dunkin' Donuts, Shakey's Pizza, Mister Donut, Wimpy's, Coca-Cola, Pepsi, and Budweiser beer seem to be everywhere. In addition, United States Aid for International Development (USAID) has funded a number of business establishments. In the Philippines, for example, the large Olongapo City Market was built with USAID money.

The sale of women's sexual labor has historically been at the base of economic systems of considerable proportions, though seldom to the benefit of the women themselves.[66] This pattern continues today around the military bases in the three countries of our study, as well as in the areas of tourist prostitution that have become big business for the governments, elites, and businesspeople of the Philippines, Thailand, and Korea.

The tourist playgrounds and U.S. military base towns have considerable similarities, because the R&R centers developed by the U.S. military during the Vietnam War became the model for the development of the tourist prostitution industry in Asia.[67] Some of the more famous tourist playgrounds are found in Manila, Chejudo, and Bangkok. The power relationship between industrialized countries and the Third World is integral to the sale of sexual labor in tourist areas and in base towns. Essentially, the rich buy and the poor sell. Those who play in the R&R playgrounds, whether tourist or military, are primarily men from Northern Europe, North America, Australia and Japan; those who work in the playgrounds are Third World women and children.[68] The primary economic exchange is the sale of sexual labor, and the system ensures that the women receive a meager portion of the money earned in the business. Power lies in the hands of those doing the purchasing and those running the business. If either is not satisfied, the women are easily discarded because poverty guarantees a steady supply of young women.

But playgrounds are only one arena in which Third World women's sexual labor is the primary economic exchange. The international exchange of Third World women as prostitutes, domestic servants, and wives is another aspect of the power relationship between industrialized countries and the Third World. Women who work overseas as domestic servants often find that they are required, with or without their consent, to provide sexual labor to their bosses on a regular basis. They are raped. The mail-order bride system provides women for men from industrialized countries who cannot find or do not want women from their own country. These men are purchasing both sexual and domestic labor. Both the mail-order bride business and recruitment for overseas employment are sometimes used to trap women into selling their sexual labor in other countries.[69]

When discussing potential marriage to an American, women in Olongapo often comment, "What he wants is a maid." This is not without a material base. A Navy guy will often pay a woman's steady bar fine while his ship is in Olongapo, usually for about five days. During that time he stays with her. She provides both sexual labor and the labor of a domestic servant—doing his laundry, cooking for him, and bathing him.

The Women: Maintaining the Distance—Image and Complexity

Bathing is an instructive example of a complex situation. Although it is done in a way that makes the men feel they are being served and cared for, bathing is a precaution taken by the woman to make sure that the men are clean and to get rid of offensive odors. Bathing is one small aspect of the lives of the women whose sexual labor is being purchased, but it exemplifies how different something appears when seen from the perspective of the women. Their lives, however, have rarely been spoken about or photographed with much depth or sensitivity. It is almost as if a shroud of silence has hovered over them in Vietnam, the Philippines, Korea, Thailand, Taiwan, Okinawa, and in Japan. The silence exists both because prostituted women in the Third World are not considered important enough to take note of and because the U.S. does not want publicity about the GIs' off-duty hours.

When the silence is broken and journalists, academics, and others write about this topic, two dominant and seemingly disparate images come into play. Photographs or cartoons depict a woman in the bikini worn by ago-go dancers. She is striking a seductive pose and has very large breasts.[70] She appears to be enjoying herself immensely—the happy hooker. She is often shown happily chasing U.S. servicemen or waiting for them at the gate to the base. The contrasting image is that of the victim—the woman so desperately poor that she has no other alternative but to sell her sexual labor. Depending on the political slant of the article, she is either the symbol of imperialist oppression or she is being helped by the presence of the base through the job or money provided; if the base were not there, she would starve.

Both images perpetuate stereotypes and treat these women and their lives superficially. The images of the ago-go dancer who appears to be having a good time reflects a judgment: she is enjoying her work and is, therefore, morally reprehensible—just as "we" believed all along. Or if not morally reprehensible, she is politically hopeless because she is bound to be pro-bases as a result of her work. The image fails to recognize or convey the nature of the work. A woman must appear happy, lively, and seductive to attract and keep customers. It is part of her work, and it must look authentic. A repeatedly used phrase in Olongapo is "I'm laughing on the outside and crying on the inside." As in most stereotypes, however, there is also a grain of truth. There are times when the woman is genuinely having fun. Oppressed or exploited people do usually find ways to laugh.

As a victim, the woman is absolved of her "crime" in the eyes of some, at least intellectually. But she will still carry the stigma of being or having been a prostituted woman. Whether she is ostracized or adored as a victim, she will be distanced—still the Other, and still powerless, with little control over her own life. To gain legitimacy through this image, the woman certainly must not be perceived as enjoying her work. The grain of truth in the victim image is that poverty, violence, and discrimination against women are all part of the woman's journey—before coming to the club, while working in the club, and after she is no longer there. Although poverty is not the cause, it is one of the roots.

The simplistic and superficial treatment of prostituted women constantly communicated to the public through the use of the ago-go and victim images is a continuation of the historical misogynist gaze that reduces all prostituted women to one stereotypical woman, thus doing injustice to the variety and complexity of the women's lives.

One aspect of the complexity of their lives is age. Women working in the clubs range from as young as thirteen to as old as fifty. A young woman of thirteen or fourteen, like Lita, will behave rather differently and have different responsibilities and fewer life experiences than a woman of forty-five or thirty-five, like Linda, who comes to the bars having been married and with five children. Lita is a teenager and, during part of her time in Olongapo, behaves like a teenager, choosing to spend her money rather irresponsibly to have a good time. Linda is less interested in a good time as she has five children to feed and put through school. One of her main concerns is that her children, who are old enough to figure things out, will find out what her work is.

The women also cope with the bar culture in very different ways. These reflect differences in age, time spent in the bars, and personality. Victim imagery presents a saintly woman doing her best to survive. Happy-hooker imagery presents an evil woman who will do anything for money and enjoy it. Neither saintly nor evil, the women choose vastly different methods of survival. Linda's friend Marlyn, for example, chooses to take advantage of opportunities to steal money from customers. Linda, however, is uncomfortable with the idea of theft.

The judgment of the women as hopelessly pro-bases that is implicit in the ago-go dancer image is also unjustly simplistic. This image is usually bolstered by accounts of pro-bases demonstrations in Olongapo or Angeles, where women from the bars participate in large numbers. In fact, in Olongapo, women will be fined a substantial sum by the bar owners if they don't participate. The fine will be deducted from their commission before it is given to them. In more extreme cases, women have lost their jobs for refusing to participate. It may be true that a majority of women in the clubs favor the retention of U.S. bases, but digging deeper one again sees complexity. The same women who favor retention of the bases also prefer not to be working in clubs. They would like other work. If the question is changed from "Do you want the U.S. bases to stay?" to "If you were able to have other work after the U.S. bases left, would you want them to stay?" The result might be very different responses.

Most women from the clubs realize that with a low educational level, finding other work in the Philippines or Korea is very problematical. Not only are jobs scarce but the stigma of having worked in a club also makes it difficult to find other work. In Korea, the stigma is greater for those who have U.S. military personnel as customers. The existence of children also intensifies the difficulty of leaving the work. A child fathered by a U.S. serviceman is living evidence of what a woman's work is or has been. Amerasian children present more difficulties in the very homogeneous culture of Korea than in the Philippines with its variety of peoples and languages. It has been common in Korea to put these children up for adoption. In the Philippines, if the child is Euro-American, acceptance is greater than if the child is African-American. Being lighter skinned in the Philippines is an indication of belonging to a higher class and/or being closely associated with the colonial power.

The hopelessly pro-bases image also overlooks the significance of education in the political development of an individual. The women in the clubs generally have not had the opportunity for education and information about the bases, the political and economic situation in the country, and feminism, to mention a few areas. Most of their information comes from their customers or bar owners who have particular viewpoints and analyses. It is only with organizing efforts growing in these countries that small numbers of women in the clubs are receiving information and education that counters what their customers and bar owners say. The AIDS petition written by women in Olongapo exemplifies the way in which women are enabled to act when they have access to information and support.

A primary function that such images as victim, ago-go dancer, and diseased—to add one more—serve is that of creating and maintaining distance. Whether she is morally reprehensible, politically hopeless, a victim of poverty, or diseased, she is Other. She is in a different class, the class of women required by the U.S. military for the morale of its boys. Such distance is important for the continuation of the bar areas and control over the women. Maintaining the distance is the reason that those in power do not want the silence broken or the images changed. They do not want anyone educating the public about the bar areas and they do not want anyone educating the women in the bars. The women must be kept in an isolated enclave. Thus, the red-baiting of centers that work with the women and harassment of organizers.[71]

The ago-go–dancer image passes judgment on the women. They will therefore be left to their own devices. Distance is maintained. The victim image may provoke a social-work type of response which will take a few women out of the clubs but will not challenge the structure significantly. Distance is maintained. And there are plenty of fresh young women available to take the place of those removed by social workers. But if the empowerment process begins, if the women become educated and begin organizing, they may soon threaten the power structures.[72] And if the distance is overcome, if other women are in solidarity with the women in the clubs, a crisis may occur in the power relationships.

The Women: Poverty and Maldevelopment

The southern part of Korea is a popular example of a newly industrialized country (NIC); the Philippines is well known as a poverty-stricken country. Yet, the women's stories have certain parallel themes: origin in an agricultural region, rural-to-urban migration, and anti-female violence and discrimination. The connection between poverty and the sale of sexual labor is clear but simplistic. The context is actually a much broader web of connections and international relationships.

Colonialism and neocolonialism—empire expansion and maintenance—have directly or indirectly created massive agricultural dislocation and environmental destruction in Korea and the Philippines. The consequent poverty and rural-to-urban migration provide a large urban labor pool for factories, the service sector, and the sale of sexual labor.

The relationship is not geographically or historically unique. Nineteenth-century Europe experienced a great increase in the sale of women's sexual labor, in the metropolitan areas and around military outposts. Consolidation of land holdings and changes in land use brought by industrialization and colonization forced large numbers of people off the land. Women migrating from the rural areas found work in the cities in the service sector or in factories.[73] A good number of them ended up selling their sexual labor.[74] Development often turns out to be maldevelopment for women from agricultural regions, be they nineteenth-century Europeans or Third World women in the last half of the twentieth century.

The rate of rural-to-urban migration in the southern part of Korea is the highest in the world.[75] Those who have not migrated to urban areas have gone deeper and deeper into debt.[76] One of the culprits in the erosion of Korean agriculture—

necessary, however, to empire expansion and maintenance—is the U.S. dumping of agricultural surpluses in the Third World and the U.S. demand of import liberalization as quid pro quo for continued access to the U.S. market for NIC-manufactured exports.[77]

Nan Hee is a woman who spent several years working in factories in Korea before selling her sexual labor. She finds the work difficult with very long hours and the wages extremely low. She is one component of what Korea's rapid industrialization was built on: long working hours, cheap labor, an efficient system of production, and minimal investment in safe working conditions.[78] Factories hire unmarried women between the ages of sixteen and twenty-five with at least a middle-school education because they are more disciplined and cheaper than men by about 50 percent.[79] When a woman marries and/or becomes pregnant, she is dismissed. The government–big business slogan for rapid industrialization has been: "Growth first, distribution later."[80] The distribution has not come for Nan Hee and other women.

During the first three years of the Aquino presidency (1986–89), the Philippine GNP grew, and government economic planners forecast that the economy was on its way to catching up to Taiwan and the southern part of Korea as a newly industrialized country. But in 1988, 70 percent of Filipinos were still reported living in absolute poverty.[81] As in Korea, agricultural dislocation has resulted in massive rural-to-urban migration and provided large numbers of young women to work as domestic helpers and/or in the clubs.

Agricultural dislocation in the Philippines is largely due to the export-oriented development policy that came with U.S. colonization.[82] Large U.S. agribusinesses, such as Dole and Del Monte, which developed pineapple and banana plantations in Mindanao, are the latest vehicles for this export-oriented development policy. Massive logging, legal and illegal, and the sugar plantations in Negros are others. The consequences are land grabbing, monopoly control, and incredible environmental destruction leading to further dislocation. When world sugar prices fell dramatically, the ramifications of an export-oriented development policy became international news with images of starvation in Negros that resembled those of East Africa.

Small farmers who have not lost their land are often unable to work it due to Marcos's, and Aquino's, "total war" policy against the revolutionary forces. A revolution has been in process and steadily growing in the Philippines for twenty years. The revolutionary forces are the National Democratic Front (NDF), the Communist Party of the Philippines (CPP), and the New People's Army (NPA), the armed wing of the NDF. The NDF claims to have the support of 20 percent of the nation's barrios with an alternative political infrastructure already in place in some areas.[83] The "total war" against the revolutionary forces has been war against the people with tactics similar to those used in the rural areas of Vietnam.[84] The U.S. gives military aid in the form of weapons, money, and training to the Philippine military in return for the use of Philippine land for U.S. bases. This military aid is used in the militarization of the countryside, creating further dislocation of farmers.

In November 1986, Brenda was able to travel with a woman from Olongapo to her barrio in Samar. Her father had some land but was unable to farm due to a 6:00 P.M. (sundown) curfew in the barrio. Anyone caught in the countryside after 6:00 was considered either NPA or an NPA supporter. In order to farm the land, the family needed to stay out for several days at a time as it was too far to travel back and forth each day during sunlight hours. Consequently, they were not farming the land at all. In this family, the oldest daughter was married with children and the next three daughters were working in the clubs in Olongapo and sending money to the family to put the two younger boys through school.

Samar could be called the "Third World" of the Philippines.[85] Many barrios in Samar have few young women or men left in them. In Lita's barrio virtually all the young women are in Olongapo. All the more substantial houses in the barrio were built from money earned by these young women. Other areas of the country are rapidly becoming more like Samar with environmental destruction of catastrophic proportions. Only an estimated 10 percent of Philippine virgin rain forests remain and only 25 percent of the coral reefs are still alive.

The Women: Work, Duty, Violence

A study on migration in the Philippines found that daughters are more likely to be sent to the city than sons because daughters have traditionally maintained closer ties with the family and are taught to be more responsible, whereas sons are given more freedom and independence.[86] Images come to mind: five-year-old girls cooking and cleaning and five-year-old boys playing, a woman running a sari-sari store and men hanging out on the street drinking, a woman working in a club and sending money home for her brother's education.

The dutiful and responsible daughter is a dominant theme in the women's stories. Ms. Pak raises her younger brothers and one sister, selling her sexual labor in order to put them through school and feed them. Lita sells her virginity to pay off a debt on the land. Madelin sells her virginity to pay for health care for an ill sister. Janet goes to Okinawa to help pay for family expenses and put younger siblings through school. Very often women who sell their sexual labor are doing so as part of their role as dutiful daughter—the responsible one. Young women who are socialized to be responsible for their families have fewer options with respect to the job world than their brothers and receive lower wages. As one woman in Olongapo put it, "For women with little education, what can they do? They can be maids or waitresses. But men, they can be carpenters or drive a jeepney or taxi."

The sale of a woman's virginity is not a small matter. In both the Philippines and Korea, a woman must be a virgin when she marries. Once she has lost her virginity, her hopes for marriage are significantly lowered and she is stigmatized. Rape is one way that a man forces a woman to marry him, as happened with Linda and Ms.

Pak. If a woman goes to the clubs a virgin, the sale of, or the taking of, her virginity is a significant turning point for her. Afterward, there is a sense of inevitability to her being there. This is articulated most clearly in Lita's story. Women sometimes say they want to marry U.S. servicemen because they care less about virginity. Through such marriages, the woman is able to become legitimate again. Many, however, prefer not to marry U.S. servicemen but might nevertheless consider marriage, should the opportunity present itself, as a way to provide a better future for their children.

In industrialized countries, studies abound correlating violence and/or sexual abuse against a woman and her becoming a prostituted woman. Prostitute groups, however, contend that the statistics do not back up the theory. Gail Pheterson comments: "Childhood sexual abuse is not a distinctive feature of prostitute women; it is a common feature of female oppression."[87] Little or no research has been done in the Philippines or Korea on such correlations, but the prevalence of violence against women globally, regardless of race, class, profession, marital status, or sexual orientation is clear. Women experience violence and sexual abuse before and after entering the clubs. Nan Hee, after finally leaving an incredibly abusive husband and living with violent Americans, concludes that men are all alike.

Prostituted women have little recourse when they are raped—and they are raped—because the common mythology is that a prostituted woman cannot be raped. And, the men believe that they paid and therefore are entitled to whatever they want. Many of the women in Olongapo prefer to take their customers home rather than to a hotel because at home, due to the crowded conditions of urban-poor living, there is always someone around to hear and help if he is abusive. In a hotel, there may be no one to come to her assistance. In Korea, women have rooms at the back of the bars, and the coming and going of customers is controlled by *mamasans* and Korean security. Key women or women like Nan Hee who move in with Americans are more at risk.

The women in Olongapo comment that, when drunk, white men are wilder or crazier than black men. Marines, however, regardless of race, are almost unanimously considered the worst. Many women do not want to go on bar fines with a Marine for fear of being abused. When stories of abuse are told, the first question is: "Was he a Marine?" Given the more intense socialization and training of the Marines, it is not surprising to find they are more violent toward women.

The Men: On Duty in Asia—Work and Play

Who are the guys? They are the members of the all-volunteer military, in place since 1973 when the draft was abolished due to domestic opposition to the Vietnam War. They are young—the vast majority ranging in age from seventeen to twenty-five. The young men are typically members of the Rapid Deployment Forces, infantrymen, airborne, or sailors. Their youth also reflects the high turnover rate in the military, with only about 50 percent reenlisting.[88] For many of the men, it is their first time outside of the U.S.; and the journey from enlistment to being stationed in Asia has been a swift one.

To secure its interests in the Pacific, the United States has more than 380,000 military personnel stationed at various bases spanning the area from the American West Coast to the Indian Ocean. In the area of our immediate concern, 43,000 are stationed in the southern part of Korea, 16,000 in the Philippines, and 30,000 on Okinawa. Another 70,000 on 90 ships with 550 aircraft are on duty with the Seventh Fleet.

Almost all the guys are single, in practice if not in fact. Very few are married and, if married, it is extremely rare for the military to allow a man to have his family with him. This is obviously true of Navy personnel at sea. It is also true of the Marines and Army. Of the approximately 43,000 troops stationed in the southern part of Korea, only 2,000 have "command sponsored status" that allows them to bring their families with them on their tour of duty.

The nature of the military bases in the three countries of our study varies. Subic is headquarters of the U.S. Seventh Fleet that patrols the Pacific Ocean from the western coast of the United States to the east coast of Africa. Subic has excellent supply-and-support systems, with three floating dry docks for repair work. Its Filipino work force is highly skilled but is paid the lowest wages of any indigenous work force employed by the American military in the area.

Camp Hansen, the Marine base in Kin, Okinawa, trains Rapid Deployment Forces. These are highly mobile combat units that give the U.S. military the ability to project a presence as needed on the Asian continent, in Southeast Asian island nations, and in the Middle East. In Korea, Tong Du Chun (TDC) is located in a valley, the pass of which forms one of the natural roads from the south to the north. The Army troops stationed there are constantly on the highest state of alert in the U.S. military.

Wherever they are stationed, the guys train constantly. An infantryman in TDC or a Marine at Camp Hansen often spends two to three arduous weeks in the field. In Korea they perform forty-five-mile marches with seventy- to eighty-pound packs up the "stairway to heaven" or hike for ten hours straight over a "grim" mountain range. In Okinawa, they parachute, practice amphibious landings, and sweat it out in the jungle with its high temperature and humidity. They may also go to Olongapo, where the indigenous Aeta people provide intense jungle survival training inside Subic Naval Base.[89] In the Navy, aboard ship, there are drills, weapons training, alerts, and maintenance. It is hard, physical, work. All the guys report that they work harder than they ever did stateside.

When they get time off, it is party time. As the guys partying in Tong Du Chun one night put it:

Boy, what do we do in the field? We go up and down more mountains than the Korean Army does. We bust our balls. That's why when we come back we gotta relax somehow. So we go down range and get drunk. We come down here to release pressure . . . just go to a bar and have a good time and everything . . . you know, we've been in the goddamn field two and a half to three weeks, almost a month, all we've been around is slutie clothes, smellin' like crap. You know, haven't had a shower . . . eating MREs, like eatin' crap, ain't even had a decent meal. So you come down here, drink your OBs, start feelin' good and about like say: Hey, I can go another . . . how many months I got here? Hell yes, I'm drunk all right . . . so is everybody else in goddamn TDC. When we get back from the field we're a bunch of drunken sons-a-bitches . . . face it. [90]

Party time means guys drinking together, talking it out, being one with hard-rock music reamed all the way up. And party time means purchasing the sexual labor of women. The bars, the strip, the brothels, hotels, and women's living space are right outside the gate of each base. So pervasive is this scene wherever the U.S. military is stationed, it is evident that it is the policy of the U.S. government to have it this way.

This arrangement provides the military with complete control over the guys: they are either busting ass while on duty, or drunk and/or in bed with a purchased sexual reward when off. There is little else. The guys do not know the local language; they don't attempt to use language phrase books. In each of the countries they are quite uninformed about the value of local money, except how much it costs to purchase liquor, a pizza, a woman, or a night at a hotel. The use of local transportation is limited. In Olongapo, the guys use tricycle cabs or jeepneys in the immediate area. Rarely will they take a public bus out of the area. In Korea and Okinawa, they do not use the public transportation system, except taxis. And in that event, there are the ubiquitous arguments with drivers over the rates.

Being in another country, another culture, is very threatening to the guys. They are not sophisticated in this regard, and they have been told stories by their peers of guys having been robbed, or beaten up by local males. Chaplains, while taking for granted that guys will have sex, warn of the dangers of "bad" women who are out to seduce them, to get them to marry, and to support them and their families. And they hear military announcements on the armed forces radio stations that speak of terrorists. In Okinawa, a radio commercial with an authoritative male voice-over cautions: "Just take a few easy precautions and deter terrorism, too. Like keeping doors and windows locked, outdoor lights on, emergency numbers by your telephone."[91] Or in the Philippines, with *Twilight Zone* music in the background and another authoritative male voice-over: "Marty and Rick are proud to be Americans, but they don't flaunt who and what they are because to do so might attract those, including terrorists, who are bent on exploiting Americans. This is one reason they try hard not to stand out . . . one reason why they enter the 'inconspicuous zone.'"[92]

The guys know little about the economic, political, social, cultural, or historical realities of the host country. They don't comprehend the antiwar demonstrations in Okinawa or the national movement of the Philippines. With respect to the almost constant demonstrations of the last fifteen years or so in the southern part of Korea, they tune in to its anti-American component. But without knowledge or tools of analysis, they interpret it personally:[93]

I was supposed to go to Germany. My orders got changed. Now, I'm an infantryman. That's what I'm paid to do, that's what my country expects me to do, that's what the contract says. I'm gonna do it, for my country. That's what I signed up to do. I know damn well what I was doin' when I signed up. I come here to Korea and I'm doin' my job. To be honest with you, I don't like the U.S. Army, you know. But I'm very patriotic, I love my country. When somebody says "Fuck America," that makes me feel bad. The only thing they want is our money.

If you look at it, the fact is we spent so much money comin' down here. We spent so much money payin' these construction workers on post, payin' these honchos on post, payin' those house-men on post, payin' these whores down here, payin' these businesses. Without us they'd cease to exist. We're spending our money comin' down here and then they have the nerve to sit around and say "Fuck America."

We're over here for one reason, one political reason, just like we're over in Germany or any other country we're in. The only reason we're here is to deter the communist aggression. Period. That's it. The ROK Army depends upon the Americans. Sure. Their weapons are ours. Their equipment is ours. Their vehicles, we gave them, not sold, but gave them. The chains are ours. Everything is ours. We're needed over here. We're protectin' the interests of South Korea. South Korea right now is democratic because the United States is here. The president of South Korea knows that.

The Men: Militarized Masculinity

U.S. military doctrine and applied strategy focus on Third World countries, with one of the principal lessons of Vietnam being that swift intervention and massive force are to be used to ensure the maintenance of U.S. interests. Instilling a militarized masculine identity, where raw aggression is equated with the entire military mission and where the soldier's view of reality becomes that of the military, is the prescription for action under the extreme stress of contemporary warfare.[94]

In military terms, being a man, being masculine is equated with aggression and domination over others. Basic training prepares recruits for combat, both physically and psychologically. The guys are taught to kill in a number of ways, are urged to kill, to feel it, to want it. And to survive doing it. It's an extremely difficult transition for the recruit to make. The key ingredient is the internalization of unquestioning and immediate obedience to orders. That is how a military man functions in the world.

Basic training uses violence—physical, psychological, verbal—to engender this masculine identity. It builds on the young man's social and economic marginality in civilian life. The decline in the availability and quality of education, health, and welfare services in the urban and rural areas of the United States, coupled with the rise in the number and kinds of drugs on the streets, and the loss of blue-collar jobs during the 1980s give recruitment a contemporary twist. The military has always functioned as an employer of last resort for lower-, middle-, and working-class youth; today, recruits are increasingly from the Third World areas of the U.S.[95]

The Men: Gender, Pornography, Racism, Power

One of our concerns with the military socialization process, and the reasons for its being as it is, is its potential impact upon gender relations. We know, for example, that feelings associated with being soft, with what is taken to be feminine, are meant to be crushed, eradicated during this socialization. This often has a homophobic or misogynistic component: "You pussy," "You faggot," "You girl" are phrases commonly screamed at those who fail. Cadence counts are filled with negative female images:

"This is my rifle . . . this is my gun . . . this is for fighting . . . this is for fun."

"I don't know . . . but I've been told . . . Eskimo pussy is mighty cold."

"Rape the town . . . kill the people . . . that's the thing . . . we love to do."

Manipulation of objects with female images is also central: ships, planes, tanks, weapons, equipment, and systems are given women's names—usually those of popular sex objects—and recruits are to gain skills, power, and dominance in using them.

The use of derision and manipulation with respect to things female builds on a young male consciousness that is between adolescence and adulthood. A recruit's knowledge of male-female social relationships has been informed by TV, film, advertising, humor, popular magazines, pornography, and the media, as well as relationships within his own family, his peer group, and his community. At best this socialization exaggerates already skewed traditional male socialization, which fails to stress the verbal and social skills needed to negotiate gender differences. At its worse, it teaches disrespect and devaluing of the female, along with an acceptance and use of violence to solve conflicts.[96]

Upon entering the bar areas around the bases, the guys enter a subculture where anything can be bought and the senses are bombarded with pornographic consumables. Hats and T-shirts revel in graphic detail. In the bar areas the misogyny of militarized masculinity can be lived out to whatever degree and in whatever way the individual male chooses. This may be the hypermasculinity of ever-ready, phallocentric domination. It may be the paid-for-rape, for the line between rape and purchase is as thin as a fine membrane. It may be having sex with a variety of partners and no attachments. It may be the power high of having the youngest and cheapest woman. It may be some form of violence against a woman whose sexual labor has been purchased. However it is expressed, this passing on of abuse and domination is a reflection of the male's public power coupled with a lack of private, authentic personal power.

For military men slated for combat, sex with prostituted women is the cap to the socialization process. It is after the unit's first experience of being on leave or liberty together that they gel. The key elements that bind them are getting drunk together and having sex with prostituted women.[97] Through this ritual each guy becomes the "fuckin-hey-right" soldier ready to lay down his life for others in his unit.

This is sexual imperialism, worked out on the bodies of women selling their sexual labor. This imperialism has a strong racist component. In addition to the well-known epithets of "slope," "slant," and the like, the guys historically and commonly use racist terms to describe the women. In Korea, during and after the war, the GIs referred to all indigenous women as "moose." In the southern part of Vietnam, those working as "key" women were called "house-mouse."[98]

In the Philippines, the guys call the women "Little Brown Fucking Machines Fueled by Rice," or LBFM for short. Guys comment continuously on how brown the women are, how many they can have, or have had, how cheap they are, how they will do anything, and how young they are. And one hears: "I just had some mother-fuckin' awesome sex." "I've got a sex appointment." "Pussy, that's what the Philippines is all about." On a Sunday afternoon, with the sun fully ablaze, one can see a guy seated with his zipper down and penis erect, right hand on his hip and left hand holding a Red Horse quart bottle of beer, and a woman at work on her knees, towel held up by her hands, stretching over the top of the penis, licking up and up and up with the whole of her upper body. Seven feet away around the corner is the bar, with a woman cleaning. Her four-year-old Amerasian daughter is helping her.

The bar area is one place where the militarized masculinity of the guys may be taken to its logical conclusion. Central to U.S. military culture is a fundamental lack of responsibility that may extend to anything and anyone. This includes children the woman may bear. They are her responsibility alone. It is extremely difficult to find a guy who expresses any bonding emotion, let alone responsibility, for a child that he's the natural father of. The men see the women as vessels to be filled up. In social situations—the bars, the streets, the jeepneys, the restaurants—the guys are talking to one another, relating to one another. The women are props—they are for playtime, which is singularly defined by its sexual component.

It was only on Okinawa that gender relations were different to any degree. Although the guys were constantly training in the field, they were stationed at Camp Hansen and would return to the bar area again. Some of the Filipinas working in the bars and some of the guys had dating relationships in which they began to know each other. Some of the guys were sensitive to the situation of the women—why they had to leave home and work in another country, their duty to family. And some of the women understood that some of the guys had also come from harsh backgrounds.

It may be that relationships in Okinawa were somewhat better because both the Filipinas and the guys were away from their home countries and both worked hard and often under quite oppressive conditions. Yet, the women are still in much more vulnerable positions than the men. They are the ones exposed, they are the ones who see constant pornographic images of themselves and experience the contradictory messages of desire, contempt, fantasy, humiliation. They are selling their sexual labor and are objectified in ways in which the men are not. And if the woman is beaten and/or abused in other ways, to whom can she turn? In her own country, she speaks the language, has friends and neighbors. In Okinawa, if she is very lucky, she'll have a relationship like Rowena's and can call upon that. Otherwise, nothing— as was the case with Janet.

Wherever they are, the guys have great power vis-à-vis the women. Their power is physical and it's economic. And the guy's mobility increases this power factor. He can use force, be abusive, demand and get what he wants, when he wants it, how he wants it, and as often as he wants it. If those terms are not met, he can get his money back. And he's here today and gone tomorrow, even when he's stationed in country. The woman has virtually no knowledge of his life and certainly no claim on or control over it. This is the nature of reality in gender relations around the military bases in the three countries of our study.

Lily, a woman who worked in the clubs in Olongapo, once said, "All of our lives we women must be strong inside. We must fight. We must not be afraid."

Lily and her daughter Elaine, at home in Olongapo

1. Gabriela is a national coalition of women's organizations at the forefront of fighting for the empowerment of women in the Philippines.

2. Proceedings from the First World Whores' Congress.

3. Laurie Bell, *Good Girls, Bad Girls: Feminists and Sex Trade Workers Face to Face* (Toronto: Seal Press, 1987), 84.

4. Susan Brownmiller, *Against Our Will: Men, Women and Rape* (New York: Simon & Schuster, 1975), 391–92.

5. Kathleen Barry, *Female Sexual Slavery* (Englewood Cliffs, N.J.: Prentice-Hall, 1979), 271.

6. Ibid., 163.

7. Barry, Bunch and Castley, *International Feminism: Networking against Female Sexual Slavery* (New York: International Women's Tribune Center, 1984), 27.

8. For a more extensive critique of both viewpoints and some additional analysis of sexual labor, see Thanh-Dam Truong, *Sex, Money and Morality* (London: Zed Books, 1990). Truong does an excellent job of looking at and critiquing the various theoretical ways of viewing sexual labor not covered in this essay.

9. Takazato Suzuyo, "Women in Relation to the Base Situation in Okinawa," unpublished manuscript presented at the International Abolitionist Federation, 2nd International Congress, Vienna, Austria, 3–6 September 1984. In recent history, it is only the socialist governments of Vietnam and China that have tried to deal comprehensively with rehabilitation. The policies of the Vietnamese government after withdrawal of U.S. military forces in 1975 was quite clear. Rehabilitation included medical treatment for venereal diseases and drug addiction and job training. The issue was seen as political, not personal: the women's work came as a result of the U.S. policy—with its destruction of villages, houses, and people—bringing the war to Vietnam. See: Melanie Beresford, *Vietnam: Politics, Economy and Society* (London and New York: Printer, 1988), 182–83. Like other aspects of socialist domestic policy carried forward or begun at this historic juncture, full implementation was not possible due to the war with Khmer Rougue–controlled Kampuchea that formally began in 1978. In late 1991, this war showed signs of being settled. In the People's Republic of China, established in 1949 after Chinese Red Armies successfully defeated both the Japanese and the Guomindang armies, the socialist government carried out extensive rehabilitation of more than a million women who had been selling their sexual labor in areas under Japanese occupation (1931–45) and in areas under Guomindang control. Red Army units closed down the brothels, arrested the owners, and put the women in hospitals to be treated for venereal diseases, drug addiction, and malnutrition. Perhaps upwards of 90 percent of the women had venereal disease, many of them in advanced stages. This was step one of the process. Step two was building of factories (most were textile or other light-industrial factories) for the women to work in and dormitories for them to live in. Many were married to men of poor peasant or working-class backgrounds who had been unable to marry before because they were not able to pay the necessary bride price. Rehabilitation of the women was a priority of the Chinese socialist state. It had the backing of the Communist party, the Chinese women's movement that had grown strong during the wars against the Japanese and the Guomindang, and rehabilitation fit in with the building of an industrialized state. It was one of those rare times when conscience, commitment of resources, and political power informed both policy decision and its implementation.

10. Gail Pheterson, *A Vindication of the Rights of Whores: The International Movement for Prostitutes' Rights* (Toronto: Seal Press, 1989), 94.

11. Truong, 87.

12. Veena Talwar Olenburg, "Lifestyle as Resistance: The Case of the Courtesans of Lucknow, India," *Feminist Studies* 16 (1990): 259–87.

13. Ibid., 283.

14. *Female Sexual Slavery*, 266.

15. Motoe Terami-Wada, "Karayuki-san of Manila: 1890–1920," *Philippine Studies* 34, (1986): 287–316. Both Filipina and Japanese women worked selling their sexual labor. Although a few Japanese women had been going to the Philippines prior to 1900, it was in that year that the first large group of sixty-four went.

16. Ibid.

17. Officers also provided their men with chemical prophylactic after each sexual exposure. See: Allan M. Brandt, *No Magic Bullet: A Social History of Venereal Disease in the United States Since 1880* (New York: Oxford University Press, 1985), ch. 2.

18. One of the problems was to acquire African-American women for African-American soldiers. See: Ibid., ch. 3.

19. Ibid.

20. Ibid.

21. Hearings before the Committee on Military Affairs, House of Representatives, Seventy-seventh Congress, March 1941, on H.R. 2475: A bill to prohibit prostitution within reasonable distance of military and naval establishments. Andrew J. May, Chairman of the Committee and from Kentucky, complimented Chaplain Arnold on his "very fine statement."

22. The government also began inducting men with uncomplicated cases of gonorrhea, syphilis, and chancroid. See Brandt, ch. 5.

23. The exception is a chapter in Arlene Eisen Bergman's *Women of Vietnam* (San Francisco: People's Press, 1974).

24. In another area of the world, Mary Ellen Mark's work stands alone. Her sensitive color photographs give the viewer a sense of the work lives and glimpses of the personal lives of women and transvestites selling their sexual labor in Bombay, India. See Mary Ellen Mark, *Falkland Road: Prostitutes of Bombay* (London: Thames and Hudson, 1981).

25. Samuel P. Huntington, "Squaring the Error," *Foreign Affairs*, July 1968. In this essay, Huntington advocates exhaustive U.S. terrorist bombing of civilians as the means of denying popular support given by peoples in the countryside to the Vietnamese revolutionary forces. This method of "denying the fish the water in which to swim," stands as a classic in academic sanctification of a policy of genocide.

26. Gloria Emerson, *Winners and Losers: Battles, Retreats, Gains, Losses and Ruins from the Vietnam War* (New York: Hartcourt Brace Jovanovich, 1976), 357.

27. Ngo Vinh Long, "Prostitution in Vietnam," draft manuscript, 1990, 16.

28. The men are butterflies, going from flower to flower. "Butterfly" is the common terminology used in the bar areas. From the woman's perspective, she looks at men who are butterflies with some disdain and tries to find customers who are not butterflies.

29. Brownmiller, 96.

30. Ibid., 95.

31. Takazato Suzuyo, unpublished manuscript.

32. Ibid., Takazato Suzuyo reports that at the time of reversion in 1972, the advance loan system had resulted in a woman having a debt of $2,000 on the average and $17,000 maximum (rate of exchange in 1972 was $1 = 360 yen).

33. Brownmiller, 93.

34. This policy of the "barrier" use of Filipinas has come under criticism from the women's movement in Okinawa and Japan. As yet, the men are not listening. Masahide Ota is the new governor elected in 1991 on a platform that included the demand that the United States close down its bases and leave Okinawa. Coupled with this stance are statements that prostitution is not as serious a problem as it had been in the past (during Vietnam), that U.S. military guys are better "behaved." This point of view would indicate that the "barrier" system is working well. See *New York Times*, 22 April 1991.

35. The origins of the name "Social Hygiene Clinic" date back to the early 1900s. Surgeons and physicians, alarmed at the rise of VD in the U.S., organized a Social Hygiene movement. They took as a given that men would purchase women's sexual labor and advocated state regulations of the diseases through control and examination of the women. John D. Rockefeller, Jr., in 1911 provided financial backing for the movement. With World War I, the U.S. government established the Social Hygiene Board in 1918 to formulate and administer policy designed to protect U.S. troops from venereal disease. A number of those who had been part of the Social Hygiene movement from the turn of the century were involved in this work. In 1922, after the war was over, the Social Hygiene Board was disbanded. See Brandt, ch. 4.

36. Soon after AIDS testing began in Olongapo, Brenda went with a local journalist to interview one of the first six women to test HIV positive. She was eighteen years old and soon after we began talking with her, it became clear she had no idea what AIDS was. All she knew was that the SHC took her to a hospital in Manila every three months for further tests. Several months later, the same journalist and Brenda returned to see the woman a second time. This time we took a Tagalog photocopy of information about AIDS. When she received it, she immediately began reading and did not look up until she was finished, when she said, "May I keep this?" This was the first time she had been given any information about AIDS. After having tested positive, she continued to work in the club and go on bar fines with Americans. She also had a Filipino lover.

37. In preparation for writing the article that was published in *The Nation*, 3 April 1989, Saundra interviewed three women who had tested HIV positive. Each had continued to work in the bars and go on bar fines after having tested positive. Two of the three women subsequently became pregnant. At the time of the interview, one woman had delivered and her boy was approximately one year old. She was told he had tested HIV negative. The other woman was nine months pregnant. The interview took place at the SHC, in the presence of a senior staff doctor. During the interview, one of the three women told Saundra that several other women, whom she knew personally, had tested HIV positive. She reported that at least one of the women was working at the Rolling Stones, a bar on Magsaysay.

38. The U.S. does not provide funding for the clinics in Korea, and the image presented is that the clinics are locally administered. However, when Brenda wanted to interview someone from the clinic administration in Tong Du Chun, she had to go through the U.S. military base to obtain permission for the interview. Two U.S. military personnel came to the interview, clearly to monitor the questions asked and the responses from the Korean administrator.

39. A night-off pass is the slip of paper given to the woman when her bar fine is paid. If she is employed by a club but tries to take customers independently of the club and keep all the money, she will also be fined and/or

put in prison. Many women however, take the risk. See Linda's story, p. 153.

40. Bar owners in the Philippines may also be retired U.S. servicemen, particularly in Barrio Barretto and Subic City. A small number of bar owners are Filipinas.

41. Two Filipinas died in a fire in the Upper Lima club in 1983 because their rooms were locked and the windows barred. When Saundra and Brenda were in Okinawa in 1989, the Filipinas working at the Upper Lima knew nothing about the fire and the women who died. In a similar incident in Thailand, in 1984, five Thai women were locked inside their rooms in a Phuket Island brothel. It burned down, killing all five. See: *South China Morning Post*, 6 November 1986.

42. Women's groups internationally, both prostituted women and nonprostituted women, are almost unanimous in their agreement that legalization of prostitution is not beneficial to women. It is decriminalization that is needed and should be fought for. Legalization results in handing greater control over to the police and bar and brothel owners.

43. For this reason, work in Okinawa was very difficult. It did not take long for Rowena's bar owner to tell her not to talk to us. We had to meet away from the bar where she would not be seen talking with us. The first time we went to the Champion bar, the women were friendly when they discovered Brenda spoke Tagalog. However, they were also obviously warned away: on later visits to the Champion, they would not speak with us at all and clearly kept their distance.

44. Lita and her cousin Terri were threatened with losing their jobs for accompanying Brenda to a Gabriela march on International Women's Day in 1987. Instead, they were fined and all the women were told they would be fired if they were caught talking with Brenda inside the club. In another incident, several women from the bars in Olongapo and Manila were interviewed on a popular TV talk show in 1988. They had to have their identities hidden through the use of shadows for fear of losing their jobs or being harassed by the police.

45. The peoples and governments of Japan and Okinawa have become increasingly convinced that it is the foreigners, principally the Americans, who have brought AIDS into the country. The U.S. military has taken heat on this issue. Seeking to avoid any blame, U.S.

military in Okinawa ordered its personnel not to donate blood for use in local hospitals. At the same time, the military maintained that none of its personnel were HIV positive. See William Wetherall, "Japan Curses Gaijin and AIDS Still Spreads," *Far Eastern Economic Review*, 9 April 1987, 111–113.

46. Ibid. *Far Eastern Economic Review*, 9 April 1987.

47. Saundra Sturdevant, "The Military, Women and AIDS: Bar Girls of Subic Bay," *The Nation*, 3 April 1989.

48. Ibid. It is known that it is easier to transmit the AIDS virus from male to female in heterosexual intercourse than it is from female to male. It is also true that the physical health, level of sanitation, frequency and type of intercourse, and number of partners are factors affecting the ease or difficulty with which the virus is transferred. See: *The Lancet*, 8 March 1986, 529. Debi Brock, "Prostitutes are Scapegoats in the AIDS panic," *Resources for Feminist Research* 19 (June 1989), raises the issue of Europeans being the source of a new virus, HIV4, among women selling their sexual labor in Senegal, West Africa.

49. Ibid., *Far Eastern Economic Review*, 9 April 1987.

50. What happens after evacuation, though, is unclear. Are the men discharged? If so, with what counseling and medical benefits? Are the hospitals of the Veterans Administration providing care? And what of the families, friends, and lovers of the military man who has tested positive? Is counseling provided? Of what kind and for how long? These questions need to be addressed, especially in light of the July 1992 study of the Centers for Disease Control, which reported that the largest number of new AIDS cases in 1991 was in the rural areas, especially in the southern United States. In the South alone, there were 15,761 new AIDS cases in 1991 (up 10.2 percent, from 14,301 in 1990). The second highest increase in new cases was in the Midwest, up 8.6 percent with 4,418 new cases reported. See: *New York Times*, July 3, 1992.

51. The first documented case of AIDS was a British sailor, twenty-five years of age, who died of the disease in 1959. See: *New York Times*, 24 July 1990, quoting *The Lancet*, 7 July 1990.

52. Saundra Sturdevant, "Talks with the Guys," TDC, August 1989 (unpublished interviews).

53. According to women in Olongapo, photographs of women who tested HIV positive were tacked on a bulletin board at the gate of the base where off-limits notifications are placed. This was done so that the guys could avoid these women: they were off-limits.

54. See: Appendix I for the text of the AIDS petition.

55. Some groups in the U.S., such as the Mennonite Central Committee and Jubilee, wrote letters to the U.S. Navy and Defense Department raising the issue of the U.S. military bringing AIDS to the Philippines. They also raised the question of the U.S. Navy taking some financial responsibility for those women who test positive. One response, a letter from Lewis H. Seaton, Vice Admiral, Medical Corps, Department of the Navy, reads: "We are concerned about the public health of the women of Olongapo and Angeles. While not obligated to provide monetary support for those women who test positive for the HTLV-III antibody, we do provide medical and technical consultation to the Ministry of Health of the Republic of the Philippines through a jointly sponsored social hygiene clinic."

56. Brandt, ch. 3. The venereal-disease rate for the U.S. military doubled from 1897, when the incidence was 84.59 per 1,000, to 1910, when it reached 196.99 per 1,000. Approximately one-third of the duty days lost had their origins in venereal disease.

57. Judith Walkowitz, *Prostitution and Victorian Society: Women, Class and the State* (Cambridge: Cambridge University Press, 1982), 49.

58. Ibid., 74.

59. Ibid.

60. Ibid., 49.

61. Maria Luisa T. Camagay, "Prostitution in Nineteenth Century Manila," *Philippine Studies* 36 (1988): 241–55.

62. Walkowitz provides a brilliant study of the enactment of this legislation, resistance to it, and extension of the legislation to deal with other targeted groups.

63. Concerned with increasing rates of venereal disease among its troops, Italy in the nineteenth century instituted a weekly system of inspecting women who sell their sexual labor to military men. Each Sunday, enlisted men were also inspected. Officers were excluded from this system. See: Mary Gibson, *Prostitution and the State in Italy, 1860–1915* (New Brunswick, N.J.: Rutgers University Press, 1986), 24.

64. Looking at the rise in VD rates during the Vietnam War (1965–75), gonorrhea cases tripled, and in 1975 syphilis was the third most common communicable disease after gonorrhea and chicken pox. See Brandt, ch. 5. What percentage of the VD cases were resistant to standard antibiotic treatment is not clear, but by 1980, authorities admitted that this was a considerable problem. Those in the military had known this for some time. The impact upon women is dramatized by the fact that in 1976 alone some 22 million American women were hospitalized with pelvic inflammation, a complication rising directly from untreated gonorrhea. Brandt also points out that with over 100 million cases worldwide, gonorrhea is still the most prevalent bacterial infection in the world. This situation reflects both direct transmission of the disease and the funding for war and war-related enterprises, with its consequent reduction in budget and personnel for education and treatment.

65. Street vendors of this sort were absent in Tong Du Chun and Okinawa. Although English-language newspapers were available in Seoul and Naha, they were not to be found in the bar areas.

66. In Seville, Spain, during the sixteenth century, this labor not only provided alternative employment for the women but it supported innkeepers and other landlords, secondhand clothiers, pimps, and an array of commercial enterprises. See: Mary Elizabeth Perry, "Lost Women in Early Modern Seville: The Politics of Prostitution," *Feminist Studies* 4 (1978): 195–214. In nineteenth- and early twentieth-century America, Isei males took the money from the sale of Isei women's sexual labor and laundered it into legitimate business enterprises, such as land acquisition. See: Yuji Ichioka, "Ameyuki-san: Japanese prostitutes in 19th century America," *Amerasia Journal* 4 (1977): 1–23. In the Philippines during the early years of the twentieth century, the sale of the sexual labor of Japanese women to U.S. military fighting and occupying the country supported small stores, boardinghouse and hotel keepers, jewelry artisans, kimono material dealers, and hairdressers. See Motoe Terami-Wada. These examples pulled from existing studies are few, but they emphasize patterns that are evident in our work. Research needs to be done on this topic, and Bruce Cumings's introduction,

"Silent but deadly," provides insights into the degree of resistance to efforts of this nature that may exist in the academic world.

67. We are indebted to Thanh-Dam Truong for her lucid analysis of the factors that have gone into the development of the contemporary tourist prostitution industry in Asia and its connection to the R&R model. Her case study is that of Thailand. Basically, Thanh-Dam Truong argues that the end of the Vietnam War and the withdrawal of large numbers of U.S. military left the region with economies facing difficult times. These economies had become highly dependent upon income generated as a result of U.S. military guys' purchase of women's sexual labor and expenditures in the bar areas. International corporations employ a highly mobile, almost exclusively male labor force, which is similar in structure. It too is provided with re-creational opportunities in the manner of the U.S. military; it subsequently became the primary purchasers of women's sexual labor in tourist prostitution. Advantages enjoyed by the corporations and their employees are similar to those enjoyed by the U.S. military as an organization and the men as workers. Moreover, indigenous national and local governments gain through taxes and other sources of related income.

68. Japanese sex tours are now well known throughout Southeast Asia. As work incentives to increase productivity, Japanese companies send managerial-level men to Southeast Asian countries in groups. They go to beach resorts and tourist areas. Included in the tour is women's sexual labor, the cost of which is about equivalent to the purchase of an after-dinner brandy in Japan.

The purchase of Filipino boys by male tourists is also common in Manila and Pagsanjan. Pagsanjan is a small town south of Manila. Prior to the filming of *Apocalypse Now* there, it was known primarily for its beautiful waterfalls. But the town is now even more well known for its young boys and some young girls whose sexual labor is available for purchase. In the early 1970s, when the town and surrounding mountains were being used for filming, many of the film crew members were said to have purchased the sexual labor of the young boys in the area. See Emilio R. Aquino, *Tourism and Child Prostitution in Pagsanjan*, (Rural Organization and Assistance for Development, United Church of Christ in the Philippines, 1987), 28. This account is verified by personal communication to Brenda Stolzfus from a Filipina who acted in the film. Emilio R. Aquino also reports that during the late 1980s, Pagsanjan had roughly 3,000 pom poms (a term coined by American GIs during the liberation of Manila for female prostitutes but contemporary use is for young boys) selling their sexual labor. On ordinary days, some 500 to 600 foreign visitors would arrive in Pagsanjan. On weekends and holidays, the number would rise to 2,000. After finding a boy (usually at a hotel set up for maximum ability to observe various boys swimming in a pool), some male tourists will pay for his education and give money to his family. In return, he must be available to provide sexual services while the tourist is in the country.

69. One well-known case is a Filipina, Nena, who was recruited by a Dutch businessman, supposedly to work in his hotel in Holland. She was taken to his farmhouse in Holland, where she was held prisoner and forced to sell her sexual labor. Nena and some of her friends were able to escape with the help of the Foundation Against Trafficking in Women in the Netherlands. She filed charges against her recruiters, resulting in a 2.5-year term of imprisonment for the club owner. Cited in Mila Astorga-Garcia, "Trafficking in Women," *National Midweek*, 6 September 1989, 38. See also: Chrizz Diaz Nagot, "Tricked into Prostitution," *New Directions for Women* 17 (November–December 1988): 10–11. Also, women who marry and move to another country and whose marriages break up sometimes begin selling their sexual labor in the country they have moved to.

70. In Taiwan and Japan and perhaps other countries, prostituted women who have the money will have silicone implants to make their breasts larger and therefore more attractive to their foreign customers.

71. In March 1986, the women in a bar in Barrio Barretto (outside Olongapo) went on strike against forced female boxing. The bar owner was American. On Palm Sunday of that year, at about 5:00 in the morning, one of the organizers was shot in the head and killed. The killer was caught: he had been hired by the bar owner, who was already out of the country. The strike continued and eventually the Olongapo City Council banned female boxing in the bars. See also Lita's story (p.

83) for a description of the boxing.

72. In September 1989, prostituted women from Olongapo held the first seminar of their own with no outside resource people. Pearly and Linda, staff at Buklod, gave input on the national situation, and they discussed Olongapo and the sale of sexual labor. During the plenary session, the women quickly reached a consensus that they should go on strike. However, only twenty out of some nine thousand women were present, so they concluded that more organizing was necessary first.

73. See: Eric Hobsbawm, *Industry and Empire* (London: Penguin, 1968).

74. See Perry and Walkowitz. Each of these works provides excellent studies of the changing relationships of production and distribution, and their impact upon women and working-class peoples. Perry's work describing this similar process in Spain during the mercantile era is especially interesting.

75. Walden Bello and Stephanie Rosenfeld, *Dragons in Distress: Asia's Miracle Economies in Crisis* (San Francisco: The Institute of Food and Development Policy, 1990), 77.

76. Ibid., 86.

77. Ibid., 11–12.

78. Ibid., 24.

79. Ibid., 25.

80. Ibid.

81. Quoted in Aida Fulleros Santos and Lynn F. Lee, *The Debt Crisis: A Treadmill of Poverty for Filipino Women* (Manila: Kalayaan, 1989), 22. "Absolute poverty refers to that income level below which people cannot buy for their families recommended nutrient requirements, cannot provide two changes of garments, cannot permit grade-six schooling for their children, cannot cover minimal costs of medical care and cannot pay for fuel and rent."

82. See also: "Gathering the Dust: The Bases Issue in the Philippines," Aida Santos's introduction to the Philippines.

83. Thomas O'Brian, M. M., *Crisis and Instability: The Philippines Enters the Nineties* (Davao City: Philippine International Forum, 1990), 30. The Philippine International Forum (PIF) is a network of foreign residents of the Philippines committed to solidarity with the Filipino people.

84. Filipinos have pointed out that the U.S. military previously used these tactics on Filipinos in the Philippine-American War (1898–1906) that followed Spain's defeat in the Spanish-American War and Spain's turning of the Philippines over to U.S. control. In American history, the Philippine-American War (1898–1902) is termed an "insurgency."

85. Aida Fulleros Santos and Lynn F. Lee further describe Samar: "It has always been hard to make a living from the land but now even more so as the effects of logging are destroying agricultural land, food crops become so scarce and prices rise, there are few industries and so few jobs to generate other income. The government's prioritizing of industrialization at the expense of the agricultural sector and its priority for debt servicing in the budget over all other government programs, is institutionalizing acute poverty in rural areas and most particularly in the inland barrios of Samar; where old women with responsibility for their grandchildren can only watch as loggers engaged in "productive" activities earning export dollars destroy their livelihood and help to drive away their sons and daughters" (44–45).

86. Jennifer Lauby and Oded Stark, "Individual Migration as a Family Strategy: Young Women in the Philippines," *Population Studies* 42 (1988): 485.

87. Pheterson, 70.

88. 62.1 percent of African-Americans reenlist and 37.6 percent of Euro-Americans reenlist. See *New York Times*, 7 August 1991.

89. Aetas are hired by the U.S. Navy to provide this training, which takes place in some of the only virgin forest left in the Philippines and on land that was once sacred to the Aeta people.

90. Saundra Sturdevant, "Talks with the Guys."

91. Ibid.

92. Ibid.

93. Ibid.

94. R. Wayne Eisenhart, "You Can't Hack It, Little Girl: A discussion of the Covert Psychological Agenda of Modern Combat Training," *The Journal of Social Issues* 31 (1975): 13–24. This is a very concise and focused presentation of the socialization process.

95. One Army survey showed 65 percent of recruits citing the military's promise of college education or marketable training enabling employment in civilian life as the reason for joining up. *New York Times*, 13 November 1990. As one young Marine from Puma, Arizona, put it: "The military is left for us poor boys . . . and all those rich college kids out there know that." Lance Cpl. Joseph E. Smyth, twenty-one years old, quoted in the *New York Times*, 31 May 1991. This is especially true of African-Americans, whose representation in the military is disproportionate to their percentage of the population. Constituting some 12 percent of the population and 14 percent of eighteen to twenty-four-year-olds, African-American males account for 21 percent of the 2 million men on active duty. African-American females account for 31 percent of the 223,000 women on active duty. See: the *New York Times*, 7 August 1991. Martin Binklin, military analyst at the Brookings Institution estimates that in 1990, 33 to 35 percent of all qualified young black men have served in the military, compared with 14 percent of the same age group of Euro-Americans. See the *New York Times*, 25 January 1991. Not only are they disproportionately represented, but military commanders also often report that African-Americans tend to be more centered, better educated, and more highly motivated than Euro-Americans, most of whom are from the south and southwestern parts of the United States. What may be happening is that a good number of young African-Americans are being lost to the streets. Many of those who survive go into the military.

96. See Shirley Litch Mercer, "Not a Pretty Picture: An Exploratory Study of Violence against Women in High School Dating Relationships," *Resources for Feminist Research* 17 (1988): 15–23.

97. Saundra Sturdevant's discussions with a senior-grade officer who had extensive soldiering experience dating from the Korean War. He was one of the senior officers who originally developed the concept of Green Berets and put that concept into practice.

98. The origin of the term "house mouse" is not certain; that of "moose" has different explanations. The GIs at the time said it was obvious: the women were ugly, they looked like moose. It may be, however, that the origin of the term stems from the Japanese colonial period, from the Japanese word for unmarried/virgin woman, which is *musame*.

GLOSSARY

Aete —a cultural minority in the Philippines, also often referred to as Negritos. The land now occupied by Subic Naval Base was once their sacred land. Anthropologists believe the Aetas to be the original inhabitants of the Philippine Islands.

ate —in its most literal sense, elder sister. As in most traditional cultures, elder sister, or *ate*, may be used for females several years older than oneself (but not old enough to be a parent) who are not blood relatives. The term conveys affection, as one would ideally feel affection for an older sister, but also is an acknowledgment of authority (also true of older sisters in traditional cultures). In the bar culture, then, the women call their female managers *ate* whether or not they feel affection toward them.

bakla —gay or effeminate man.

bangka boat —a small boat in the Philippines used for fishing.

baranguay captain —a *baranguay* is the smallest geographical division, either urban or rural. Each *baranguay* has an elected official called a *baranguay captain*.

barkada —a group of close friends who usually spend a great deal of time together. A *barkada* may either be a supportive group or one with a negative impact on an individual's behavior.

carabao —a water buffalo.

chinelas —rubber thongs sometimes called slippers.

Chusok —a traditional Korean holiday in the fall of the year celebrating harvest.

dalaga —a Tagalog word that may mean a virgin or an unmarried women. It may be tied to whether or not a woman has had sexual intercourse, but this is not necessarily the case. A woman who is "older" and has had sexual intercourse but never married may still be called a *dalaga*, probably *matandang dalaga* (old maid).

halo-halo —a summer snack made from ice mixed with sweet bits and sugar, sometimes with a dip of ice cream on top. The word *halo* means to mix. During the summer, it is sold on street corners.

kano —the women's term for an American customer.

kumpare/kumare/pare/mare —used for the godfather/godmother of one's child or for the father/mother of a child one is godfather/godmother to. *Pare* and *mare* are also used when one is speaking to someone whose name is not known.

kuya —in its most literal sense, elder brother. As in most traditional cultures, elder brother, or *kuya*, may be used for males several years older than oneself (but not old enough to be a parent) who are not blood relatives. The term *kuya* conveys affection, as one would ideally feel affection for an older brother, but is also an acknowledgment of authority (also true of older brothers in traditional cultures). In the bar culture, then, the women call their male managers *kuya* whether or not they feel affection toward them.

Magsaysay —in Olongapo, the street leading away from the main gate of the base which is lined with bars, massage parlors, restaurants, money exchanges, and souvenir shops.

mamasan —a term used in the bar areas of all three countries with variations in meaning. Filipinos use it in both the Philippines and Okinawa to refer to female bar owners. In the Korean bar area, the *mamasan* is the female pimp or the woman who does the cleaning and laundry.

naku —a Tagalog expression of surprise, wonder, fear, pain, and so on.

NDF —National Democratic Front. The NDF is an underground revolutionary coalition founded in 1973. Included in the coalition are the New People's Army (NPA), the Communist Party of the Philippines (CPP), the Christians for National Liberation (CNL), and various sectorial organizations. The NDF program calls for "genuine land reform, nationalization of major industries, termination of foreign business privileges in order to return the economy to national hands, cancellation of the Military Bases Agreement and other unequal treaties with the United States, pursuit of a nonaligned foreign policy, and guarantee of full civil and human rights to Filipinos." (From "A Letter of Concern from U.S. Missioners in the Philippines to the Christian Churches of the United States," produced by the Philippines International Forum [PIF], July 1986)

negro —an English term that has been incorporated into Tagalog. Such incorporation is called Taglish. The term refers to African-Americans and is commonly used by Filipinas in the bar areas.

NPA —New People's Army. The revolutionary armed wing of the CPP.

ondo —Traditional method of heating used in Korea and in northern China. It involves a fire pit situated outside on one side of the room and an opening for the exhaust located outside on the opposite side of the room. Running under the room, a flue connects the fire pit and the exhaust. The air heated by the fire flows through this flue, heating the floor of the room and emerging through the exhaust on the opposite side.

OPM —Office of the Provost Martial. Both OPM and SP are U.S. military police in Olongapo. OPM has a permanent office just inside the gate of the base. They mediate problems between U.S. personnel and Filipinos and take Americans back on base if they are out of control.

papasan —a term used in the bar areas of all three countries to refer to male bar owners and/or managers.

side dish —a small dish of vegetables and/or meat, to accompany rice. Side dishes are a part of each meal throughout Asia.

SP —Shore Patrol. Shore Patrol work with the OPM, performing the same function, but are from the ships docked at Subic.

stay-in —in the Philippines, when a woman lives in a room above or behind the bar, she is called *stay-in*. Generally the rooms are small, perhaps nine by twelve and occupied by two to three women. Some clubs may have slightly larger rooms, but these are occupied by more women. The conditions vary with respect to rent.

tuba —an alcoholic drink common in the rural areas of the Philippines.

ulam —any side dish eaten with rice.

yakuza —The underworld, or Mafia, of Japan. A 1983 National Police survey showed 98,771 *yakuza* divided into 2,330 distinct groups. The origin of the name *yakuza* is from a card game, similar to blackjack but with 19 being the desired number. *Ya-ku-za* are Japanese words for 8–9–3, which total 20—useless. See Clyde Haberman, "TV Funeral for Japan's Slain Godfather," *New York Times*, 1 February 1985. The *yakuza*, however, are far from useless. In existence since at least the late nineteenth century, they emerged during the post–World War II period as one of the few organizations that had remained intact. Their role in Japanese financial and political structures—including their centrality to prostitution, drugs, entertainment, and the control of labor—has been detailed by Alec Dubro and David Kaplan in *Yakuza* (San Francisco: Centre for Investigative Reporting, 1986). Japanese authorities have prohibited this book from being sold in Japan, primarily because of the thoroughness with which Dubro and Kaplan document the links between the *yakuza* and the ruling Liberal Democratic party, the only party that has held political power in the postwar period.

BIBLIOGRAPHY

Aquino, Emilio R. *Tourism and Child Prostitution in Pagsanjan*. Manila: ROAD, UCCP, 1987.

Ballhatchet, Kenneth. *Race, Sex and Class Under the Raj*. London: Weidenfeld and Nicolson, 1980.

Barry, Bunch and Castley. *International Feminism: Networking Against Female Sexual Slavery*. New York: International Women's Tribune Center, 1984.

Barry, Kathleen. *Female Sexual Slavery*. Englewood Cliffs, N.J.: Prentice-Hall, 1979.

Bell, Laurie. *Good Girls, Bad Girls: Feminists and Sex Trade Workers Face to Face*. Toronto: Seal Press, 1987.

Bello, Walden, and Stephanie Rosenfeld. *Dragons in Distress: Asia's Miracle Economies in Crisis*. San Francisco: Institute for Food and Development Policy, 1990.

Beresford, Melanie. *Vietnam: Politics, Economy and Society*. London and New York: Printer, 1988.

Bergman, Arlene Eisen, Women of Vietnam. San Francisco: People's Press, 1974.

Bernheimer, Charles. *Figures of Ill-Repute: Representing Prostitution in Nineteenth-Century France*. Cambridge: Cambridge University Press, 1989.

Brandt, Allan M. *No Magic Bullet: A Social History of Venereal Disease in the United States Since 1880*. Oxford: Oxford University Press, 1985.

Brock, Debi. "Prostitutes are Scapegoats in the AIDS Panic." *Resources for Feminist Research* 19 (1989): 13–17.

Brownmiller, Susan. *Against Our Will: Men, Women and Rape*. New York: Simon & Schuster, 1975.

Camagay, Maria Luisa T. "Prostitution in Nineteenth Century Manila." *Philippine Studies* 36 (1988): 241–55.

Chrizz Diaz Nagot. *New Directions for Women* 17 (1988): 10–11.

Cronin, Richard. *Japan's Expanding Role and Influence in the Asia-Pacific Region*. Washington, D.C.: Congressional Research Service, 1990.

Dijkstra, Bram. *Idols of Perversity: Fantasies of Feminine Evil in Fin-de-Siècle Culture*. New York: Oxford, 1986.

Eisenhart, R. Wayne. "You Can't Hack It, Little Girl." *The Journal of Social Issues* 31 (1975): 13–24.

Emerson, Gloria. *Winners & Losers: Battles, Retreats, Gains, Losses and Ruins from the Vietnam War*. New York: Hartcourt Brace Jovanovich, 1976.

Enloe, Cynthia. *Bananas, Beaches and Bases: Making Feminist Sense of International Politics*. Berkeley: University of California Press, 1989.

Friedman, George, and Meredith Lebard. *The Coming War with Japan*. New York: St. Martin's Press, 1991.

Gerson, Joseph, and Bruce Birchard, eds. *The Sun Never Sets*. Boston: South End Press, 1991.

Gibson, Mary. *Prostitution and the State in Italy, 1860–1915*. New Brunswick: Rutgers University Press, 1986.

Hearn, Jeff, and David Morgan, eds. *Men, Masculinities and Social Theory*. New York: Unwin Hyman Ltd., 1990.

Hobsbawm, Eric. *Industry and Empire*. London: Penguin, 1968.

Ichioka, Yuji. "Ameyuki-san: Japanese Prostitutes in 19th century America." *Amerasia Journal* 4 (1977): 1–23.

Lauby, Jennifer, and Oded Stark. "Individual Migration as a Family Strategy: Young Women in the Philippines." *Population Studies* 42 (1988): 473–86.

Mark, Mary Ellen. *Falkland Road: Prostitutes of Bombay*. London: Thames and Hudson, 1981.

Matsuura, K. "Administering Foreign Aid: The View from the Top." *Economic Eye* (1989): 12–13.

Mercer, Shirley Litch. "Not a Pretty Picture." *Resources for Feminist Research*. 17 (1988): 15–23.

Motoe, Terami-Wada. "Karayuki-san of Manila: 1890–1920." *Philippine Studies* 34 (1986): 287–316.

O'Brian, Thomas, M. M. *Crisis and Instability: The Philippines Enters the Nineties*. Davao City: Philippine International Forum, 1990.

Olenburg, Veena Talwar. "Lifestyle as Resistance: The Case of the Courtesans of Lucknow, India." *Feminist Studies* 16 (1990): 259–87.

Perry, Mary Elizabeth. "Lost Women in Early Modern Seville: The Politics of Prostitution." *Feminist Studies* 4 (1978): 195–214.

Pheterson, Gail. *A Vindication of the Rights of Whores: The International Movement for Prostitutes' Rights*. Toronto: Seal Press, 1989.

Pollock, Griselda. *Vision and Difference: Femininity, Feminism and Histories of Art*. London: Routledge, 1988.

Santos, Aida Fulleros, and Lynn F. Lee. *The Debt Crisis: A Treadmill of Poverty for Filipino Women*. Manila: Kalayaan, 1989.

Scott, Anne Farrer. "Women and War." *Hungry Mind Review* (1991): 23.

Truong, Thanh-Dam. *Sex, Money and Morality*. London: Zed Books, 1990.

Vogel, Steven. *Japanese High Technology, Politics, and Power*. Berkeley: Berkeley Roundtable on the International Economy, 1989.

Walkowitz, Judith. *Prostitution and Victorian Society: Women, Class and the State*. Cambridge: Cambridge University Press, 1982.

Worsley, Peter, and Kofi Buenor Hadjor, eds. *On the Brink: Nuclear Proliferation and the Third World*. London: Third World Communications, 1987.

Appendix I

In July 1986, prior to the launching of Buklod Center, a two-day seminar was held with the women from the clubs during which the decision was made to have a center. In September 1986, the first health seminar was held with the women. By that time, AIDS testing had begun in Olongapo and was becoming a much-discussed issue. Several weeks after the health seminar, about ten women from the clubs gathered at Brenda's house and wrote the following petition. Although the gathering was initiated by Brenda, the women wrote the petition. They then made photocopies and took them around to their bars. A total of 600 signatures was gathered.

PETITION ON AIDS

We are the women who work in Olongapo as entertainers and waitresses. We are in agreement that AIDS comes from the Americans.

Therefore we ask that:

1. The U.S. military support each victim of AIDS in Olongapo and Angeles with the following:
   a. Income for the women victims of AIDS adequate to support those who depend on her;
   b. The medicine she needs and regular checkups in order to maintain her health;
   c. The Philippine government and people should not have to spend any money on the disease AIDS.
2. The Americans should be tested before leaving the base in order to lessen the spread of AIDS. They should also have evidence or ID to show they are free of AIDS.

We are doing this with our signatures for the good of all who work in the bars here in Olongapo and Angeles and for the Americans.

Appendix II

The following statement was written by Alma Bulawan, a member of the staff at Buklod and formerly a waitress in a club, to present at a consultation on alternatives to the bases. Before Alma wrote the statement, she carried out a small survey, talking to women at Buklod and other friends and neighbors from the bars.

WHAT ARE THE ALTERNATIVES TO A MILITARY BASE?

Alma Bulawan and the Women of Buklod

Presently, there are significant questions being raised about the continued existence of the U.S. bases here in our country. Many consultations are also being held in order to discuss these questions. At first glance, the primary problem and stumbling block would be the loss of work for the large numbers of Filipinos who work inside the base.

This issue is being seriously considered by the government and the large and strong sectors of the country. I wish to make known to everyone that there is one more sector that is in need of an alternative if the bases leave. This sector is the 9,000 women who work in the hospitality industry.[1] I am here therefore because I want to pass on to everyone, and to you, the fact that there is a responsibility to make decisions about their serious needs. Please listen for a moment and consider what the women in this trade would like to have passed on.

Based on our questions and our knowledge as of now, one alternative to the U.S. bases is to make a free port at Olongapo City. We believe that this is not the answer to our situation and that, rather, the situation would become even worse. If many different ships came into port, there would simply be different kinds of customers— a situation that would induce many more women to work in the hospitality trade. This would add to the loss of suitable ways of caring for and control of the foreigners who arrive.

One more alternative being considered is an industrial complex. This would mean that the women would work in factories. This is a possible answer to the situation if the regulations and conditions were just: for example, a proper salary, time away from the job for the different duties and responsibilities of women, benefits that respond to the situation of women, support for their needs in caring for their children and families, and the assurance that management would not make assessments according to high levels of education and experience. If this is not accomplished, nothing will change because the work in the factories will only lead to exasperation and frustration; and if the earnings are not sufficient, it is possible that the women will return to what they did before.

Our questioning indicated that if the government provided an alternative, a number of women would like to have some capital in order to start a small business. Perhaps this is one of several possible solutions to the problem and should be studied in detail. If so, there are additional considerations that need to be addressed: drawing from our limited experience, we know that many of the women who borrow even a small amount of capital are not able to repay it. There are at least three reasons for this: first, lack of business experience; second, lack of knowledge about the system of business dealings; and third, perhaps, a certain lack of responsibility. If there were capital available for business loans, proper training and experience would have to be provided as well. The training and experience should respond to the entirety of what is needed for the advancement of women. These are the following:

1. Consciousness raising so that the women may understand that it is not right to lose one's choice of livelihood and also feel forced to barter this valuable resource (sexual labor) in order just to eat and stay alive.
2. Training about the rights and responsibilities of women.
3. Focus on an understanding of reproductive health and other health training.
4. The importance of nationalism and self-reliance.
5. Education and training in business: being careful, orderly, and clean; saving for the future; and recognizing the importance of work and one's fellow human beings.

Equally as important as education and experience is the methodology of implementation. The methodology must be suitable to the progress of the women's consciousness.

Finally, and perhaps of greatest importance, is the eradication of society's low regard for the women who have been forced to work in the hospitality trade. We must all endeavor to accept them without exception and without doubt as valuable members of the country of the Philippines.

When all this has been accomplished, we will be able to say that there are genuine alternatives for our women in Olongapo.

The women of BUKLOD
Olongapo City

---

[1] The figure of 9,000 used here refers to registered women in Olongapo. Estimates of the number of registered and unregistered women together in Olongapo are around 16,000.

Technical Notes on the Photography

Three Nikon cameras were used: two F3s and one FM2. The lenses were Nikkor 28mm f1.2, 55mm micro f2.8, 85mm f1.4, and 135mm f1.2. In addition, a Widelux camera was used for selected wide-angle shots. A Metz 60CT2 flash system was used for shots inside the bars and inside factories, on the streets at night and sometimes inside houses.

Kodak Tri-X film, rated at 400 ASA, was used almost exclusively. Kodak 3200 ASA, pushed one or two stops, was also used.